AGEING, HEALTH AND CARE

Christina R. Victor

This edition published in Great Britain in 2010 by

The Policy Press
University of Bristol
Fourth Floor
Beacon House
Queen's Road
Bristol BS8 1QU
UK

t: +44 (0)117 331 4054
f: +44 (0)117 331 4093
tpp-info@bristol.ac.uk
www.policypress.co.uk

North American office:
The Policy Press
c/o International Specialized Books Services
920 NE 58th Avenue, Suite 300
Portland, OR 97213-3786, USA
t: +1 503 287 3093
f: +1 503 280 8832
info@isbs.com

British Library Cataloguing in Publication Data
A catalogue record for this book is available from the British Library.

Library of Congress Cataloging-in-Publication Data
A catalog record for this book has been requested.

ISBN 978 1 84742 087 9 (paperback)
ISBN 978 1 84742 088 6 (hardcover)

Cover design by The Policy Press
Front cover: image kindly supplied by iStock.com
Printed and bound in Great Britain by Hobbs, Southampton

The Policy Press uses environmentally responsible print partners.

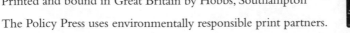

Contents

List of tables

Acknowledgements

The gestation of this book has been somewhat longer than anticipated as a consequence of 'turbulence' in my professional life following the review and subsequent closure announcement of the School of Health and Social Care of which I was Head at the University of Reading in 2008/09! The initial work on this volume started while I was Professor of Gerontology at the University of Reading and has been completed since my move to Brunel University, West London, where I am now Professor of Gerontology, Director of the Healthy Ageing Programme in the Brunel Institute for Ageing Studies (BIAS) and Director of the Doctorate in Public Health (DrPH) programme. I would like to take this opportunity to thank my colleagues in the School of Health Sciences and Social Care and BIAS at Brunel for giving me the opportunity to complete this project. I owe a considerable debt to the staff at The Policy Press, especially Ali Shaw, Emily Watt, Laura Greaves and Kathryn King for their sensitivity in dealing with my job change and for their expert and professional input, and to Professor Judith Phillips for her support and encouragement. Most importantly I would like to take this opportunity to acknowledge my friends, colleagues and students in the School of Health and Social Care at the University of Reading. It was a great privilege to have been Head of the School and to have worked with such a professional, motivated and enthusiastic staff team. This book is dedicated to you all as a way of saying 'thank you' for your support, friendship and loyalty.

Perspectives on ageing, health and care

Perceptions of old age

There are many negative perceptions about old age and later life. These include the idea that 'all old people are alike', that the old cannot learn and that older people are lonely and socially isolated, leading lives of no value and neglected by their family, friends and society more generally. Such distorted representations of a specific social group are termed 'stereotypes' and they serve to represent a set of universal characteristics that apply to the specific group in question – in our case, older people. These stereotypes obscure variations between individuals and suggest that all older people are alike, thereby eroding the individuality of each older person, suggesting a universal set of needs that can be met by a universal service response. A survey conducted in the US by the Pew Research Center (2009) demonstrates the veracity and pervasive nature of these stereotypes. Of adults aged 18-64, 57% expected to experience memory loss in old age, 42% expected to have a serious illness in old age, 42% thought that incontinence was inevitable in old age and 34% thought that loneliness accompanied old age.

These stereotypes are not new as we can see them encapsulated in the following quotation attributed to Phat-hotep who lived in Egypt in 2500 BC. He wrote:

> How hard and painful are the last days of an aged man! He grows weaker every day; his eyes become dim, his ears deaf; his strength fades; his heart knows peace no longer; his mouth falls silent and he speaks no word. The power of his mind lessens and today he cannot remember what yesterday was like. All his bones hurt. Those things which not long ago were done with pleasure are painful now; and taste vanishes. Old age is the worst of misfortunes that can afflict a man. (de Beauvoir, 1972: 104)

The ancient Egyptian hieroglyph for 'old' was a bent figure leaning on a staff, a representation not dissimilar to the Highway Code sign in the UK alerting to the possibility of older people crossing the road ahead, and in 550 BC the Ebers Papyrus suggested the existence of 'debility through senile decay' (Morley, 2004).

In this rather gloomy description of old age, and the views of adult Americans (who in this respect are little different from their UK and European cousins), we can see depicted the most common of all stereotypes of old age and that is its association with poor physical and mental health. There is a widespread presumption among the population at large that the experience of old age and later life is characterised by ill–health, failing mental and physical capabilities and generalised physical decline. We can see these negative stereotypes about old age and later life attributed to populations that are ageing. Indeed, population ageing is often represented very negatively, with 'ageing populations' characterised as being backward looking, not willing to innovate or develop and characterised by the burdens of supporting a sick and frail population. This image is illustrated by the Health Advisory Service (1982) report titled *The rising tide: Developing services for mental health in old age*. This presented the very important issue of planning mental health services for an ageing population as a social disaster of cataclysmic proportions, as the report title implies.

Until the mid–19th century, 'old age' was largely conceptualised as an almost supernatural phenomenon outwith the control of humankind. Gruman (1996) describes how, from ancient times until the early 1800s, death was conceptualised as the result of either impact of cosmic or supernatural forces or the punishment of God for the sins and folly of humankind. As late as the 1830s, preachers in the US were representing 'infirm old age' as the reward for a sinful life.

The view that ageing was not a supernatural phenomenon linked to the moral quality of an individual's life was articulated in the 1840s by the Belgian statistician Adolphe Quetelet who stated: 'Man is born, grows up, and dies, according to certain laws which have never been properly investigated, either as a whole or in the mode of the mutual reactions' (Quetelet, 1968: 5). He demonstrated that the duration of life varied according to the environment in which individuals lived and with sociodemographic factors such as gender. At an international exhibition on health held in London in 1884, Francis Galton measured 17 different bodily functions for 9,377 males and females aged 12-84 who all paid a fee to participate (but received a copy of their measurements in return). He was the first to pioneer statistical association (correlation) between two variables and showed that on selected measures such as grip strength, performance decreased with age while variability increased with age. Benjamin Gompertz (1825) – a British actuary – described the relationship between age and mortality as an exponential equation. Each of these three quantitative researchers demonstrated an association (but not causation) between chronological age and health and function, which perhaps fuels the negative stereotypes noted earlier but careful description is a prerequisite to understanding! In this book these common stereotypes are subject to challenge and rigorous scrutiny and are demonstrated to be, at best, partial in their accuracy.

Studying health and care in old age

Gerontology is the branch of science concerned with the study of the social, psychological and biological aspects of ageing. The introduction and origination of the term is credited to Metchnikoff in 1903 and it is an area of research that is explicitly multidisciplinary and which focuses on understanding the complexity of ageing and later life. Gerontologists are concerned with studying a broad range of questions about old age and later life, including:

- the physical, mental and social characteristics of older people and changes in these parameters as they age/grow older;
- the ageing process and the links between 'normal' ageing and age-related disease;
- the effects of population ageing at a societal/global level.

The focus of this book is on:

- providing an overview of the health status of older people;
- understanding how older people define and understand the meaning of health in old age;
- the nature and extent of health problems in old age and the policy and service response to the health issues of older people;
- looking at health at a population level and examining the variability of health experiences in later life with key elements of social structure, most notably gender, age, socioeconomic status and ethnicity.

As such, this constitutes a 'public health' rather than clinical perspective on the health of older people. Thus, this book complements existing texts that focus on the clinical management of the health problems characteristic of old age (see Evans et al, 2000; Redfern and Ross, 2005).

Gerontology is distinguished from geriatrics or geriatric medicine, which is the branch of medicine (or healthcare more broadly) concerned with the treatment of the diseases of old age and older people. The term 'geriatrics', to describe this area of healthcare, was coined by Nascher (1914) in his book *Geriatrics: The diseases of old age and their treatment* while it was in the post-war National Health Service (NHS) that an age-related speciality for older people, as envisaged by Warren (1943: 190) was realised (see Morley, 2004). One result of the close link between gerontology and geriatric medicine, with the latter's concern for pathology and disease, is the conflation of pathology, disease and illness with 'normal' ageing. Thus, it is easy to see how such a close academic link can reinforce ideas about the inevitability of ill-health in old age.

However, an interest in health is not confined to older people. The survey by the Pew Research Center (2009) demonstrates that good health contributes to happiness for both young and old alike. Healthier adults are happier than those who are less healthy, and this is true across all age groups. Among older adults who say they are in excellent health, nearly half (49%) are very happy with their lives; of those in good health, a third (32%) are very happy, compared with only 16% of those in fair or poor health.

Given the centrality of health to quality of life in old age, this book provides an overview of the experience of health and care in later life and shows the links between health, daily life and past lifestyle choices. The book also examines how health constrains the opportunities that older people have and the choices they can make and how these constraints are also linked to key social variables, most notably social class, gender, ethnicity and age. The book does not examine the clinical aspects of specific diseases – rather, the aim is to provide an overview of physical and mental health status in later life and consider the appropriateness (or otherwise) of the key stereotypes about the health of older people. The book also shows how policies help or hinder. One key test to establish the veracity of links between age and health status is if we see the same levels of (ill-) health across very different populations (eg in Europe and Australia) and similar variations in terms of, for example, gender. Consequently, wherever possible, international data are examined so that the situation in the UK can be compared with a range of other countries.

Structure of the book

In undertaking this task, health is examined from a range of perspectives and a range of different approaches is employed. Within each chapter, there are a number of common features, including key definitions of terms and concepts, activities, further reading and useful websites. Chapter One, as well as providing the demographic context that serves to frame the debate about health in old age, considers how 'health' and 'illness' are defined and more specifically focuses on how older adults understand and conceptualise their health. The chapter also considers how 'old age' is defined and looks at some of the assumptions implicit within the use of a single chronological age to define 'old age'.

Chapters Two and Three consider the different aspects of physical health in old age and examine the evidence of the 'all old people are ill/unhealthy' stereotype. In particular, the chapters consider the methodological complexities of studying health in old age, the use of key epidemiological terms such as incidence, prevalence, mortality and morbidity, and examine the evidence for the stereotype that the health experiences of older people are undifferentiated.

Chapter Four develops these themes by focusing on mental health in later life. In particular, it argues that, while dementia and cognitive impairment are important, there are also important issues around more neglected mental health problems such as depression and suicide.

Chapter Five examines issues around health and lifestyle in old age. Allied to the 'traditional' focus on issues of diet and exercise, it also examines issues of 'anti-ageing' medicine and the 'long history of trying to live longer'.

Policy and provision for later life is an important element of any analysis of the experience of health in later life and Chapter Six considers health and social care provision for older people and the relationship with the care and support provided by family and friends.

Chapter Seven looks forward to the likely health experiences of the next generation of older people. Are we living longer but in worse health? Is life expectancy increasing at the expense of quality of life? Is a short life a happy one? The chapter also looks forward to the potential impacts of population ageing on health and care in a global context. Population ageing is now a global phenomenon and the chapter concludes by laying out some of the challenges that an ageing world possesses for practitioners, policy makers and older people and their families.

ACTIVITY 1: Try these quizzes to find out how much you know about ageing

▶ Healthy Ageing quiz: www.mydr.com.au/quiz/healthy-ageing-quiz

▶ What do you know ageing?: http://cas.umkc.edu/CAS/AgingFactsQuiz.htm

▶ How old are you? Establish your 'biological age': www.growyouthful.com/quiz.php

▶ Global ageing quiz: www.isu.edu/nursing/opd/geriatric/friday/Global_Aging_Quiz.pdf

ACTIVITY 2: Stereotypes

▶ Look at newspapers, magazines, television, birthday cards and advertisements. How are older people depicted? How many positive depictions of old age are there and how many negative ones? What do these representations tell us about how society values older people and old age?

▶ Stereotypes are not limited to old age and older people. Think about how some other groups such as teenage mothers or young men are depicted in the media.

Further reading

de Beauvoir, S. (1972) *Old age* (trans. Patrick O'Brian). London: Andre Deutsch.

Ebrahim, S. and Kalache, A. (eds) (1996) *Epidemiology in old age*. London: BMJ Books.

Evans, J. Grimley., Williams, T., Beattie, L., Michel, J. and Wilcock, G.J. (2000) *Oxford textbook of geriatric medicine* (4th edition). Oxford: Oxford University Press.

Pew Research Center (2009) *Growing old in America: Expectations vs. reality*. Washington, DC: Pew Research Center (available at http://pewresearch.org/pubs/1269/aging-survey-expectations-versus-reality).

Redfern, S. and Ross, F. (eds) (2005) *Nursing older people* (4th edition). Edinburgh: Elsevier Press.

Tallis, R. (1998) *Increasing longevity: Medical, social and political implications*. London: Royal College of Physicians.

Townsend, P. (1962) *The last refuge: A survey of residential institutions and homes for the aged in England and Wales*. London: Routledge & Kegan Paul.

Townsend, P. (1963) *The family life of old people: An inquiry in East London*. Harmondsworth: Penguin.

Useful websites

• *British Society of Gerontology:* www.britishgerontology.org

• *Centre for Policy on Ageing*: www.cpa.org.uk/index.html

• *Tom Kirkwood's 2001 Reith Lectures. 'The end of age':* www.bbc.co.uk/radio4/reith2001/lecturer.shtml

- *The Mortal Immortal – Scientific and Social Aspects of Ageing:* www.ebi.ac.uk/ Information/events/ageingresearch/

ONE

Introduction to the key concepts

Key points

In this chapter we consider the two underlying conceptual foundations of this book: (a) understanding what we mean by terms such as 'old age' and ageing and the link with population ageing and (b) how we define and understand health.

- What does a chronological age mean?
- How well does the age of 65 (or 75) define the start of 'old age'?
- What is population ageing and what are the factors that explain it?

What is old age?

Across the developed world, a range of chronological ages, from 50 to 70, is used to determine the onset of 'old age'. In many cases this is an 'arbitrary' definition linked to the age at which individuals attain eligibility for a range of state/privately funded pension benefits and entitlements. For example, in the UK, men become eligible for the state retirement pension at 65; the over-sixties are entitled to free swimming in public baths while the over-eighties receive a supplement to the state pension. The use of a defined chronological age, linked to benefit entitlement, to determine the 'onset' of old age can be traced back to the 1875 Friendly Societies Act, which defined old age as 'any age after 50' (Roebuck, 1979). The use of a specific calendar age to mark the threshold of old age assumes this has a direct equivalence with biological age: chronological age and biological age are conceptualised as interchangeable. However, biological ageing is played out within a specific historical, environmental and social context. Thus, chronological age and biological ageing are not necessarily synonymous and the link between them undoubtedly varies within the broader socioenvironmental and historical context (see Bytheway, 2002, 2005a, 2005b, 2005c, 2006; Bytheway et al, 2007). Chronological age is not the only way of defining old age, although it is the most widely used within developed countries. There is a range of other social indicators that could fulfil this function, such as retirement, widowhood, the birth of (great) grandchildren or the changes in capabilities resultant from health problems. However, such indicators, along with notions such as 'functional' age, are extremely difficult to operationalise empirically for the purposes of research, policy or practice. In this book we use a chronological definition of old age as this enables us to explore the wealth of empirical data describing the health experiences of this population. However, we recognise the limitations of this approach and seek to explore the heterogeneity of the experience of health in old age disguised by the use of this rather blunt definition.

ACTIVITY 1: Which of these characteristics do you think defines the 'onset' of old age:

▸ retirement from work;

▸ birth of a grandchild;

▸ death of a spouse/long-term partner;

▸ can no longer drive a car;

▸ has grey hair;

▸ reaches the age of 65/75/85;

▸ can no longer live independently at home;

▸ has a major health event such as a stroke or heart attack?

To see what other people think about the link between these factors and the 'onset' of old age, see Pew Research Centre (2009).

The demographic context of ageing

Central to any discussion of old age and later life is the demographic context. Britain, like many other developed (and developing) countries, is characterised by an 'ageing' population. By this we mean that the population is distinguished by a high absolute and relative representation of older people (aged 60/65) within the total population. This demographic imperative is one of the key drivers for the policy interest in older people and later life, largely because this group is a major user of health and social care services (see Chapter Six). In thinking about the profile of older people within our, or indeed any other, population, we need to consider both the absolute number of people within a specific age group – for example those aged 100 and over – and the relative size of the group, that is, what percentage of the total population the group represents. Debates about the changes in the absolute and relative size of the older population (or indeed other population subgroups) are invariably viewed through the prism of public policy. In this section we cover the key issues that contextualise our analysis of the health status of older people (for a more detailed exposition of the demography of old age and population ageing both nationally and globally, see Harper, 2006; Victor, 2010a).

In thinking about old age and later life it is important to remind ourselves that there have always been older people present in our population. Haycock (2008) observes that, while death rates were high in early modern England, those who survived the health hazards of infancy and childhood could achieve what he termed a 'reasonable' lifespan. In Stratford upon Avon between 1570 and 1630, about 30% of men and 20% of women lived to the age of 60 or over and around 1700, 10% of our population was aged 60 and over (Haycock, 2008). There are also a number of instances of individuals characterised by extreme longevity. Perhaps the most famous of these individuals was Thomas Parr. He was introduced to King Charles 2nd and died at the putative age of 152 years and nine months in November 1635 (Haycock, 2008). William Harvey conducted his autopsy; the report of which was published in *Philosophical Transaction* in 1668 (and which is available online at http://rstl.royalsocietypublishing.org/content/3/33-44.toc). In recognition of his great celebrity, Parr was buried in Westminster Abbey. While we might be sceptical as to the precise claims of Parr's age, given the problems of verifying dates of birth, there are certainly examples of individuals achieving very long lives. For example, Christopher Wren was (probably) in his nineties when he died.

What does mark out contemporary Western societies is in both the absolute and the relative numbers of people achieving 'old age' and as a consequence our populations are characterised as 'ageing'. We can demonstrate this by the use of a summary statistical measure known as the 'median age'. This describes the age at which 50% of a given population are older and 50% younger. In 1841 in England and Wales, the earliest date for which the measure may be reliably calculated, the median age was 22.4 years as compared with 38 in 2005 (Sanderson and Scherbov, 2005). We can also illustrate the changes that have taken place in the age structure of our population by looking at the percentage of various birth cohorts who survived to the age of 85. For the cohort born in 1851, 3% of men and 7% of women would reach the age of 85 compared with 42% and 57% respectively for the 1950 birth cohort. Our social expectations have changed radically since the 1900s. While Pete Townsend may have wanted to die before he grew old, the majority of us do not. We now all presume we will reach old age, even if we do not embrace the notion with enthusiasm and do not demonstrate a penchant for pension planning or saving for our retirement.

Box 1: Key terms in demography

- *Median age:* the age that divides a population into two numerically equal groups; half the people are younger than the index age and half are older. It is a single index that summarises the age distribution of a population. Median age ranges from about 15 in Uganda to over 40 in Japan.

- *Mean age:* the mathematical average. This can be distorted by the presence of outliers (that is, lots of very young or very old people) and so this measure can be problematic when describing the overall population. We often calculate mean age at birth of first child or mean age at retirement.

- *Modal age:* this defines the most frequent age in a distribution. So in Chapter 7 we consider the modal age of death or the age at which most deaths occur to be currently approximately 86 years in England and Wales.

The demographic structure of our population

ACTIVITY 2: **What do you know about population ageing in Britain?**

▶ In 2010, what percentage of our population is aged 65 and over?

▶ What percentage was aged 65 and over in 1901?

▶ How many centenarians (people aged 100 and over) are there in Britain in 2010?

▶ What percentage of those aged 65 and over live in the community?

▶ What reasons explain the 'ageing' of our population?

The key data source in enabling us to track trends in the size and composition of the population of Britain is the Census. These have been held every 10 years since 1801 with the exception of 1941 and, since 1841, completion of the Census form has been compulsory. Jefferies (2005) provides a succinct overview of the transformation of our population over the last 150 years. Here our specific focus is on the changes in the age composition of our population. Demographic and other 'official' statistics used in this book are provided from a range of administrative units. These vary according to the purpose of the data and issues of governance, which are now made more complex by the development of devolved government in Wales, Scotland and Northern Ireland. Some data are available for the UK (this consists of England, Wales, Scotland and Northern Ireland); some for Great Britain (England, Wales and Scotland), some for England and Wales and some for just England. Readers need to be alert as to which administrative unit data are being provided for and accept that the inconsistencies in these across the book reflect availability but that this should not affect the logic or flow of the arguments advanced.

In 1900, the population of the UK was approximately 38 million, of whom 5% were aged 65 years or older. By 2008, this percentage had quadrupled to 20% and the total population was 60 million. In absolute terms, this represents an increase from approximately 1.9 million in 1900 to 9.6 million in 2008. Barring fluctuations brought about by epidemics, the percentage of what we would now categorise as older people was approximately stable up until 1900. Thus, in Britain, population ageing is predominantly a 20th-century phenomenon.

Key features of the older population

The population aged 60/65 years and over is not homogeneous but is differentiated according to several key sociostructural variables, most notably age, gender, class and ethnicity. In addition, several other key characteristics, such as civil status and household composition, are also important contextual variables when considering both health needs and the services and interventions designed to respond to those needs. Here we very briefly consider these parameters in order to facilitate a more enlightened understanding of the health data presented in subsequent chapters. For a more detailed exposition of these topics, see Victor (2005) and Higgs and Jones (2009).

The 65–74 age group accounts for 51% of the 9.6 million people aged 65 and over (see Table 1.1) with those aged 85 and over accounting for 12%. However it is, perhaps, the growth in the number of nonagenarians and centenarians that is emblematic of population ageing. It is estimated that there are currently (2009) approximately 9,330 centenarians in England and Wales, of whom 87% (8,130) are women, and 390,000 nonagenarians. We see the 'traditional' excess of women across all of the older age groups but these gender-based differentials in survival into old age are decreasing. For example, in 1991, for those aged 65–74 there were 77 males for every 100 females and 52 males per 100 females for those aged 75–84. In 2008, the respective ratios were 90 and 73. Thus, over a comparatively short time period the 'taken-for-granted' gender differential in old age has been reduced in response to changes in male/female mortality rates. However, this serves to illustrate two important points when considering the experience of old age and later life. First, it illustrates how aspects of old age and later life that we take as 'normal' or 'natural' may, in fact, be the result of the complex interplay of social, cultural or environmental factors as well as biology. Second, it demonstrates that old age is a dynamic experience and we cannot presume that patterns observed in the past will be maintained.

Table 1.1: Population of the UK 2008 and projections to 2051 (000s)

Age	2008		2021		2051	
	M	F	M	F	M	F
All ages	29,694	30,893	33,252	33,938	38,426	38,810
65-69	1,293	1,398	1,582	1,700	2,019	2,105
70-74	1,086	1,252	1,571	1,738	1,646	1,790
75-79	849	1,110	1,178	1,357	1,492	1,687
80-84	564	892	813	1,014	1,427	1,692
85-89	273	547	496	693	1,102	1,400
90+	106	317	274	484	997	1,388
Mean age	39.9		41.9		44.3	
Median age	39.8		41.8		44.1	

Note: In all the tables, M = male and F = female.

Source: Bray (2008)

There are two very important sociostructural factors that, for different reasons, are not as widely studied in terms of the experience of ageing and later life within the UK and these are socioeconomic position and ethnicity. The measurement of socioeconomic position, which in the UK is intimately linked with occupation and the labour market, is problematic for a group who are largely excluded from employment. However, it is also clear that such a major axis of social differentiation is not rendered null and void upon entry into 'old age'. Inequalities in life chances based around social class are longlasting and any rigorous analysis of the experience of ageing and later life needs to engage with the issue of class. Ethnicity is a much more recent dimension of differentiation within the UK. At the 2001 Census, 7.6% of the total population came from minority ethnic groups: 16% of the white population were aged 65 and over compared with 9% of the African Caribbean group, 6% of the Indian group and 3% of those from Pakistani, Bangladeshi and Chinese backgrounds (Blackwell, 2000; White, 2002). The 'ageing' of minority ethnic populations represents one of the most significant changes that will characterise our population over the next two decades.

Civil (or marital) status is also an important factor in the experience of ageing as it is a vital link into social support and social networks. This parameter too shows variation over time, with the emergence of the 'divorced' as a social category for both men and women, the decrease in the percentage classified as single (never married) for women and the decrease in the percentage of women experiencing old age as a widow (see Table 1.2). As a result of improved male mortality rates, couples are now more likely to experience old age together, women are less likely than they were to be widows and the age at which widowhood becomes normative for women has been pushed back.

Table 1.2: Civil status of the population aged 65+, Great Britain, 1971-2007 (%)

Civil status	1971		2007	
	M	F	M	F
Single	7	15	7	5
Married	73	35	70	45
Widowed	20	50	15	43
Divorced	0	0	8	7

Source: ONS (2009, table 1.1)

The final contextual factor we need to consider here relates to household composition or household size. In percentage terms, the highest rates of 'living alone' in Great Britain are demonstrated by the 65 and over age group. In 2007, 35% of men aged 75 and over and 61% of women aged 75 and over lived alone compared with 14% of those aged 45-64, 12% of those aged 25-44 and 2% of those aged 16-24. Focusing on the population aged 65 and over, the vast majority of people live with their spouse (65%), while 33% live alone and a very small minority (around 2%) live in multigenerational households. However, we must be very careful not to infer that those who live alone do not have access to a supportive social network. This was a point well made by Sheldon (1948) in his study of Wolverhampton where he noted that, while older people were classified as living alone, they were embedded within a network of kin and friendship care and support networks.

What has brought about the ageing of our population?

What are the factors that have brought about this change in the age composition of our population? The absolute and relative numbers of any given age group within the total population reflect the interplay of birth rates and death rates.

Total births and birth rates

The number of births in any given year is important because it establishes the size of any specific birth cohort, for example the number of people born in 1914 or in the period 1914-19. However, the number of live births is also important as it establishes the size of the total population within which older people form a component part. If there are fewer babies being born then older people will, by definition, represent an increasing relative part of the population. If the numbers of children being born in successive cohorts are declining, then the relative size of the older age groups will increase without any other factors such as death rates changing. Hence, a long-term decline in fertility has been one of the key drivers of population ageing in Britain (and elsewhere).

In 2008, there were an estimated 5,058,000 people aged 65-74 years in our population, which reflects two factors: (a) the number of births 65-74 years ago and (b) rates of mortality (or deaths) at birth, infancy, childhood and adult life. In 1938 (these people would be 74 years in 2008), there were 621,204 live births, while in 1943 (these people would be 65 in 2008) there were 684,334 live births in England and Wales. These figures illustrate one very important feature of demography and demographic analysis: that in any individual year there are fluctuations in the total numbers of live births. In 1838, the first complete year of live birth registration in England and Wales, there were 463,787 live births – plus a not inconsiderable number of still births. Annual fluctuations in live births can be substantial. The largest number of live births recorded in a single year in England and Wales was in 1920 when there were 957,782 births, 265,344 more than in 1919! In 2008, there were 708,000 births in England and Wales compared with 580,000 in 2005 (ONS, 2009). The occurrence of several years of high numbers of births, within an overall pattern of declining births, is colloquially termed a 'baby boom': the most famous of which is that which occurred in the aftermath of the Second World War and resulted in the attribution of the label 'baby boomers' to an entire birth cohort. This phenomenon was most keenly observed in the US but is evident within the UK. The ageing of the baby boomer generation is a topic that has generated considerable academic research and policy debate and is an issue to which we will return in Chapter 7 (Biggs et al, 2008).

However, the absolute number of births is of only limited utility as a demographic indicator. Fluctuations in the numbers of births may simply reflect variation in the numbers of women of 'childbearing' age. Thus, in interpreting changes in the numbers of births, we need to have a measure of total births (the numerator) and the relevant denominator – either the total population (which describes the crude birth rate) or the number of women of childbearing age. The crude birth rate can be used to establish broad trends in fertility. This has fallen from 32.3 live births per 100 population in 1841–45 to 12.1 in 2005; since then there has been a modest increase in the birth rate to 12.7 in 2008 and total births increased by 15% between 2001 and 2008 (see Tromans et al, 2009). Total Period Fertility Rate (TPFR) is a more specific measure of fertility, which describes the average (mean) number of children per women for specific time points. This is a very crude statistic but it does summarise succinctly the changes that have taken place in terms of family size in Britain over the last century and a half. This was fairly stable at about five children per woman from about 1600 up until the end of the 19th century, then declined consistently to reach a low of 1.64 in 2001 but has since increased to 1.94 in 2008, which is still below the replacement level of 2.1. These generally low and declining birth rates have been interspersed in the UK with two post-war 'birth bulges' – one in the period 1945–55 and another in the period 1961–65 when the TPFR was 2.8, which translated into over 800,000 births a year (ONS 2009; Tromans et al, 2009). These trends towards low fertility are not unique to the UK. There are 90 countries in the world where the total fertility rate is below the 2.1 replacement level threshold, including Austria, Germany, Hong Kong, Italy, Japan, Singapore and several countries from the 'old' Soviet bloc states including Belarus and Ukraine. At the opposite end of the spectrum, the 'average' woman in Mali or Niger will have seven children (see Victor, 2010a).

Death rates

Once the size of a specific birth cohort has been established, then the second element to be considered is the survival of cohort members (to old age). Thus, death rates (or mortality rates) across the lifespan also influence population ageing because they affect the probability of birth cohorts living long enough to grow old. As with births, we need both to know the absolute numbers of deaths and to be able to express this in terms of the 'population at risk', which can be the total population (which generates the crude death rate) or specific age groups (which generates age-specific mortality rates). The rates are calculated by dividing the number of deaths (the numerator) by the size of the relevant population (the denominator). Deaths within the first year of life are calculated separately. This is termed the 'infant mortality rate', with the denominator being the total number of live births. Infant mortality is a touchstone indicator of development. It is widely used to profile and rank the health status of populations globally and to identify variations within, and between, countries. In order to calculate these rates (and the measures of fertility), we need accurate records for both the numerator and the denominator. Within Britain these are provided by the compulsory registration of births and deaths and the decennial population Census, the next one of which is scheduled for 2011.

Decreases in mortality rates have been an important driver of population ageing. Across Western Europe and the developed world mortality rates have been decreasing consistently over the last 150 years, meaning that the probability of surviving to old age for any given cohort has been increasing (see Bloom and Canning, 2005; Harper, 2006). Population ageing is our reward for reducing mortality across the lifecourse: in infancy, childhood and adulthood. However, lest we become complacent, mortality rates can increase and reduce the size of specific cohorts or whole populations. This is very clearly demonstrated by the example of AIDS and its impact on the population structure of many sub-Saharan African countries.

Crude death rates in Britain, that is, deaths per 1,000 of the total population, have declined steadily since the 1830s. For the period 1841-45, the crude death rate was 21.4 per 1,000 of the population compared with 9.6 per 1,000 in 2008. This is an impressive decline. The crude death rate is influenced by the absolute and relative numbers of older people within the population, which, in the case of England and Wales, have quadrupled over this time period. To illustrate the magnitude of this change, mortality rates have halved while the size of the key population group 'at risk' has quadrupled. We need to be able to describe changes in mortality rates independent of changes in the age composition of the total population. We can do this by calculating the standardised mortality ratio (the SMR), which takes into account the changing nature of the population. First, we need to establish the population structure and mortality rates that we wish to use as our reference or index point and this is given the value of 100. We can then calculate rates for different time periods with reference to this. Values of more than 100 indicate 'worse' mortality rates than those described for the reference population and those below 100 'improved' rates. If we establish Britain in 1950 as our reference standard of 100, the SMR in 1841-45 was 344 and 55 in 2005. Thus, overall mortality rates, when we take out the influence of population change, have roughly halved in the 60 years from 1950. A similar summary measure is the age-standardised mortality rate. In the UK this decreased by 46% from 1976 (rate of 10,486 per million) to 2008 (a rate of 5,915 per million) (ONS, 2009).

Again a broader context helps us to interpret these figures and put them into a wider perspective. In 2008, there were eight countries with crude death rates above 20 per 1,000 of the population: Swaziland (30.7 per 1,000), Angola (24.4), Lesotho (22.3), Sierra Leone (22.2), Liberia (21.4), Zambia (21.3), Mozambique (20.2) and Niger (20.2). These are very high death rates and we need to reassure ourselves that they are not simply an artefact of inaccuracies in the numerator and/or denominator. While there may be some inaccuracies in the size of the denominators in particular, these are probably not of sufficient size to inflate and distort death rates to the levels observed in these countries. The global mean crude death rate for 2008 was 8 per 1,000 and the lowest rates recorded were all from countries where the population aged 65 and over was under 3% (demonstrating the influence of age structure on mortality rates noted earlier). The countries with crude death rates of under 3 per 1,000 were United Arab Emigrates (2.1 per 1,000), Kuwait (2.3), Qatar (2.4), Saudi Arabia (2.4) and Jordan (2.7) (see www.nationmaster.com/graph/peo_dea_rat-people-death-rate for crude death rates by country).

Age-specific deaths have also demonstrated a substantial decline, especially those observed in infancy and childhood. As Kermack et al,(1934) note, survival of childhood is key to the ageing of the British population, and indeed other contemporary societies. Here we focus on the indicator that has most profoundly influenced survival and that is infant mortality. Hicks and Allen (1999) report that in 1900, the infant mortality rate for the UK was 140 per 1,000 live births and 151 per 1,000 for England and Wales. Expressed in another way, this means that 15% of live born children in England and Wales died within the first year of life. Hence, of the 927,062 children born in England and Wales that year, 129,788 would have died before reaching their first birthday. If these rates are applied to the 794,400 births in the UK in 2008, then 119,100 would have died compared with the 3,700 actual infant deaths: a rate of 4.7 per 1,000. This is a remarkable decline when we take into account the increased number of multiple and low birthweight babies that have occurred over this period.

Death rates across childhood have also declined. Using the period 1861-65 for England and Wales as our reference point, the death rates per 1,000 were 36.8 for ages 1-4, 8.4 for ages 5-9 and 4.7 for ages 10-14. For 2007, the latest data available, the respective rates were 0.2 per 1,000, 0.1 per 1,000 and 0.1 per 1,000 (ONS, 2009). So, as Victor (2005) observes, these reductions in infant and childhood death rates have changed the 'epidemiology' of death. In 1901, 40% of deaths were accounted for by children aged under 15 compared with 1% in 2008. At the opposite end of the age range, 83% of deaths in 2008 were accounted for by those aged 65 and over compared with 44% in 1901. Improvements in survival at later ages have also been important in increasing the chances of people surviving into old age and we consider these in more detail in Chapter Two as, historically, it is the reductions in childhood and early adult mortality that were the initial drivers of population ageing. However, in thinking of the future it is likely that reductions in late-life mortality will assume increasing importance within the context of a population characterised by low fertility and low general mortality.

Again a broader perspective serves to illustrate how well the UK performs within the international context in terms of mortality in infancy and childhood. There are seven countries where infant mortality in 2008 was above 10% (100 per 1,000): Angola (192.5), Afghanistan (165.9), Mozambique (137.0), Liberia (130.5), Niger (122), Mali (117.9) and Guinea-Bissau (101.2). While again we may have some doubts as to the accuracy of numerators and denominators for these countries, it is unlikely that these high rates are simply the result of recording errors and (probably) not an artefact. At the opposite end of the spectrum, 11 countries recorded infant mortality rates of less than 4 per 1,000: Czech Republic (3.83), Malta (3.79), Norway (3.61), Anguilla (3.54), Finland (3.5), France (3.36), Iceland (3.25), Hong Kong (2.93), Japan (2.8), Sweden (2.75) and Singapore (2.3) (see www.nationmaster.com/graph/peo_dea_rat-people-death-rate). Thus, the infant mortality rate recorded in the UK in 2008 of 4.7 per 1,000 is not 'good' enough to get us into the 'top 10' list of 'best rates worldwide'!

Box 2: Key terms in demography – birth and death rates

- *Crude death rate:* total deaths per 1,000 total population (for example, 50 deaths for a total population of 2,000 aged 1 to 99 = a crude death rate of 25 per 1,000).
- *Standardising death rates:* comparing crude death rates for populations (or areas) with different age structure is problematic because the age composition affects the crude death rate. To overcome this we adjust or standardise the mortality rates to take account of differences between population age structures. The two main forms of standardisation are standardised mortality ratios (SMRs) (also called 'indirect standardisation') and age-standardised rates (ASMRs) (also called 'direct standardisation').
- *SMRs:* compare the number of observed deaths in a population with the number of expected deaths if the age-specific death rates were the same as a standard population. It is expressed as a ratio of observed to expected deaths, multiplied by 100, thereby enabling us to compare death rates in 2010 with those for 1950. An SMR equal to 100 implies that the mortality rate is the same as the SMR. A number higher than 100 implies an excess mortality rate whereas a number below 100 implies below-average mortality.
- *The ASMR for a population:* summarises the number of deaths per 100,000 that would occur in that population (Britain in 2010) had the same age structure as the standard population (Britain in 1950) and current mortality rates applied for each specific age group.
- *Birth rate:* total live births per 1,000 population (calculation follows same procedure as crude death rates).
- *Total Period Fertility Rate (TPFR):* the average (mean) number of children per women for specific time points, for example 1970-79.

ACTIVITY 3

▸ How long can the average Briton expect to live?
▸ How long can the average South African expect to live?
▸ What factors might explain the difference?

Expectation of life

Expectation of life, especially at birth, is often used as a proxy for the overall health status of populations and is widely used to make comparisons about health status within, and between, populations and over time where the data are available. Expectation of life is a statistical construct and is an aggregate-level measure: we cannot make inferences about the actual length of specific individuals' lives on the basis of life expectancy data. Thus, expectation of life at birth expresses the number of years that the average child could be expected to live if current mortality rates apply across their lifetime. We can also calculate life expectancy for other specific ages, not just at birth. Life expectancy at, for example, age 65 expresses the average number of years of additional life a person of 65 would live if current age–specific mortality rates continue to apply.

> ## Box 3: Key terms in gerontology
> - *Life expectancy:* The number of years that an average individual is expected to live from a specified age. This is usually calculated at birth but can be calculated from any age.
> - *Maximum life span:* the maximum lifespan observed in a group. Jeanne Calment (1875-1997, 122 years, 164 days) was the oldest person whose age has been verified by modern documentation and so she defines the modern human lifespan.
> - *Longevity:* the average lifespan expected under ideal conditions. This term is often used more colloquially to describe a 'long life'. There are innumerable mythical examples of individuals achieving advanced longevity and most cultures have myths and legends about very long-lived individuals and ideas of 'the fountain of youth'. Various Biblical characters lived to beyond 900, including Methuselah (age 969) (Genesis 5:27), Noah (age 950) and Adam, the first man (age 930).

There are two broad methods of calculating life expectancy statistics: period-based calculations and cohort-based calculations (see Table 1.3). Period expectation of life is simply the average (mean) number of years of life an individual of a given age may expect to live if current death rates for the year of birth are maintained across their lifecourse. Hence, this measure rests on the assumption that existing age-specific rates of mortality will continue to apply unchanged in the future (that is, the assumption is that rates will neither increase nor decrease but will remain constant). Thus, when we are looking at projected period life expectancy for the future, we must take heed of the very important presumption of the continuation of current levels of mortality. Cohort-based life expectancy calculations incorporate predicted/known changes in age-specific mortality and thus model the effect of projected changes in mortality rates into calculations of life expectancy. This is clearly a more dynamic measure but its accuracy rests on the robustness of the extent, timing and predictability of mortality changes (for either better or worse). Thus far we have observed that the pattern of death rates in Britain has been one of continuous improvement and these would be included in cohort-based life expectancy projections. However, there may well come a point at which this trend for continuous improvement in mortality reaches a plateau or even reverses as a result of major epidemics of infectious diseases or if the increase in levels of obesity results in an increase in mortality rates.

Given the significant changes in both overall and age-specific mortality, it is unsurprising that life expectancy has also changed for the better in the UK over the last 150 years. Without the benefit of complete records, estimates of life expectancy in Britain before the mid-19th century are inevitably somewhat speculative. As a very rough guide, life expectancy at birth in Britain between about 1500 and 1800 was estimated to be in the range of 40 and 45 years (Thane, 2005, 2000). However, this estimate could fluctuate because of the influence of epidemics of infectious diseases, which were the major sources of mortality during this historical period. Around the turn of the 20th century, period life expectancy at birth in the UK was about 48 years for men and 52 years for women compared with 77.1 years and 82.5 years respectively for 2008 (ONS, 2009). Thus, over a relatively short historical period – approximately a hundred years – life expectancy at birth in Britain increased by 60% for men and 56% for women, largely as a result of the changes in infant and childhood mortality rates described earlier. Since the 1980s, period-based expectation of life at birth has increased by two years (approximately) per decade (see Bray, 2008). There are significant differences in the period- and cohort-based estimates of life expectancy (see Table 1.3). For 2006, period-based life expectancy at birth was 77 for men compared with 88 if we use the cohort-based estimates based on the assumption of continuing improvements in mortality, especially in later life. We can, however, compute life expectancy for other ages – as noted above it is not a statistic that is confined to birth and infancy.

Table 1.3: Cohort- and period-based life expectancy by gender, UK, 2006

Expectation of life	Period-based calculation		Cohort-based calculation	
	M	F	M	F
At birth	77.2	81.5	88.1	91.5
Age 15	62.0	67.0	71.8	75.3
Age 65	17.2	20.0	20.6	23.1
Age 75	10.4	12.4	11.9	13.5
Age 85	5.7	6.6	5.9	6.7

Source: Bray (2008, table 7.5)

For those who actually managed to survive the hazards of childhood and infancy then, in 1841, a 65-year-old male in England and Wales could expect to live another 11 years compared with 17 years in 2006. For females the increase over the same period was from 12 to 20 years. While these increases are not so spectacular in absolute terms, they still represent a relative increase of about 60% and demonstrate the impact of a steady decrease in late-life mortality rates, which we discuss in Chapter 2. In 2008, data for the UK indicate that the 'average' male aged 60 could look forward to another 21 years of life, at age 70 another 13 years of life and at age 80 another eight years of life; for 'average' women the figures were 24 years, 16 years and nine years respectively (ONS, 2009). At age 85 years the 'average' person has a life expectancy of six years. Another way of expressing this point is to look at the age at which the average life remaining is 15 years. In 1901, this was 55 years for men and 58 for women; in 2004/05 the comparable ages were 68 and 71 respectively.

How do these life expectancies compare with other developed countries? For women, the 20 years' expectation of life at age 65 is bettered by 13 of the 26 countries of the Organisation for Economic Co-operation and Development (OECD), with Japan reporting 3.2 years more life for the average 65-year-old woman and Turkish women having 15 years more life. The differentials for men range from 13 years for Turkey to 18 years for Iceland, Australia and Japan. These variations indicate that life expectancy is clearly sensitive to the socioenvironmental and historical context.

How does life expectancy in Britain compare with the rest of the world? In 2008, the estimated period global average life expectancy was approximately 67 years (65 years for males and 70 years for females) but this overall average masks profound variations between countries. There were 15 countries where period-based expectation of life at birth was over 80 years; Japan had the highest life expectancy at birth of 82.6 years (79 years for males and 86 years for females). Iceland was the only country where life expectancy was above 80 years for both males (80.2) and females (83.3) and 81.8 overall. The UK was ranked 26th, with an average of 78.7 years. At the other end of the distribution, Swaziland had the lowest life expectancy, with an average of 39.2 years and there were four other countries where life expectancy was under 42 years: Lesotho (42.6), Sierra Leone (42.6), Zambia (42.4) and Mozambique (42.1) – levels that were typical (or slightly worse) than Britain in the 1840s. Given that these are national averages, we may reasonably speculate that there will be some areas or groups within these countries where life expectancies are (probably) below these already low rates.

We have thus far documented a situation in which life expectancy, along with death rates, has demonstrated a trend of continual improvement. We have cautioned that when thinking about future patterns of mortality and life expectancy we are 'forward projecting' current trends. We are also presuming that things will stay the same – if not improve; we do not think (or plan) on the assumption that health statistics will deteriorate. Unfortunately, there are examples of countries where life expectancy has decreased – examples include Russia but perhaps the best (or worst) example is Zimbabwe. In the 1990s, life expectancy in Zimbabwe was around 60 years – this has now decreased to around 36 years, reflecting an increase in the infant mortality rate, which has climbed from 53 to 81 deaths per 1,000 live births and other mortality rates have similarly increased.

What will population structure of the UK look like in the future?

We have briefly summarised the factors that have shaped the composition of the UK's current population age structure. For many social commentators the key issue is how the size and composition of our population will change in the future. In examining the likely size and age composition of our population we are 'forward projecting' current trends, albeit using a series of 'worst' and 'best' case assumptions. However, as noted above, when interpreting these projections we must be mindful that they are based on the continuation of existing trends and these may be subject to change and modification over the next 50-75 years (these issues are cogently discussed by Bray, 2008).

The population of the UK was estimated in 2008 to be 60.5 million people and is expected to increase to 71.2 million in 2031, with a longer-term estimate of 85.2 million in 2081. The dynamic nature of population projections, which are sensitive to changes in assumptions about mortality, fertility and migration, is illustrated by considering that the 2004 population projection for 2031 was 4 million fewer than the 2008 estimate. For example, the 2004-based estimate of life expectancy at birth for 2031 was 81.4 years for men and 85 years for women compared with 82.7 and 86.2 respectively for the 2008 estimates (Bray, 2008). The population is expected to increase by 25 million over the next 80 years, of which half is projected to be as a result of migration. The number of people aged 65 and over will increase from 9.6 million (2006) to 22.8 million (2081) – an increase of 237% – while the number of those aged 80 and over will triple from 2.7 million (2006) to 10.3 million (2081). These increases are reflected in the predicted rise in the average (mean) age of the population from 39.6 in 2006 to 42.6 in 2031.

Projecting life expectancy for future cohorts is clearly problematic. However, it is a vital element of the demographers' and actuaries' role and it is clear that for planning purposes we need to be able to estimate a range of differing demographic parameters, including future life expectancies, birth rates, fertility and net-migration. However, such projections are not precise and inevitably contain some degree of error. Only hindsight reveals the direction and size of the error. If we use period-based life expectancies at birth in 2031, these will be over 80 years of age for both males and females but if we use cohort-based life expectancies, which factor in assumed improvements in mortality rates, then the life expectancy at birth will be over 90 years. Indeed, cohort-based life expectancies at birth for 2006 are 88 years for men and 91 years for women as opposed to 77 years and 81 years respectively for period-based calculations. Thus, there is almost a decade's difference in potential life expectancy for those children who were born in 2006, which illustrates the reductions in mortality that the demographers are expecting will be achieved. Although the differences between cohort- and period-based life expectancies are less marked for the 65 and over age groups, they are still evident.

If we examine population estimates for the older population in more detail we can see the growth of the nonagenarian population (see Table 1.1). In 2006, there were an estimated 420,000 people in the UK aged 90 and over – this is projected to increase to almost 2 million by 2051. The growth of those who are 'very old' (or in deep old age) is a phenomenon of many Western populations as the ageing population itself 'ages'. In the focus on the increasing number of people surviving to old age and very old age, we are sometimes guilty of failing to notice other changes in the composition of this population. As shown in Table 1.1, we can see the gradual but clearly demonstrable change in the gender ratios as more men survive into old age. Thus, in 2008 for the 65-69 age group, there were 92 men for every 100 women and 33 men for every woman by the age of 90 and over. If we look at the situation in 2051, the female predominance, while still present, is less marked. For the 65-69 age group, the ratio has improved to almost parity, with 96 men per 100 women. However, at advanced ages the differential – while still present – is closing such that there are projected to be 71 men for every 100 women. Analysis of time series period life expectancy data at birth suggests that the 'gender gap' reduced from six years in 1980 to four years in 2006. Future projections suggest that this will reduce to 3.6 years in 2011 and 3 years in 2081 (Bray, 2008). This is not a simple point of interest merely to demographers and actuaries: it has implications for health in that there are gender differentials in the experience of health, access to healthcare and the receipt and provision of social care.

This potential change in the gender balance in old age also reminds us that the experience of later life is dynamic and fluid and changes as different groups or cohorts move into old age. We now have the ageing of the baby boomers and the generations that created the post-war 'consumer society' (see Jones et al, 2008). One feature that will change in coming decades is the ethnicity distribution of the population. It is still the case that the vast majority (96%) of those aged 65 and over are essentially 'White British' in terms of ethnicity. At the 2001 Census, 15% of people from non-White minority ethnic groups were aged 50 and over compared with 33% of the overall population. Currently, 9% of the Black Caribbean population are aged 65 and over with 15% in the 50-64 age groups. This will be the first group of migrants to move into old age followed by the Indian, Pakistani and Bangladeshi groups over the next 50 years. Again, given the differential health experiences of minority populations, this may not (or may) have implications for the overall health of the older population and the identification of healthcare needs. However, there are many uncertainties here, not the least of which is whether our migrant communities will choose to grow old here or return to their homelands. Again, these changes help us to appreciate the dynamic and evolving nature and composition of the group labelled as 'older people' and to appreciate that they are a diverse population: not a homogeneous group with a uniform set of health and social care needs that can be met by a single, universal policy response.

What is health and why is it important in old age?

ACTIVITY 4

‣ How would you define health for yourself and for an older person?
‣ What factors influence the health of individuals?
‣ How important do you think good health is for a 'good' old age?
‣ What do you think quality of life means in old age?

Issues relating to 'health' are central to the study of ageing and the experience of old age and later life at both macro (societal) and micro (individual) levels. At the macro level, key debates in the policy area emphasise notions of active and successful ageing as a mechanism for promoting the health status of older people thereby (in theory at least) reducing the perceived 'burden' of an ageing population. At a micro level, notions of 'successful ageing' stress the importance of health for quality of life in old age (see Bowling, 2005, 2007, 2008; Bowling and Gabriel, 2007). Role models of very active individuals in advanced old age are held up for admiration such as the 2008 London Marathon finisher Buster Martin – aged at least 94 or possibly older (his claim to being a centenarian was not accepted by those who verify such things). However, such individuals are presented as 'exceptional examples' of old age and later life, which do little to combat the pervasive negative stereotype of old age as a time of (virtually) universal ill-health. Health status, either actual or perceived, is consistently associated with quality of life in old age. Those in good health, or who perceive their health to be good, consistently report good quality of life compared with those whose health is poor or whose family members have poor health. The onset of poor health may be seen by many as a 'cue' signifying entry into 'old age' or that, at least, they are growing older.

The health experience of any specific individual reflects the complex interplay between five main factors:

- genetic heritage;
- individual behaviours (such as exercise, diet, alcohol consumption and the management of long-term conditions such as diabetes);
- environmental and occupational exposures;
- sociodemographic factors such as class and ethnicity; and
- access to, availability and quality of healthcare (both therapeutic and preventative).

The precise contribution made by each of these sets of factors remains hotly debated and the balance of 'power' between these explanations may vary historically, across the lifecourse and between different social groups. Currently, explanations for individual and population patterns of disease emphasise the importance of genetics – the importance of choosing 'good parents', defined by their genetic profile both in terms of longevity and genetic markers for a range of chronic diseases and disabilities. We would argue that health status at any age is much more complex than simply genetic heritage, as this is 'played out' within a socioenvironmental context and an infrastructure of healthcare services and interventions. Thus, health in old age and across the lifecourse reflects the interaction between individual-level factors and macro-level socioenvironmental influences. However, this is a very static perspective and in examining health in later life we need to incorporate the temporal dimension. Our experiences of health as we grow older reflect the cumulative interplay and dynamic interrelationships of these factors over time. The health of older people reflects contemporary influences – most obviously the availability of modern healthcare services and medical/surgical/pharmacological interventions such as joint replacements, dialysis, lifestyle factors such as diet and exercise and potential 'genetic'-based interventions and therapies. However, the health experiences of our current generation of older people also reflects historical influences such as diet in early childhood, living conditions, occupational and/or environmental exposures and the health and nutritional status of their mother. The importance of the last of these was argued in the Barker (1995) hypothesis – that under-nutrition in the middle and late phases of gestation are linked to coronary heart disease in mid to later life. Subsequent research has confirmed the importance of the health of mothers for the lifetime health of their children, especially in terms of coronary heart disease in men (Barker et al, 1993; Barker, 1998; Frankl et al, 1996; Stein et al, 1996).

We can argue about the specific details of the robustness and implications of the Barker hypothesis, for example the emphasis on heart disease rather than other health outcomes or the focus on men. However, it is certainly biologically plausible that experiences in infancy and early childhood can influence health status in adulthood and later life. We would not argue for the highly deterministic position that health status in adulthood is determined solely by childhood and the gestational environment. This is self-evidently a very limited position, which denies the importance of numerous other influences and modifiers that shape health status (Bury and Wadsworth, 2003) post infancy. Rather, the point that we wish to make is that the health status of older people reflects the influences of both the historical period into which they were born and subsequent experiences across the lifecourse. Determining the relative importance of these explanatory frameworks remains a challenge to researchers given that the balance is almost certainly dynamic and will vary over time. Within epidemiology and public health there is an increased interest in understanding the pattern of diseases within populations from a lifecourse perspective (see Ben-Shlomo and Kuh, 2002). These authors define the lifecourse approach to disease as:

> the study of the long term effects on chronic disease risk of physical and social exposures during gestation, childhood, adolescence, young adulthood and later adult life. It includes studies of the biological, behavioural and psychosocial pathways that operate across an individual's lifecourse, as well as across generations, to influence the development of chronic diseases. (Ben-Shlomo and Kuh, 2002: 285; see also Aboderin et al, 2002; Wadsworth, 2003)

In proposing a lifecourse approach, Ben-Shlomo and Kuh (2002) identify the importance of both the accumulation of 'risks' and exposures across the lifecourse as a contribution to health in old age. They also argue for the importance of 'critical events' in understanding the distribution of health within (and between) populations. The central premise of the 'critical period model' is that exposure(s) experienced at a specific time period may compromise the biological integrity of the individual, resulting in permanent and irreparable damage. This proposition is the basis for the 'fetal origins of adult disease' hypothesis developed by Barker

(1995) noted earlier and which proposes that poor growth in utero leads to a variety of chronic disorders in mid to later life such as cardiovascular disease, non-insulin-dependent diabetes and hypertension as well as poor health in childhood (see Guralnik et al, 2006; Kuh et al, 2006a, 2006b). The distinctive features of the 'critical period' element of the lifecourse explanation of health status are that the period is time limited and the damage rendered to the biological integrity of the individual is beyond repair. An infamous example of this concept is the effect that the drug thalidomide had on the children of mothers who took the drug for morning sickness.

However, as the name implies, the lifecourse approach to understanding health adopts a broader perspective than the simple Barker hypothesis. First, the approach accepts that there are, if only in theory, 'critical periods' other than those *in utero*: exposures and experiences in puberty might potentially fall into this category. We might hypothesise that exposure to certain (illegal) drugs in puberty may result in changes in the brain that might render the individual more vulnerable to psychoses in adulthood. Similarly, exposure to (passive) tobacco smoke in infancy or childhood may irreparably damage the cardiovascular and respiratory systems. Second, the approach recognises that experiences across the lifespan can (and indeed do) influence health. While such experiences or exposures may be reversible, unlike those characterising the critical period explanations, accumulated exposures across the lifecourse undoubtedly influence the health experiences of older people. However, it is worth noting that such exposures may be positive as well as negative. Hence, while we predominantly discuss the effects on health of poor diet, a sedentary lifestyle and over-indulgence in alcohol, we must also be mindful that lifestyles based on 'good habits' can bring longlasting beneficial effects. Too often in epidemiology exposures are conceptualised in the negative (for example, exposure to a poor working environment) rather than in the positive. In thinking critically about the critical events hypothesis, it is clear that such events are defined in terms of biological parameters. We would wish to argue that critical *social* events such as redundancy, stress or bereavement may also have negative health consequences for individuals and the impact of such experiences can be both negative and longlasting.

As well as a focus on understanding the onset of specific, mostly chronic diseases such as diabetes or heart disease or the health status of specific subgroups such as older people, the lifecourse approach seeks to integrate the biological, social and environmental influences into this explanatory framework. A lifecourse approach to the understanding of health seeks to integrate the major factors that have empirically been linked to health outcomes but have often been considered in isolation. For example, relationships between ethnicity, gender or class and health status are considered separately when, in reality, individuals occupy a social location that includes all three of those attributes (plus of course a chronological age). These explanatory factors reflect both individual-level influences (such as 'genetic heritage', health behaviours and broadly socioenvironmental factors such as occupational health issues) and macro-level factors (such as developments in healthcare and the ability to access these). While in Britain healthcare is free at the point of delivery, this is not the case for older people in all countries.

The dynamic temporal element that is at the centre of the lifecourse approach is important when trying to understand the current health status of older people and to predict or project the health status of future generations of older people. Understanding health in old age or later life requires an understanding of the experiences of people across their lifetime in terms of both individual experiences and behaviours and the broader macro-sociodemographic context. Individual lives are played out within the historical, political and social welfare context and these factors influence health status and experiences. For example, the creation of the post-war welfare state in Britain, with the creation of a 'free at the point of delivery' healthcare service, means that access to healthcare is very different for those people moving into old age now as opposed to their grandparents where access to healthcare was much more limited.

What is health?

Before proceeding further to consider the health experiences of older people, we first need to establish our 'terms of reference' by considering what we mean by older people and how we define health. To deal with the latter point first – what do we mean when we talk about the concept of 'health' within either an academic context or popular discourse? Like many commonly used words or terms, there are a multitude of different meanings and interpretations encompassed by the term 'health' depending on the context – academic debate or popular discourse – within which it is being used (see Bury and Gabe, 2004). Hence, the term 'health' is used in a variety of different settings, by differing constituencies of users and therefore carries a multitude of differing meanings. Bury (2005) neatly encapsulates the two key elements underpinning the concept of 'health' within the academic arena: orientation and breadth of the definition. So to take the former point first, in terms of orientation we can use the term 'health' in either a positive or negative way – we can be in good or bad health. As we shall see in the substantive chapters dealing with the health status of older people, this positive/negative polarity is reflected in the various measures that we use to describe health at a population level. We can define health very narrowly in terms of a specific organ, such as the heart, or body system, such as the circulatory or respiratory system. Alternatively, we can adopt an expansive perspective by considering the health of a specific population group such as young people or those from specific minority groups or we can use the term at the level of whole societies. So specific populations (or subgroups) may be characterised as 'very healthy' or very unhealthy – an example of the latter being young people in Britain who are characterised as having poor health because of high rates of sexual activity, sexually transmitted diseases, illegal drug use, depression and binge drinking, especially in comparison with their European contemporaries. Again, the breadth of the definition used is reflected in the types of measures we use to record the health of populations.

Before proceeding to the substantive chapters of this book, or defining in detail the population of interest, we first need to summarise the main approaches that academics, policy makers and individuals use to define and understand the term 'health'. This provides the foundation for a critique of the current state of knowledge about the health of older people and debates about the likely health of future generations of elders. This is a necessarily short introduction to a complex subject and interested readers are directed to texts such as those by Bury (2005) for a more detailed exposition. There are a number of different approaches to the definition of health. Here we focus on two key perspectives – the medical model and the sociological approach – as these perspectives are both the most relevant and the most important in shaping our knowledge and understanding of health in later life. They stand as exemplars of the different ways that we can think about health, have broadly informed the theoretical frameworks within which health–related research is conducted and underpin the definition of health in research, policy and practice. As such, they help us to understand and evaluate what we know about health in old age and, perhaps more importantly, what we do not know.

The medical model

One of the most influential ways of thinking about health is the 'medical model'. Medical science and medical knowledge are central to our evidence base concerning health in later life. It is both plausible and defensible to argue that the medical model dominates debates about health and is the dominant paradigm in terms of influencing the research and policy agenda and our evidence/knowledge base about health in old age. This model emerged in the 19th century as medicine and biomedical researchers responded to developments in the scientific understanding of infectious diseases; perhaps the key health challenge researchers then faced (Bury, 2005). The premise of the medical model is the search for the identification of the pathological changes or 'causes' that result in the diseases manifest in individuals. The focus of medical science and research is to identify the pathology of internal organs/bodily functions that generate the symptoms demonstrated by individual patients and to develop interventions and treatments that will ameliorate the identified pathology. As the 20th century progressed, the level at which 'pathology' within the body was identified changed. The initial focus was on whole systems such as the respiratory system, through specific organs such as the lungs to the now contemporary cellular or sub-cellular approach – with specific diseases often being linked to specific genetic defects and the 'solutions' posited to such pathology being similarly microscopic and genetic in nature. Interventions to 'cure' the identified pathology are usually either surgical or medical (that is, pharmaceutical treatments) in nature and specific organs, genes or systems are investigated and 'treated' in isolation from the 'rest' of the body.

The medical model is important both for the dominance of this way of understanding issues to do with health and disease and for the types of knowledge and explanations generated. The focus is on the individual; explanations for disease are sought within the 'body' of that individual. This approach is inherently individualistic and little weight is given to the importance of social and environmental factors in explaining health and disease. The central thrust of the medical model of health is a clear emphasis on health and disease as issues that relate to the individual with little, or no, relationship to the broader socioenvironmental context within which that individual lives. We are encouraged to see health matters as our personal responsibility rather than in a more collective fashion and with structural social, environmental or occupational factors given much less importance in explaining the distribution of (ill-)health across and within populations. This is also a highly reductionist approach to understanding health. Explanations for the presence/absence of disease are sought exclusively in terms of deficits of the body's physiological and biological functions with little, or no, reference to the social, environmental or occupational context. The medical model sees health as divorced from broader psychological processes. Thus, we can see a theoretical situation in which individuals are categorised as healthy/unhealthy by the imposition of an external label (or diagnosis) attributed by a doctor based solely on 'objective' physiological indices, regardless of the state of perceived wellbeing of the individual concerned. Bury (2005) considers that this individually centred reductionist critique of the medical model is overstated. He notes that, although this is probably the dominant explanatory framework, we should not ignore the fact that most contemporary Western societies have an established public health function that focuses on measures to promote and enhance the health of specific populations – such as older people – or indeed whole societies. While this is a valid observation, the role and function of 'the public health' approach within contemporary societies is, unfortunately, marginalised compared with the pre-eminence of the traditional medical model.

A key feature of the medical model is that the treatment of 'health problems' is characterised as being the (sole) province of the medical profession. This focus on health at the individual level, the emphasis on bodily processes and functions and the vesting of authority to 'treat' and care for these conditions in the medical profession constitutes what Foucault (1973) termed the 'medical gaze'. This perspective excludes or marginalises the role of patients such that they are offered merely a 'passive' subservient role in the diagnosis, treatment and management of their condition. By de-emphasising the contribution of 'non-medical' knowledge about health and illness, the medical profession has established medical dominance as the pre-eminent influence on the nature and delivery of healthcare. As a consequence, 'lay 'perspectives and non-medical discourses about health are, at best, marginal.

The emphasis on pathology and the focus of health expertise in the medical profession has led to what Illich (1975) termed the medicalisation of 'natural' processes and events. The most obvious example is childbirth but it also applies to mental illness, the menopause, death and dying and sexuality. Taking the emblematic issue of childbirth and pregnancy, feminists argue that a natural process such as pregnancy and childbirth has been appropriated by the medical profession and a natural, normal part of women's lives has been redefined as an 'illness'. The result is that a 'normal' part of life has become highly regulated and controlled by the medical profession and a manifestation of how women's lives are regulated and controlled within the context of a patriarchal society. This argument emphasises how 'normal' or 'natural' events and processes such as the menopause become redefined as 'abnormal' or 'pathological'. They then become both the province of 'experts' and the subject of research focusing on 'cures' and/ or palliative/therapeutic interventions.

We can argue that 'ageing' and old age demonstrate aspects of this process of medicalisation. A normal process – ageing – has been appropriated by the medical profession and reconstructed as a medical problem requiring medical/expert knowledge and medical solutions (see Estes, 1979, 1989, 2001; Binney et al, 1990). This perspective is paralleled in much of the work in the British gerontological tradition of research, which seeks solutions to the 'problems' of old age as defined by experts (see Victor, 2005). Both Vincent (2003a, 2003b, 2006) and Tulle (2008a) have noted the dominance of biology and medical sciences in the understanding of the ageing body, in the emphasis on pathological aspects and in finding 'cures' for the health problems associated with old age and, also, ageing itself. Estes and Binney (1991) similarly argue that 'ageing' has been medicalised, with the result that older people and old age itself are 'pathologised'. Ageing is constructed as a medical problem with a consequent emphasis on medical research and medically based 'solutions' to the problems of an ageing body, which is seen as (at best) problematic because it does not conform to the norms that are established with reference to the young (male?) body. Tulle (2008a, 2008b, 2008c) develops this argument further by noting that the ageing body is seen as a 'malfunctioning' body and that the focus of research (and debate) has been around mapping the decline of the body and, less actively, in searching for interventions to arrest this decline (and restore function to pre old-age levels). She then proposes that this narrative of decline is applied, by extension, to other spheres of later life and ultimately to older people. Hence, much of the research about ageing and ageing bodies has focused on identifying solutions to a problem – not with understanding the basic processes or looking at aspects of later life that are not 'problems'. 'Medicalisation' of later life can, therefore, be seen to have had a much wider impact than a restricted focus on 'medical matters'. The dominant focus on decline and problems has seeped out from the healthcare sphere to influence wider aspects of old age and later life and influence the broad social context such that old age is 'always' a problem, for both societies and individuals. Old age becomes conceptualised as a problematic stage of life dominated by a discourse of decline and decay and a search for solutions to the problem of pathology (we return to issues of anti-ageing medicine in Chapter Five).

We can see the recent growth of 'anti-ageing' medicine as a manifestation of this process in which we are seeking solutions to the (medical) problem of the normal process of ageing/old age. However, we need to differentiate the process of ageing – that is clearly 'normal' and (currently) inevitable and which starts at birth (!) – from the diseases or pathologies that are manifest by older people (age-related or age-associated diseases). The pioneers of the practice of geriatric medicine in the UK, clinicians such as Marjorie Warren and Lionel Cosin, demonstrated that many of the older people languishing in the-then public hospitals and long-stay wards had treatable medical conditions and were not suffering from the 'inevitable' consequences of old age. The infirmity of this population, they argued, reflected untreated conditions – such as heart failure or a failure to provide rehabilitation after a stroke – rather than the effects of ageing per se. Hence, they were attempting to distinguish between ageing and the diseases associated with ageing. They were focusing on combating a widespread 'health' problem, that is, the neglect of older people, the failure to treat or rehabilitate this population and the failure to distinguish between ageing and pathology. In this instance, we could argue that medicalisation, or at least interest being expressed by the medical profession, was a 'good thing' in that it enabled older people to access health services, get treatment for their health problems and thereby have an improved quality of life and return to the community to live independent lives (and, of course, not to impose a burden on the public purse by living in institutional care settings). As a result of the activities of Warren and colleagues, geriatric medicine became a recognised (or perhaps tolerated) medical specialty that resulted in the creation of Academic Departments of Geriatric Medicine in some medical schools and the appointment of a cadre of high-profile Professors of Geriatric Medicine – in Birmingham (Bernard Isaacs), Cardiff (John Pathy) and Manchester (John Brocklehurst) – who did much to advance the status and understanding of the medicine of old age.

This positive view of the benefits of 'geriatric medicine' is certainly the position held by Ebrahim (2002). He argues that the medicalisation of old age resulted in positive outcomes for older people and proposes that contemporary generations of older people in the UK are being disadvantaged by the de-medicalisation of 'old age' as clinicians have withdrawn from involvement in research, care and treatment of older people. Ebrahim (2002) advances the interesting, if controversial, view that two trends in contemporary healthcare have resulted in the de-medicalisation of old age, with consequent negative outcomes for older people in terms of both healthcare and their status within the healthcare environment. He suggests that hospital-based healthcare has been substituted by care in nursing home settings, provided by less qualified (non-medical) staff and without the infrastructure for rehabilitation etc provided in the modern hospital environment. Problems that were previously defined as being related to 'health' and for whom the appropriate response was care and treatment within a healthcare setting (mostly but not exclusively in hospital) have been redefined as 'social' problems and a different model of care has been invoked. Ebrahim (2002) considers this a retrograde step, in which medicine is denied a legitimate role in the provision of established treatment of older people with clear medical problems (although not defined in those terms). He sees this as a result of medical disinterest in older people, a failure of the medical profession to be interested in the medical problems of old age, and the popularity of the social model of disease. We can also see this as a response to the tightening of the boundaries of medicine, especially in hospitals. There is a greater focus in hospitals on acute illnesses where the emphasis is on cure; active management rather than the palliative care of (irremediable) long-term conditions or managing the multiple pathology so commonly manifest by older people. He argues that the medicalisation of old age is a good thing in so far as it focuses on the treatment of illness, is not fatalistic or accepting of disease in old age, and gives access to healthcare, both palliative and restorative, to a group with significant needs.

What other challenges have been made to the medical model of health? The model is often characterised as a negative one because it focuses predominantly on the identification, diagnosis and treatment of disease but we must recognise the circumstances in which the medical profession operates – people rarely consult a doctor when they are feeling in 'good health' (Bury, 2005). The term 'disease' is usually used to refer to defects or abnormalities in function or structure of any part, process or system of the body. Hence, the explanations of disease within this perspective are conducted in terms of the pathology or suboptimal functioning of bodies. The inherently 'negative' aspect of the medical model is that health is defined by what it is not; that is, health is not having a disease: if you are not 'sick' then you are 'healthy'. This does not articulate a very 'positive' way of thinking about health and the dominant discourse of disease is focused on human biology and its deficits. An implicit (if not explicit) distinction is drawn between the 'objective' signs and symptoms illustrated by a body and how that individual feels about these and their health status more broadly. Within the frame of reference of the medical model it is the objective signs and symptoms that are central to the definition of (ill-)health, not how the individual feels.

At its most simplistic, the medical model of disease understands these as having a specific, and usually, single cause or aetiology. Bury (2005) suggests that this reflects the origins of the medical model in the search for the causes of, and effective treatments for, infectious diseases. He notes that while we can all clearly see this 'traditional' medical model at work in research examining the influences of specific genes in relation to a range of diseases, the contemporary context has modified this approach. He argues that as the majority of contemporary health threats are posed by chronic and degenerative diseases, the 'medical model' now accepts (and indeed embraces) the idea that diagnosis may be probabilistic rather than definitive; that treatment may be palliative rather than curative; and that 'cause' may be multifactorial, complex or even 'unknown' rather than specific. However, this may be an overly optimistic reading of contemporary debates when the dominant explanatory paradigm for so many diseases focuses on genetic factors.

We may conclude this brief summary of the medical model approach to health by illustrating it with the issues of falls and fractures for older people. Falls are a major problem, with 25% of those aged 65 and over reporting that they have fallen in the previous year. There are many sequelae of falls, one of which is fractures. At a simplistic individual or biological/medical level, osteoporosis – a decrease in bone density or bone health that is largely demonstrated by post-menopausal women – is advanced as a 'cause' of fractures in older people. Biologically this is plausible and this then sets a research agenda that focuses on developing a treatment or intervention, often pharmacological, to prevent or reduce osteoporotic bone density loss (and restore bone density). If we look more widely than at the physiologically based bone health of individuals and ask 'what are the causes of osteoporosis in older people?', a new research agenda emerges that considers, for example, the nutrition of older people because adequate dietary calcium is important in protecting against osteoporosis. Thus, we may need to consider the financial resources available to older people as this influences their opportunities to access an adequate diet or to participate in exercise; we may consider issues of mobility or access to food shops. This is a rather different research agenda than the very narrow, specific search for a relationship between bone health and fractures that is characteristic of a 'medical model' approach.

The sociological perspective

It is both simplistic and naïve to label this section 'the sociological perspective'. The sociology of health is a vibrant and extensive discipline of sociology and it embraces many aspects of study. Here we can just highlight the key issues relating to the definition of health from a sociological perspective and some of the issues that this raises for understanding health in old age. The essentially biologically, objectively defined concept of disease, contrasts with the person-centred, subjective approach to the definition of health encapsulated by the sociological term 'illness'. This definitional strategy leaves it to individuals to determine whether they are, or are not, in good physical or mental health. The focus of illness research is to establish the perspective of individuals about their own health status, either globally, in terms of specific conditions, or in terms of acute/chronic problems. The correlation between disease and illness is not perfect. Individuals may be diseased without feeling ill and vice versa. Bury (2005) illustrates the complexity of this link with the example of osteoarthritis of the hip but the point he makes has a wider resonance. Osteoarthritis (OA), as we shall see in Chapter Two, is a disease that is very common among older people, with about 45% of those aged 65 and over reporting symptoms. Hence, individuals (and others) may attribute the signs and symptoms of osteoarthritis as part of normal ageing rather than as a progressive, degenerative disease and may not consider the symptoms to be a 'medical problem'. Individuals are highly variable with regard to when they report symptoms to a medical practitioner. The link between disease progression, as measured by degeneration present in the joint identified by X-ray, and symptoms is far from perfect. Individuals with severe degeneration may report few symptoms, pain and limited functionality of the joint, while those with little evident degeneration may report high levels of symptoms.

The sociological perspective on illness and health focuses on the social processes and forces that underpin the distribution of illness within and between populations. We can differentiate two broad strands within this perspective – the influence of social inequalities or environmental factors in the creation of illness and the production of disease and illness as a result of a complex set of social processes that contextualise the identification, diagnosis and treatment of conditions. Bury (2005) suggests that the latter approach is particularly relevant to chronic diseases where it is not always clear where 'normality' stops and chronic disease starts. This is especially relevant to the study of old age where chronic diseases are reported by about 50% of the population aged 65 and over – indeed we could construct an argument whereby the presence of chronic disease could be seen as normative.

A key debate within the sociological approach to health has been that of the 'social construction' of disability, health and illness. Within sociology there has been a trend for the 'body' to be discounted in debates about health and illness, with an emphasis placed on the influence of the broader social context and the 'social construction' of ill-health. We argue that health and illness are more than social constructs and a sociological view that relies entirely on this means that we ignore the biological, physical and embodied dimensions of the study of health. Consequently, we abandon the study of the 'physical manifestations' of illness/disability to the medical profession and do not subject the (ageing) body to rigorous sociological analysis and scrutiny. Within the field of sociology/ gerontology, several scholars have been active in developing our understanding of the importance of the embodied nature of ageing and later life (see Twigg, 2000a, 2000b; Tulle, 2003, 2007, 2008a, 2008b, 2008c) although they note that social gerontologists, and medical sociologists more broadly, have largely ignored the ageing body. However, researchers are now recognising the centrality of the body to the understanding of later life for, as Tulle (2008a) argues, it is central to understanding ageing as it provides the daily context within which older people experience their daily lives.

Regardless of age, illness presents social consequences for the individual, of which the notion of stigma or spoilt identity is of considerable importance (see Goffman, 1961, for a full exposition). Those with long-term chronic illness can come to acquire a highly stigmatised status as the extensive duration of their illness means that they cannot demonstrate the valued social attributes of independence, autonomy and self-determination. Such groups are negatively evaluated and disempowered via notions of social stigma and stereotyping. A stigmatising status may be ascribed to older people generally because of the perceived widespread prevalence of chronic illness and the way that this can compromise the prized and vital attributes of independence and autonomy in daily life. For example, Werner and Heinik (2008) examined notions of stigma for those caring for people with Alzheimer's disease, an example of stigma by association whereby the negative attributes of those with the condition are transmitted to their carers. One reason for the loss of interest by the medical profession in the care and treatment of older people noted by Ebrahim (2002) is the potential for the transference of stigma from patient to carer and the subsequent loss of status from those who choose to focus on older people in terms of professional practice, education and research.

Reconciling perspectives?

The two major approaches summarised in this chapter, the medical and sociological 'models', stand as exemplars of two approaches towards the understanding of health and illness: the attributional and the relational. The attributional approach, which is most easily linked to the medical model, presupposes that health, disease, illness and disability are attributes of the individual's physical make-up. In contrast, the relational view of health focuses on the influence of social factors and the social context in determining what Bury (2005) terms the 'pattern and expression of illness'. We can illustrate this by returning to the example of osteoarthritis. There is not always a definitive biological disease marker that unambiguously marks the onset of disease. The pathway to the diagnosis of osteoarthritis may involve a number of phases that relate to the individual concerned, including their age, the level of symptoms, their tolerance of symptoms, the assignment of symptoms to other factors, the views of family and friends and access to and involvement with the healthcare system. We can see this tension between relational and attributional definitions of health played out in how we conceptualise disability. We can distinguish between impairment – disturbances of the 'normal' functioning of the body resultant from trauma or disease – and disability – the problems individuals have as a result in performing some normal or usual activities such as mobility or self-care. Bury (2005) comments that disability has 'traditionally' been thought of as an attribute of the individual, not as a 'social construct'. More recently, writers such as Oliver (1996) have differentiated impairment and bodily malfunction from disability, which he argues is wholly relational and is a result of discrimination and oppression. This example serves to illustrate the tension that inevitably exists within these two explanatory frameworks for understanding health and illness and for setting the research agendas that underpin our knowledge of health, ageing and later life. We would support Bury's (2005) view that in order to fully understand health and illness we need to incorporate a dynamic, lifecourse approach and to recognise that both attributional and relational explanatory frameworks have a part to play in this understanding and that their relative importance may vary across the lifecourse. In the remaining chapters of this book, we examine the issues that surround age, health and care for older people – largely defined as those aged 65 and over – locating this where possible within a broader lifecourse and sociocultural context.

Key points

In this chapter we have established the age composition of the UK population and the factors underpinning population ageing. We have introduced key demographic and gerontological terms and the principles underpinning the measurement of disease in populations. We have examined key trends in life expectancy and illustrated how these vary with socioeconomic factors and globally. And we have illustrated how common terms such as 'health' and 'illness' are contested in terms of their definition and how the way such terms are conceptualised influences how they are measured and thus the information we have about the health of older people.

Further activities

▸ For your area, look up the most recent Census data and find out the number of people aged 65-74, 75-84 and 85 and over. What percentage of the total population do they make up? What other data about older people can you find out from the Census? What data can you obtain about the health of older people in your locality?

▸ The development of geriatric medicine (an age-related speciality dedicated to the care of older people) was one of the key innovations of the NHS but has now fallen out of fashion. What do you think are the advantages/disadvantages of this model of care?

▸ At what age is 50% of a birth cohort still alive? Visit http://spreadsheets.google.com/ccc?key=tUbJCqSPdjgRA2OQ1YC0maw

Further reading

Doyle, Y., McKee, M., Rechel, B. and Grundy, E. (2009) 'Meeting the challenge of population ageing', *British Medical Journal*, 339, b3926.

Gileard, C. and Higgs, P. (2009) The power of silver: age and identity politics in the 21st century. *Journal of Aging and Social Policy*, 21, 277-95.

Grundy, E. (2002) Demography and public health. In Detels, R., McEwen, J., Beaglehole, R. and Tanaka, H. (eds) *Oxford textbook of public health* (pp 807-82). Oxford: Oxford University Press.

Higgs, P. and Jones, I.R. (2009) *Medical sociology and old age: Towards a sociology of health in later life.* London: Routledge.

Higgs, P., Leontowitsch, M., Stevenson, F. and Jones, I.R. (2009) Not just old and sick – the 'will to health' in later life. *Ageing and Society*, 29(5), 687-707.

Hyde, M., Higgs, P. and Newman, S. (2009) The health profile of ageing populations. In Newman, S., Steed, E. and Mulligan, K. (ed) *chronic physical illness: Self-management and behavioural interventions.* Maidenhead: Open University Press,

Johnson, M. (ed) (2005) *The Cambridge handbook of age and ageing*, Cambridge: Cambridge University Press.

Taylor, S. and Field, D. (eds) (2007) *Sociology of health and healthcare* (4th edition). Oxford: Blackwell.

Useful websites

- *Government Actuaries Department – for population projections:* www.gad.gov.uk/Demography%20Data/
- *United Nations Programme on Ageing:* www.un.org/esa/socdev/ageing/
- *Data from the 2001 Census:* www.statistics.gov.uk/census2001/census2001.asp
- *Old age from the inside! A selection of older bloggers:* http://threescoreplusten.blogspot.com/
- www.timegoesby.net/
- http://jenett.org/ageless/
- *Ageing Britain:* www.guardian.co.uk/uk/series/ageing-britain
- *UK population data:* www.statistics.gov.uk/cci/nugget.asp?ID=949
- *Summary of official statistics about older people:* www.statistics.gov.uk/focuson/olderpeople/
- *Survey of Health, Ageing and Retirement Europe (SHARE):* www.share-project.org/

TWO

Health and mortality

Key points

In this chapter we consider:

- sources of data describing health (in old age) in Britain;
- theoretical and methodological aspects of measuring health in populations;
- patterns of mortality in later life and compare these with morbidity data;
- the extent of undiagnosed illness among older people;
- variations in levels of mortality and morbidity among older people.

'I suppose health's the main thing, cause you've got no quality of life if you haven't got your health have you?', thus wrote one of the participants in Bowling's (2005: 118) study of the definition and constitution of quality of life in old age. Consistently, empirical studies identify health as the main variable associated with wellbeing and quality of life across the age ranges. This is not an association that is seen only among older people, as the work of Bowling and Gabriel (2004) demonstrates. Why is health so important, especially to older people? We noted in Chapter One that the onset of chronic ill-health or a disability may be one of the 'cues' to indicate the onset of 'old age'. Bond and Corner (2004) suggest that, as well as reminding us all of our impending mortality, ill-health is associated with loss of autonomy and independence, which in the case of chronic conditions may be longstanding. These abstract academic concerns with notions such as autonomy and independence are put into context by comments from older people such as 'Having my health and a reasonable standard of living. Well they both give you the freedom to do what you want. You are not dependent on anyone ....' and 'I think that number one is having good health.... Because without that you are restricted....' (Bowling, 2005: 127). Poor health compromises quality of life in two major ways. First, there are the direct effects resultant from the actual symptoms and physical consequences of the condition, such as breathlessness as a result of heart failure or the pain and joint stiffness of arthritis, which can compromise quality of life as a result of pain and distress. These are real experiences, not social constructs. However, equally important are the secondary, perhaps indirect, social consequences resultant from such conditions such as limited mobility, inability to drive or not being fit enough to partake in the social and leisure activities that people want to. Good health is important in its own right but also for what it enables individuals to do especially in terms of maintaining control over daily life and in terms of autonomy and choice. Poor health is clearly a barrier to participation and engagement with daily life and is a major factor in social exclusion (see Victor et al, 2009).

However, the definition of 'health' is both complex and contested. Blaxter (2004a, 2004b) conceptualises health as a 'reserve' of three separate dimensions – vitality, fitness and strength – which enable individuals to achieve their (social) goals. From this perspective, health is both a biological attribute and a relational attribute mediated by the social, environmental and historical context. Furthermore, Blaxter (2004a, 2004b) views health as a dynamic entity that varies across both historical time and individual biological time, with different elements of the three components of 'health' varying in importance across the lifecourse. The World Health Organization model offers an idealistic vision of health as a state of complete physical, social and psychological wellbeing, which acknowledges the link between mind and body and the importance of social and environmental factors (WHO, 1946). The recognition of the importance of 'social health' for both individuals and populations is, or was at the time, highly innovative. Older people's views of health resonate with the World Health Organization model of health as a state of physical, social and psychological wellbeing and they acknowledge the link between mind (mental health and wellbeing) and body (physical health, functional performance and 'fitness'). While in this book we certainly embrace the link between physical and mental wellbeing, we review each of these dimensions individually. In this chapter we focus on physical health problems, Chapter Three focuses on disability and the consequences of (ill-) health, Chapter Four discusses mental health and wellbeing, while the final chapter examines the debates concerning the (likely) health status of future generations of older people.

Health in old age and later life (or indeed any other phase of life) reflects the complex interaction of five major factors:

- genetic heritage and biology;
- individual behaviours (such as diet, exercise and smoking);
- exposure to environmental and occupational hazards;
- social context such as gender, ethnicity and social class; and
- access to, availability and quality of health and social care services.

Health in old age represents the outcome of the complex interaction between both micro-level individual factors and macro-level social and environmental factors as well as factors concerning the organisation of health (and social) care. In this chapter we examine the health status of older people, focusing on physical health indicators, and consider how the experience of health in later life is shaped by macro (social) factors such as gender, class and ethnicity.

ACTIVITY 1

‣ How would you define healthy ageing?

‣ How would you define successful ageing?

‣ Do you think an older person would define these concepts differently and why? In what ways might they define these concepts differently?

Measuring health

As we noted in the Introduction, health is a complex and contested notion. With that complexity come difficulties in deciding how (precisely) to operationalise, empirically measure and record health status in any meaningful way. This complexity is enhanced when we integrate older people's perspectives into the empirical mix. Within the literature there are several distinct approaches to health. There are data collected on patterns of death (usually referred to as mortality) and data collected on disease, symptoms and illnesses – either physical or mental (usually referred to as morbidity). With both of these approaches there is a focus on the 'negative', with those in 'good health' being identified by the absence of the factor measured or recorded. There are also a range of generic and disease-specific health-related quality-of-life measures, which adopt a more positive approach to measuring health. In this chapter we examine mortality and morbidity for specific physical diseases and acute (short-term self-limiting conditions) and chronic (long-term) conditions at a population or group level of analysis. We do not stray into issues of diagnosis, prognosis or treatment; these are the province of clinicians and interested readers are referred elsewhere to key texts in nursing (Redfern and Ross, 2006), geriatric medicine (Grimley Evans et al, 2000) and healthcare (Kydd et al, 2009). A particular feature of our approach is providing a population perspective on the health of older people as a way of establishing broad health needs and explicitly articulating the variations within the population, which all too often is still treated as a single homogeneous group, especially in terms of identifying needs and developing interventions and services to respond to these. By differentiating the population into relevant constituent elements and examining variations in health, we can start to address the veracity of two pernicious stereotypes – that all old people are 'ill' and that all old people are alike – and, as a consequence, a single uniform service solution is all that is required.

Sources of health data

There are a range of data sources from which we can derive information about the health of older people. We can use administrative data about utilisation of services but this is problematic because not all those with a health need are known to the service provision agencies. Much of the data used to describe and monitor the health of older people in Britain is derived from large sample surveys of either the general adult population or those focusing specifically on older people (which are based on taking a statistically representative and robust sample of the population), the Census (which involves collection of data from every member of the population) and vital statistics recording systems that cover the whole population in terms of births, deaths and (re)marriages. There are a number of general issues with these data sources, which require articulation. First, with regard to the generic sources, especially vital statistics and the national Census, they are not specific to older people and therefore are not focused on issues relating to older people. Second, many of these data sources fulfil national-level policy objectives in that they are used to monitor and inform the development and achievement of social welfare policy and policy objectives nationally. For example, the origin of the Health Survey for England derives from the need to monitor achievement of the Health of the Nation targets established in 1992 as a strategic approach to improving the nation's health (for a review of this policy, see www.publications.doh.gov.uk/pub/docs/doh/exec.pdf) rather than the more expansive health survey function, which it has subsequently evolved into.

The first recognisably modern Census in Britain, including the home nations of England, Wales, Scotland, the Channel Islands and the Isle of Man, took place on the 10 March 1801. Key factors in the genesis of this social research innovation were concerns about the number of men of 'fighting age' (this was during the Napoleonic wars, and government war planning wanted to know the number of military-age men and sailors in the population) and a lack of knowledge about the size of the total population and the trajectory of change (especially in the light of the writings of Thomas Malthus and the concerns about the ability to feed the population). The example of the now compulsory decennial Census in Britain illustrates how such data collection exercises change and develop in response to the development of national policy concerns at differing time points. For example, questions relating to health have not been present in every Census sweep nor are questions asked consistently over time (although the broad topic area may remain constant). In terms of health measures, the Census has asked about a range of different factors at differing historical time points. In 1851, the questions were about sensory impairments (blindness, deafness and 'dumbness'); in 1871, the questions were about the presence of 'imbeciles, idiots and lunatics'; while in 2001, the Census asked about longstanding illness or disability, health rating as well the provision of care to dependent people. We present this as an example of how national-level data collection varies in response to changes in the social and welfare context over time. Hence, when reading and interpreting data deriving from such nationally based datasets, we need to consider why those specific questions were thought important at specific time points. It is also important to note the issues that are not addressed in such surveys and datasets as, again, this links to the perceived importance of specific health issues at particular times.

Before proceeding to provide an overview of the health of older people in contemporary Britain, a further methodological caveat relating to several of the key sources used in this book should be noted. Datasets such as the General Household Survey (GHS) in Britain, which covers all adults, the Health Survey for England (HSE), or surveys focusing on older people in Britain (the English

Longitudinal Study of Ageing: ELSA), Europe (Survey of Health and Retirement Europe: SHARE) or the US (Health and Retirement Survey: HRS) collect a substantial amount of health data via interviews and self-report. Respondents may be asked if they have been told by a doctor in the last year that they are suffering from a specific condition such as diabetes; they are not assessed individually by a doctor nor is a detailed clinical examination undertaken, although some clinical measurements such as lung function or blood pressure may be conducted. Thus, the accuracy of the level of, for example, diabetes in a community generated by this approach relies on the individual (a) having consulted their general practitioner (GP), (b) remembering that they were given a diagnosis of diabetes and (c) being able to recall this information in the interview situation and in the format required by the interview. Some surveys such as ELSA include a clinical module that will include the collection of blood samples, which will be examined back in a laboratory for key markers such as cholesterol, a record of lung function and the completion of simple tests such as measuring height/weight, timed walks or grip strength. However, these data and measurements are collected for clinical prevalence studies and are not intended to be diagnostic for the individual although, of course, there is an ethical protocol to be observed when previously undetected disease is identified. The approach in these surveys is that respondents are asked a series of questions about their health and it is responses to these questions that provide a substantial amount of the evidence base for the generic health status of older people. There is an important semantic caveat to the interpretation of these types of data. The data gathered describe syndromes or symptoms such as forgetfulness, joint pain/impaired mobility or depressive symptomatology rather than clinically diagnosed conditions such as dementia, depression or arthritis.

It is essential that the questions used to gather these health data are robust and demonstrate good reliability (that is, responses are stable) and validity (that is, the questions actually capture the concept that they are attempting to measure). In longitudinal studies we also need the questions or measures used to be sensitive to change and to be free from floor/ceiling effects. In the case of health surveys, we may be trying to record a health behaviour such as smoking or participation in physical activity; the symptoms of a specific clinical condition such as depression or dementia; or a more general concept such as chronic disease or health-related quality of life. Hence, as users of such data we need to assure ourselves that the questions used do actually measure either the specific disease entity that we are interested in or the more general health-related concepts such as quality of life or wellbeing or lifestyle/behaviours such as diet and physical exercise.

It is helpful to consider a specific example to illustrate the process that underpins the development of these health-related measures. While our examples relate to older people, the points raised have wider resonance to the study of health in populations. Depression is an important but under-recognised (and potentially under-treated) aspect of the health of older people. Researchers and policy makers are interested in establishing how many older people have depression;

what the 'risk factors' for experiencing depression are; what the 'natural history' of depression is (how long it lasts, what its severity is, etc); and what we can do to prevent older people from becoming depressed or treat effectively those who succumb to this condition. One way to determine the extent of depression among older people would be to see how many consult a psychiatrist for this problem by reviewing clinical/service use records. There are several problems with this approach because it is reliant on (a) the older person consulting their GP about depression, which requires them (or a friend/relative) to identify their condition or symptoms as a 'disease' and not a part of 'normal' ageing, (b) the GP recognising it as such and (c) the GP referring them to a psychiatrist. Similarly, relying on GP consultations or the prescribing of anti-depressants requires the older person to consult and the GP to recognise and treat the condition. Relying on such data sources to generate estimates of the extent of depression within the population is compromised by both (a) the failure of older people to consult and (b) the failure of GPs to recognise the condition and refer and/or treat. Furthermore, if we then rely on clinical/administrative records to examine potential risk factors, we are limited by the information recorded in the notes/records and such details as bereavement or ethnicity may not be systematically recorded. Clinical and administrative records are just that – they record details of the management and treatment of the patients: they are not designed as research tools although they may be used in research studies, which are inevitably limited by the original purpose of the sources used. Hence, our estimate of the prevalence of depression based on these sources will (a) (probably) be an underestimate and (b) (probably) be biased towards the severe end of the disease spectrum.

A population-based survey can overcome many of the biases inherent in relying on consultation data. We could, therefore, send a trained psychiatrist to visit every older person (or a robust statistical sample) in a specific population or locality and conduct the appropriate clinical interview. However, this would be a very expensive strategy so it is more usual to devise a set of questions that will be able to identify depressed older people and that can be used in a survey setting by trained interviewers (or for self-completion). These questions would need to be able to distinguish the depressed from the non-depressed and not misattribute general characteristics that are common among the older population, such as bereavement or living alone, as depression. Where we have a continuous score from this series of questions we need to be able to establish 'cut-off points' that accurately differentiate the group into depressed versus non-depressed. We need a measure that does not incorrectly label non-depressed people as depressed (that is, generate false positives) or depressed people as non-depressed (that is, generate false negatives). These are attributes that are a prerequisite of population screening tests, such as the cervical and breast cancer screening services, and are known as sensitivity and specificity respectively.

We can illustrate these points with reference to a widely used measure of depression in studies of older people: the Geriatric Depression Scale (GDS). The GDS is widely used in population studies of older people because it has the requisite scientific robustness, is acceptable to study participants and, with the 15-item version, takes only about five minutes to complete. It started out as a set of 100 questions used to assess depression derived from clinical interviews/ judgement, to which respondents answered either yes or no. This was clearly an extensive question list and there was the possibility of redundancy and duplication of questions combined with issues of the burden that such a long set of items imposes on respondents. Thus, researchers strived to develop measures that contained the minimum number of items required to obtain robust estimates and to maximise sensitivity and specificity. Testing and refinement resulted in the number of questions being reduced to 30 and there is now a 15-item version. The initial work in developing the scale involved comparing the performance of the measure with older people hospitalised with depression, and therefore with a secure clinical diagnosis, and those living in the community with no history of depression. Here the scale developers were testing the ability of the measure to correctly distinguish the depressed from the non-depressed. In this type of scale, the scores given for the response to each question are added up to generate an overall score with a range of 0 to 100. Consequently, a 'cut-off point score' is needed at which to distinguish between depression and non-depression. Scores between 0 and 10 are characterised as in the normal range and scores of 11 or more are taken as indicative of depressive symptomatology and this yields an 84% sensitivity rate (that is, the test/measure correctly identifies an individual with depression in 84% of instances) and a 95% specificity rate (that is, the ability to correctly classify a non-depressed person as not having depression in 95% of cases). However, we can see from these rates that the measure demonstrates some inaccuracy and this needs to be factored into any analysis and interpretation of the results so that we can establish the 'precision' of our prevalence estimates. Again, we must reiterate that a score of 11 or more on the GDS is not saying that an individual is clinically depressed but that they demonstrate symptoms suggestive of being depressed; the score is not a clinical diagnosis. In some measures the range is divided into three categories: non-depressed; borderline and depressed. The creation of a borderline category reflects some of the uncertainty inherent in these types of population-based survey measures. So when we are looking at data reporting the distribution of health problems within populations, these are the types of data that question/scale developers need to produce. For many commonly used general questions, however, such a process of development and psychometric robustness is not always undertaken. Hence, we must always exercise a degree of caution and scepticism when reviewing and analysing health data derived from population surveys.

Mortality: a paradoxical health measure

Thus far we have concentrated on some of the principles underlying how to measure health status in populations. Ideally, measures to describe the health of populations should be able to facilitate comparisons between and within groups, between whole populations (including internationally) and at different historical time points. It is the ultimate paradox of health research that the indicator that comes closest to these requirements is mortality data or information concerning the distribution of patterns of death. By using data about deaths to describe the health of the population, we are presuming that the patterns observed mirror those for the distribution of health. We assume that the distribution, in terms of age, class, gender or ethnicity and causes of mortality mirror those for morbidity. We will test the veracity of this assumption in the later part of this chapter and in Chapters Three and Four.

Official registration of births, deaths and marriages in England and Wales began on 1 July 1837. These are often collectively referred to as 'vital statistics'. Registration of deaths is compulsory and is almost certainly complete in the UK in that it is impossible to die without a certificate! The death certificate lists when and where a person died, their name, gender, date of birth (or age on older certificates), occupation and address, as well as information about the person who reported the death. The certificate records cause of death (for example, myocardial infarction), underlying cause (for example, ischemic heart disease) and contributory causes (for example, chest infection). The compiling of details drawn from each individual certificate forms the basis of aggregate national data about mortality in the UK.

Within the UK we can be confident that we hold complete data about the number of deaths. However, uncertainties can creep in around the calculation of death rates, which require both numbers of deaths (numerator) and the total number of people (in the age-gender group) (the denominator). We need accurate population data in order to develop a robust commentary on patterns of mortality. Within the UK the decennial Census establishes a virtually complete enumeration of the population. However, between censuses we rely on population estimates and these can become inaccurate the further away from the initial Census date that we progress. We might speculate that inter-Census estimates of the size of the older population are more robust than those for younger age groups in that they are less likely to be influenced by in/out migration. Finally, if we are using death certificate data to describe the types of health problems within populations then we need to be confident that the individual causes of death are correctly identified. Although the degree of error is uncertain, there are inaccuracies in death certification (Johansson and Westerling, 2000, Johansson et al, 2006, 2009; Mathers et al, 2005) and these inaccuracies are most common among the older population. This therefore reminds us to be cautious when interpreting trends in sources of mortality over time as the historical analysis of causes of death can be problematic because of variation in medical practice and knowledge and changes in how different causes of death are classified.

Describing and analysing the health of older people: patterns of mortality

During 2008, there were 509,000 deaths registered in England and Wales, of which 266,000 (52%) were males and 243,000 were females, compared with 551,585 in 1901. This serves to re-emphasise the substantial decrease in death rates that there has been in Britain over the last century. The vast majority of deaths registered in 2008 were accounted for by older people: deaths at age 65 and over accounted for 83% of the total and those aged 85 and over accounted for 35% of the total (a total of 182,000). 'Premature' mortality, deaths between the ages of 16 and 64 are increasingly rare from a population perspective, accounting for 16% of deaths with deaths in childhood accounting for 1%. Victor (2005) has drawn attention to the changing age profile of mortality and this trend is continuing, with mortality being increasingly prevalent in the later phases of the lifecourse. In 1901 in England and Wales, some 40% of all deaths were accounted for by children aged 0–14, with a further 44% accounted for by those aged 65 and over. While there may be some inaccuracies in this mortality age profile because birth registration only became a legal requirement in 1841 and potentially there could be some doubts about the true ages of this over-65 group, it is unlikely to radically distort the distribution. Indeed, if there is any error it is likely to overestimate the number of deaths of people aged 65 and over. This elegantly illustrates how reductions in deaths and death rates in infancy and childhood have served to change the distribution of death within society and the whole way that we as a society think about death. Perhaps the increasing prevalence of death in the later phases of life, rather than it being more equally distributed across the lifecourse, has contributed to the development of negative stereotypes of old age. One conclusion we can draw from the previous analysis is that the bulk of societies' health problems (as measured by mortality) are experienced by older people, and that at a population level, ill–health is comparatively rare among the rest of the population. Thus, in terms of 'health needs' we could argue that it is older people who demonstrate the 'greatest needs' and that they should form the focus of health service expenditure and activities.

We have thus far focused on examining the absolute distribution of deaths within the population. However, the kinds of changes we have observed may simply reflect the change in the composition of our population. Thus, as we started to discuss in Chapter One, we can examine how health and illness are distributed across the population by looking at age- and gender-specific death rates and, in order to do this accurately, we need to have information about the size of these differing population subgroups as noted previously. This is (relatively) straightforward for age-gender groups but becomes more problematic for other population subgroups. Using data for 2005, Table 2.1 shows that the pattern of mortality across the population demonstrates a classic J-shaped distribution. The first year of life is clearly relatively hazardous as mortality rates are (relatively) high at about 5 per 1,000 live births but then decrease and are low at less than 1 per 1,000 population until about the age of 45 from when mortality rates increase by a factor of three for each 10-year age grouping (see Table 2.1). Manton (1986, 1999) suggests that the pattern of mortality in mid and later life (that is, post 45 years) is influenced by two interacting sets of factors: senescence (or the rate of 'natural ageing') and the distribution of risk factors for specific diseases such as heart disease or cancer within populations, for example the prevalence of smoking, obesity, lack of exercise or environmental/occupational health hazards. However, it is not clear from such aggregate-level data as to the relative contribution of these differing (or complementary) explanatory frameworks or whether they operate differentially within age, gender, class and ethnicity subgroups. However, this identification of behavioural and lifestyle factors in explaining the patterns of mortality in later life suggests that senescence and/or genetic heritage offer only a partial explanation for observed patterns of health in later life. This also offers up the possibility that, if behavioural/lifestyle factors are important in influencing the pattern of mortality in later life, then this distribution may change as younger age groups, with different risk profiles, move into old age.

Another key trend is evident from Table 2.1 and that is the higher death rates demonstrated by men as compared with women. At all ages, men demonstrate mortality rates that are higher than their female counterparts. This excess is especially prominent for the 15–34 age groups (although the rates are low in both groups and absolute numbers are small). For those aged between 65 and 84

Table 2.1: Death rates by age and gender, England and Wales, 2005

Age	Rate per 1,000		
	M	F	M/F ratio
Under 1	6.0	4.0	1.5
1-4	0.2	0.2	1.0
5-9	0.1	0.1	1.0
10-14	0.1	0.1	1.0
15-19	0.4	0.2	2.0
20-24	0.6	0.3	2.0
25-34	0.8	0.4	2.0
35-44	1.5	0.9	1.6
45-54	3.6	2.4	1.5
55-64	8.9	5.6	1.5
65-74	24.0	15.4	1.5
75-84	67.4	48.1	1.4
85+	171.6	152.7	1.1
All ages	9.9	9.3	1.1

Source: ONS (2006, table 4)

years, the male mortality rate excess is in the order of 50%, with this differential decreasing to 10% for the over–85 age group. Thus, a key finding from the analysis of mortality data is that men have worse health than women and that the very young and the very old experience the highest (relative) mortality rates and thus the worst health.

As well as age and gender there are other sociodemographic factors that shape and contextualise our lives and which are associated with the distribution of health and illness within contemporary society. Marmot (2008) demonstrates very powerfully that profound inequalities in health remain a feature of the global landscape and social class-based inequalities are a pervasive and stubborn feature of British society although Wilkinson and Pickett (2009) argue that inequalities in health, and other social outcomes, are neither universal nor inevitable. Social class within the UK context is usually operationalised in terms of the classification of occupations – a system first reported nationally in 1911 and which has become an established component of British social research. Thus, there is a well-established body of empirical work demonstrating how socioeconomic status is associated with health outcomes, especially infant mortality, premature mortality and expectation of life and the probability of reaching old age (see DH, 2009). The Black Report on health inequalities (Black, 1980) is an exemplar of this approach, carefully enumerating how occupationally-based measures of social class are very strongly linked with health and other aspects of life chances such as educational achievement. As well as documenting the link between class and mortality, there is also a body of work examining whether social class gradients in mortality in the UK are increasing, decreasing or remaining stable (see Mitchell et al, 2000; Davey Smith et al, 2002; Ramsay et al, 2008). However, the focus in much of this work has been on socioeconomic differentials in premature adult mortality/ infant mortality. Socioeconomic differentials in mortality in later life have been the subject of much less attention although, as we can see, these now account for almost all of the deaths in the UK. We suggest that part of this (relative) neglect reflects the problems involved in attributing a 'social class' location to those who are no longer part of the labour force (see Grundy and Holt, 2001; Bowling, 2004). Which is the best measure of socioeconomic position to use in studies with older people? Within the UK, Grundy and Holt (2001) suggest that deprivation indicators should be paired with either class (as measured by occupation) or educational qualifications. Applying an occupationally based class typology to older women is problematic given that many may not have worked in the formal labour market or only in a very limited way. This latter issue may become less problematic as future cohorts of older women are likely to have had higher rates of, and longer engagement with, the formal labour market. Whether the type of often part-time work that many women participate in 'accurately' reflects their class position or is adequately dealt with by this type of typology is another issue. Thus, there has been a search for other indicators to use to profile what might be broadly termed 'social position' such as housing tenure or education. In addition, there has been, until fairly recently, an implicit and perhaps uncritical assumption that 'older people' can be conceptualised as a single homogeneous social category. The use of categories such as '65 years and older' in reports and policy documents inadvertently (perhaps) created an impression that this population subgroup did not demonstrate the socially based differentials in terms of age, gender and class so characteristic of the rest of British society. Given the pervasive effect of social class on a whole swathe of life chances in Britain, it seems highly unlikely that such differentials will disappear on entering old age. However, applying a social class or social status attributional system to older people is not a new issue. Albrecht (1951) raised these issues in her studies of changes in social status across the lifecourse and accurately profiling the social position of older people remains a challenge for social researchers: a challenge that is compounded when we want to make comparisons either over time or across different societies.

What, if any, is the evidence for class-based differentials in mortality being continued into later life? Using a variety of differing datasets such as 'routine' mortality data or the follow-up of specific cohorts, evidence that class-based inequalities persist into later life is robust. The precise extent of the differential is variable, reflecting the influence of the original data sources and the way that social position is defined (see Avlund et al, 2003). Nazroo et al (2009), analysing deaths reported for ELSA participants, demonstrated inequalities in mortality for both men and women aged over 50 using three measures of 'class': occupational class, educational qualifications and wealth. The mortality differentials in old age reported by Nazroo et al (2009) are not trivial. For men aged 60-74, death rates for those with a degree were (approximately) 40% lower than those without any educational qualification; managerial and professional workers had mortality rates that were 43% lower than their counterparts from manual jobs and those in the highest wealth quintile (top 20%) had a mortality rate that was a third (36%) that of the poorest group. These were reduced but still evident for males aged 75 and over where the mortality differential between the educational groupings was 32%; 22% for the class-based typology and 45% for the wealth categories. Given the established problems of employing these typologies to women, can we determine class-based health inequalities in later life? Looking first at the 60-74 age group, Nazroo et al (2009) reported mortality differentials of 63% for education 43% for social class and 84% for wealth compared with differentials of 40% for education, 32% for class and 43% for wealth for women aged 75 and over. Again, while the size of some of these differentials may be influenced by small cell counts, we cannot attribute all of these differentials to artefact or measurement error. So while differentials may decrease across old age they remain present even at the oldest age groups (see also Victor, 1991; Jyhlä and Luukkaala, 2006). The indicators used as measures of socioeconomic position are to some degree context specific. It remains to be seen whether the utility of specific measures varies as new cohorts, with differing experiences of education, occupational histories and housing markets, enter old age.

Are such differentials unique to the UK, a reflection of our specific social structure? Huisman et al (2004) present an overview of socioeconomic differential in mortality among older people in a range of European countries (Austria, Barcelona, Belgium, Denmark, England, Finland, France, Madrid, Norway, Switzerland, Turin and Wales) and attempt to (a) make comparisons across countries and (b) examine how these differentials in later life compare with younger age groups. They operationalise socioeconomic status in terms of housing tenure (essentially public versus private ownership) and education (based around qualifications and post-compulsory education) in an attempt to find indicators that have validity across a range of countries, which are appropriate to the older age group and facilitate comparison with younger populations. These authors demonstrate that there are significant socioeconomic inequalities among older people observable across countries from both Southern and Northern Europe and that these are more evident for educational status than for housing tenure. In terms of educationally based inequalities, Huisman et al (2004) demonstrate that at age 80-89, rates of mortality for the least educated men and women in Britain are 28% and 7% higher than their better-educated contemporaries. This lower differential for women may reflect the limited educational opportunities available to women of this age group where post-compulsory education was achieved by very few members of the cohort rather than the unimportance of socioeconomic status to the health experience of older women. Indeed, Huisman et al (2004: 471) observe: 'Among men, the relative inequalities (rate ratios) were lower among the elderly than among the middle aged in all populations, with the exception of England and Wales, where the largest inequalities were observed at ages 60-69'. This differential was 61%. Although we should be cautious in drawing too many inferences from this single piece of work, it does seem reasonable to conclude that while health inequality decreases with age it is not eradicated. That the maintenance of socioeconomic differentials is not inevitable is illustrated by the case of Norway where, for both men and women, socioeconomic mortality differentials decrease in old age. In generating a profile of the health experiences of older people, then, on the basis of mortality data we can conclude that (a) health status decreases with increase in age from about the age of 45 onwards, (b) health in old age is better for women than for men and (c) those at the bottom of the socioeconomic hierarchy have worse health in old age than those from more privileged backgrounds (and indeed are less likely to reach old age).

These variations in mortality rates are reflected in a differential expectation of life by occupation class in the UK. The probability of reaching 'old age' is also linked to social class (Table 2.2). There is a seven-year differential in life expectancy at birth for men (80 years versus 73 years) and women (85 years versus 78 years) between the top and bottom of the class hierarchy. For those who reach the age of 65 years, there is then a four-year differential in further expectation of life across the class hierarchy. So not only is there a differential by social class in the chances of reaching 65 years, there is also a further differential in life expectancy from this age onwards. Increases in life expectancy at birth/age 65 since 1972 have served to maintain class differentials and not reduced them. In combination with the data on mortality, the expectation of life data confirm that there is, within contemporary Britain, a significant health divide based around class in terms of achieving old age and in the amount of life to be enjoyed once having achieved old age, and there is no evidence to indicate that these differentials have decreased over the last three decades.

Table 2.2: Life expectancy by social class, England and Wales, 1972-2005

Males				
Social class	Birth		Age 65+	
	1971	2005	1971	2005
1	71.9	80.0	14.0	18.3
2	71.9	79.4	13.3	18.0
3 non-manual	69.5	78.4	12.6	17.4
3 manual	70.0	76.5	12.2	16.3
4	68.3	75.7	12.2	15.7
5	66.5	72.7	11.6	14.1
All non-manual	71.2	79.2	13.9	17.6
All manual	69.1	75.9	12.1	15.9
All classes	69.3	77.0	12.3	16.6
Females				
Social class	Birth		Age 65+	
	1971	2005	1971	2005
1	79.0	85.1	19.1	22.0
2	71.1	83.2	17.2	21.0
3 non-manual	78.3	82.4	17.9	19.9
3 manual	75.2	80.5	16.4	18.7
4	75.3	79.9	16.9	18.9
5	74.2	78.1	16.6	17.7
All non-manual	77.7	82.9	17.5	20.5
All manual	75.2	80.0	16.6	18.6
All classes	75.3	81.1	16.3	19.4

Source: ONS (2008, tables 1 and 3)

Thus, in terms of mortality, social class exerts a strong influence on the chances of reaching old age and on the health experience of older people. These data also demonstrate that health gains, as reflected in a variety of different measures including expectation of life, are rarely equitably distributed across the population. Here we can see that those from the most privileged occupational classes are the most likely to benefit from increased life expectancy. These data eloquently and succinctly demonstrate the enormous influence that social economic status has on the health experience of older people and, by extension, other aspects of later life. While there are no comparable data on ethnicity, it seems highly unlikely that increases in life expectancy, improved mortality and probability of surviving to reach 'old age' will have been shared equally across the major ethnic groups. However, the use of life expectancy as a measure is limited as it tells us nothing about the quality or health status of these lives. We shall return to this issue in Chapter Three when we consider issues of disability and dependency.

Social class, age and gender are established dimensions of social differentiation within British society. Ethnicity is a newly-emerging and developing source of health inequality, reflecting the changing nature of our population as we embrace ethnicity and cultural diversity. One of the key changes in the nature of old age in Britain is the 'ageing' of our migrant communities. There are still comparatively few older people who are drawn from the migrant communities who moved to the UK between 1948 and the 1980s. Infant mortality data are published for minority ethnic communities within the UK and hint at the types of differentials that (probably) characterise later life. In 2007, the infant mortality rate for children born to 'White British' parents was 4.5 per 1,000 compared with over 9 per 1,000 for several minority ethnic communities (9.8 per 1,000 for the Caribbean community; 9.6 for the Pakistani community; 6.0 for the African community; 5.8 for the Indian community; and 4.0 for the Bangladeshi community). Thus, with the exception of the Bangladeshi community, infant mortality rates are between 30 and 100% higher among minority ethnic communities compared with the general population. Are these mortality differentials maintained across the lifecourse and into later life? There are very well-established mortality differentials by race in the US and between ethnic groups in some European states (see, for example, Bos et al, 2004) but, as Jarman and Aylin (2004) observe, until ethnicity is accurately and completely recorded on death certificates in the UK we can only speculate as to the range and direction of inequalities in adult death rates between and within ethnic groups in the UK.

Identifying key health problems: cause of death

ACTIVITY 2

▶ What do you think are the biggest causes of death among older people?

▶ What do you think would have been the major causes of death in Britain in 1850?

We are using mortality data as a proxy measure of health on the assumption that the patterns revealed mirror those for more positive but harder-to-measure definitions of health. We can conclude that health (broadly) decreases with age; and that men are least likely to reach old age than women and experience worse health than women in old age. Similarly, the most disadvantaged within society are less likely to reach old age than their more privileged contemporaries and experience worse health in old age if they achieve this status. Evidence concerning ethnicity and health and ageing is, for the UK, less robust but we may speculate that ethnicity is also linked with both the chances of achieving old age and the experience of health in old age. Of course, this is a very univariate way of conceptualising society as we are treating each dimension of social differentiation – age, class, gender and ethnicity – separately when in fact they all intersect. The work by Bos et al (2004) is one of the few examples of the analysis of mortality that attempts to examine both ethnicity and socioeconomic status. It is a weakness of much routine data that they do not easily facilitate the multiple analysis of disadvantage when it is clear that we do not live our lives in a unidimensional fashion. It is also important to examine whether multiple disadvantage (and of course advantage) are additive or multiplicative in their effects.

We can use data about causes of death to identify the key health problems within populations. For those aged 65 years and over, data for 2005 indicate that the major causes of death and hence the biggest health problems in later life are as follows: circulatory diseases – heart disease and strokes – accounted for 39% of male deaths and 38% of female deaths; cancers accounted for 29% and 21% of deaths respectively and respiratory diseases another 15% and 16% of deaths respectively. Overall, these three causes of death accounted for 83% of male deaths and 76% of female deaths. Conversely, mental health problems accounted for about 1.5% of deaths and musculoskeletal problems considerably less than 1% of deaths. Thus, these data suggest that mental health problems and musculoskeletal disorders are relatively unimportant health problems in later life when considered at the population level, rather than individual level, of analysis. We will evaluate this conclusion when we consider issues of morbidity, disability and mental health problems in the remainder of this chapter and in Chapters Three and Four.

Health in later life: morbidity

For all the advantages of mortality rates as a robust measure of health status, there are limitations to this measure; in particular, the presumption that death rates accurately describe the health status of the population, identify the key health differentials and characterise the key health problems. More fundamentally, death rates tell us nothing about those who are not dead! So how should we measure the health status of the older age groups (and indeed other population subgroups)? What measures are available and relevant to the daily lives of older people? There are a number of different approaches to the development of morbidity indicators. In essence, we can look at symptoms/diagnoses of specific conditions (for example, cancer or digestive disorders); the distribution of broad categories of health issues such as chronic (for example, diabetes or arthritis); and the distribution of acute diseases (for example, swine flu). In the rest of this chapter we focus on acute health problems and specific diseases. Our aim is to determine the levels of physical health problems within the older age groups and the presence (or absence) of sociodemographic inequalities in the distribution of these conditions. We consider chronic illness, disability and functional activities in Chapter Three and psychological wellbeing and perceptions of health status in Chapter Four. Naturally, this is a somewhat artificial distinction and we shall endeavour to make links across these three key empirical chapters.

Describing disease in populations

Before proceeding to the substantive aspects of this section, and to establish the framework for the empirical data in Chapters Three and Four, we need to briefly introduce some key terms used in the study of population health. We need to distinguish between two key concepts in describing disease: (a) the total number of older people with a specific condition such as arthritis and (b) the number of new cases of a given disease identified within a given timeframe. The total number of cases of, for example, diabetes is known as the prevalence rate and succinctly describes the 'disease burden' within a population. This is clearly of importance because it establishes the size of specific health problems and facilitates comparisons within and between populations and over time. However, it is also relevant to know how many new cases of a specific disease or health problem are occurring within a specific timeframe. This is known as incidence and may be calculated for a range of timeframes, from a week (in the case of a highly infectious disease such as swine flu) to a year (the more traditional reference period for chronic or long-term conditions such as arthritis). These two concepts are clearly interrelated. The prevalence of any given disease or health problem at a specific point in time reflects both the incidence of the illness and the duration of the condition (which is influenced by factors affecting mortality, morbidity, prevention and treatment).

Acute health problems

It is conceptually important to differentiate between acute health problems and those of a more longstanding or chronic nature because of the differential impact these conditions are hypothesised to have on individuals and society. Intuitively, acute illnesses are much less likely than chronic conditions to impose restrictions on the daily activities of individuals and to challenge their ability to maintain an independent and autonomous life in the community. Acute illnesses are, by definition, time limited (usually a duration of three months or less) and may (in theory at least) be more amenable to medically based interventions. They are also thought to be much less problematic in terms of the impact on individuals and the implications for health and social care policy. However, the swine flu pandemic of 2009 indicates that acute health conditions can generate long-term consequences and negative outcomes for sufferers (people died of swine flu) and the costs of responding to such infectious diseases can be significant. Thus, acute illnesses are not necessarily trivial or bereft of significant and/or long-term individual/societal consequences.

Table 2.3 presents data on the prevalence of acute illness – and restricted activity within the 14 days before interview – by age and gender, derived from the community-based GHS. This survey excludes people who live in residential or nursing homes: a significant omission given that those resident in these types of settings demonstrate high levels of health problems and constitute 5% of the overall population aged 65 and over (and 20% of those aged 85 and over).

Therefore, we can use survey data such as the GHS to comment on the health status of older people living in the community – we cannot use it to characterise the health status of all older people (that is, community and residential/nursing care dwelling individuals). There is an increase in the percentage reporting acute illnesses with age, from 15% for adults aged 16-44 compared with 22% of those aged 75 and over. We can also observe a gender differential but it is the reverse of that observed for mortality, with women demonstrating 'worse' health by reporting rates of acute illness for the post 65 years age groups some 25-30% higher than males of the same age. The number of days of restricted activity also increases with age. The average person in midlife reports 37 days of 'restricted activity' per year because of acute illness: this is approximately half of the 65 days reported by those aged 75 and over. Differentials in rates of acute illness between community and residential/nursing home care for those aged 65 and over are not significant (18% for those in the community and 20% for those in care) (Victor, 2005). While acute illness is unpleasant at the time, it is not usually life threatening – although some such illnesses such as flu can become so for older people and can certainly be debilitating, as this quotation illustrates: 'I mean the year before last I went to Benidorm with XXX and we got the flu and we had a rotten six months and actually I still was going out I suppose that it took us ages to get over this flu. I hadn't got the strength....' (Victor et al, 2009: respondent 302[*1]).

Having introduced data describing the prevalence of acute illnesses within the population, it is appropriate to consider one of the key methodological issues relevant to the study of ageing and this relates to the issue of study design (see Victor, 2007). This brief review of the major research designs serves as a context within which to locate the presentation of the data-reporting aspects of the health status of older people. The data displayed in Table 2.3 are derived from a 'cross-sectional' study design. In this type of study we select participants of different ages and make comparisons between them in terms of the topic under consideration, in this case acute illness, at the same point in time. The rates of reported acute illness increase with age and we might wish to infer that 'ageing' causes an increase in the prevalence of acute illness. Unfortunately, this claim stretches the credibility of our data and methodological design. Using a cross-sectional research design we can demonstrate an age–related pattern of the distribution of disease. We can identify

Table 2.3: Acute illness by age and gender, Great Britain, 2007 (%)

Age	% reporting acute illness		Mean days of restricted activity	
	M	F	M	F
5-15	7	8	10	10
16-44	9	11	16	21
45-64	14	17	35	40
65-74	16	21	41	55
75+	19	24	56	70

Source: Ali et al (2007, tables 7.2 and 7.3)

and highlight age differences, and observe age-related or age-associated patterns in our data, but we cannot justifiably claim that these observations represent the results of ageing. This is because the distribution we observe in Table 2.3 could be explained by three different explanatory frameworks, all of which relate to different 'types' of time: biological time (age effects), historical time (the influence of living through specific historical events, known as cohorts) and calendar time (the influence of historical events such as the Depression across the whole of society, known as period effects).

These issues are explained in more detail elsewhere (see Victor, 2007). Age effects are developmental or maturational changes demonstrated by individuals with increased chronological age and which reflect the passing of developmental time. For an observed change to be accepted as an age effect it must fulfil a number of 'conditions': (a) be universal and (b) be intrinsic, that is, not the result of external factors such as environmental/occupational exposures (such as living in close proximity to high-voltage power lines) or lifestyle factors such as sun exposure, smoking, diet or exercise. Strehler (1962), a biologist, also considered that to be considered an age effect the factor under consideration had to demonstrate progressiveness and that it must be deleterious in that it reduced the ability of the organism to function. The stringent requirement for universality means that few of the health or other attributes we see demonstrated by older people can be characterised as age effects. This goal of universality has been useful in contributing to the debate about the distinction between pathology (disease and disease processes) and ageing that we introduced in Chapter One. Distinguishing between these two states is very important both conceptually and in policy terms. Thus, we may be able to accurately describe many diseases such as dementia or arthritis as age related or age associated but we cannot be certain that they are 'caused' by ageing, that is, they are not age effects.

Period and cohort effects reflect different elements of the influence of historical time. Cohort effects are usually considered to be influences related to specific (usually) birth cohorts. We discuss this further in Chapter Seven where we consider the issue of the ageing of the 'baby boom' generation. Period effects, sometimes referred to as 'secular trends', influence all age groups equally such as the rationing imposed in Britain during the 1939–45 period. It is often very difficult to differentiate between these two aspects of historical time. However, it is important to accept the premise that observed differences between people of differing ages may reflect the influence of historical rather than biological time.

Identifying these differing explanatory frameworks represents one of the great intellectual challenges of gerontological research and indicates that 'ageing' is only one of the potential explanations for differences observed across a range of parameters between people of differing ages. So if we return to Table 2.3, we can see that with this type of design we cannot distinguish between the influence of age, period or cohort effects – this is because we are comparing the characteristics of people of different ages who reflect different experiences of historical time in terms of period (general) and cohort (the specific experiences of a group born at the same time) effects. This type of study design can thus only be used descriptively, that is, differences between age groups can be described and articulated but the differences cannot be definitively explained. However, this does not mean that this is not a very useful and enlightening form of study design and can be used to raise questions about ageing and to characterise how experiences vary across differing age groups; we just cannot use this type of design to attribute any of these changes to ageing per se.

To overcome these limitations we can use a longitudinal study design, which involves the same group of research participants being followed up over a period of time. This type of design is strongly linked with (child) development research and in Britain the largest longitudinal studies involve following up all children born in specific weeks in 1946, although as these studies have continued they have turned into studies of mid-life and, perhaps, will eventually turn into studies of old age! One of the most famous longitudinal studies is the Framingham study in the US, which started in 1948 when 5,209 men and women aged 30-62 from the town of Framingham, Massachusetts were enrolled in a study of the progression of heart disease. At baseline, participants underwent a thorough physical examination and lifestyle interview and were then followed up every two years for the development of cardiovascular disease. In 1971, the study enrolled a 'second generation' group: 5,124 of the original participants' adult children and their spouses and in 2001 a 'third generation' (the children of the offspring cohort) were recruited. This study has been important for demonstrating the link between a variety of 'risk factors' such as the effects of diet, exercise, smoking and obesity on heart disease, including the reduction of disease risk by the modification of such factors (see www.framinghamheartstudy.org .)

As might be expected, there are problems with longitudinal studies. Longitudinal studies suffer from a range of potential threats to internal validity, not all of which are unique to this type of study design. We have already noted the importance of the source of the population of individuals to be included within the study – for example, including only those individuals resident in the community rather than including those resident in residential and nursing homes as well. There is also the issue of how participants in the study are identified and recruited. Some studies (and not just longitudinal ones) are based on volunteers, which is always problematic as people who volunteer are intrinsically different from the rest of the population.[2] Thus, the most robust way of recruiting samples is via random selection from the appropriate groups. This can be both difficult and time consuming but it is the 'gold standard' for ensuring that the research study is built on secure foundations (see Bryman, 2008, for a good review of general principles of social research).

In research the term 'bias' refers to the introduction of systematic (as opposed to random) errors within the data and thus the compromising of the generalisability of the results. Low (fewer than 50%) response rates to a survey can mean that the results are biased, that is, are not representative of the group under consideration. However, in longitudinal studies the loss of individuals from death, non-response, loss of contact or moving into care, poses a specific threat in that such losses are rarely 'randomly' distributed but are concentrated among particular groups. For example, we may lose the healthiest (they are too busy to participate) or the least healthy (they are too unwell to participate). Either way, this will result in the study being biased in that it will under (or over) state the health problems of older people. Furthermore, the attrition of the original study can result in the number of individuals in a study becoming so small that the results are compromised. We can illustrate these points by reference to the ELSA study where 'loss to follow-up' refers to individuals included in wave 1 of the study who do not then participate in wave 2 (or subsequent waves) for a range of reasons (for example, death, refusals or loss of contact with the study because of residential moves). These losses are important because (a) they reduce the overall size and therefore the power of the study and (b) they are rarely randomly distributed across the survey participants. Of those interviewed in wave 1, 10,770 of this group were still eligible for interview at wave 2, of whom 8,780 participated: a response rate of 82%. 'Non-response' in wave 2 is less problematic in that data from wave 1 can be used to determine the presence/absence of 'non-response' bias and then weight the achieved results accordingly so that the data become more representative of the general population of interest. Globally, there are a number of longitudinal studies of ageing conducted at both the local (Bangor, Manitoba, Rotterdam, Seattle) and national level (Australia, England, China, Italy, the US). A comprehensive listing of studies is available at www.nia.nih.gov/ ResearchInformation/ScientificResources/LongitudinalStudiesAllCurrent.htm.

Prevalence of specific diseases in later life

In this section we are concerned with establishing the extent to which older people experience specific physical diseases/conditions. We look at the consequences of these health issues in terms of ability to live independently and autonomously in the community in Chapter Three, while Chapter Four examines psychological health in old age. Both specific health surveys, such as the HSE and the ELSA survey, and more generic surveys of older people ask about the prevalence of a range of specific health conditions such as heart disease or arthritis and/or more generic symptoms. While the number of conditions may vary between studies – ELSA asks about 17 different conditions – they are usually selected because they have the potential to impair individuals' ability to function effectively and thereby retain their independence in the community and require long-term interventions and/or service support to attain this. Hence, there is a focus in these 'symptom/ disease' checklists on chronic or longstanding conditions. Clearly this is a very medically focused conceptualisation of the experience of health in later life although there is an implicit link with the concerns with older people to retain their ability to live at home. Very broadly, the specific diseases discussed relate to cardiovascular problems such as angina, heart attack, stroke, heart failure, arrhythmia and heart murmurs and indicators of such problems such as hypertension and high cholesterol; musculoskeletal diseases (arthritis and osteoporosis), cancer and lung/respiratory diseases (chronic lung disease and asthma); and sensory impairments such as problems with sight and hearing.

ACTIVITY 3: What percentage of those aged 65 and over do you think:

▸ have arthritis;

▸ experience a fall at least once a year;

▸ are incontinent of urine;

▸ have high blood pressure;

▸ have a stroke;

▸ have problems with their hearing;

▸ have problems with their sight?

In the ELSA study, whose methodology is typical of these types of studies, respondents are asked if they have ever been diagnosed by a doctor with any of the 17 conditions listed. This requires that (a) the person consulted a GP for their symptoms and (b) they can recall that they were given a definite diagnosis by their doctor. A key advantage of ELSA is that it provides data about both the prevalence of specific diseases (the total disease burden) and the incidence (the number of new cases arising between the survey waves) of these conditions as it is a longitudinal survey. The comparability of ELSA and the sister surveys in the US (HRS) and Europe (SHARE) offer the potential for robust internationally based comparisons of health problems in later life in terms of both incidence and prevalence and for their distribution within and between generations. This is very valuable as trends and patterns that are robust across different populations can be viewed with more confidence than those arising from a single, specific local study. Furthermore, by investigating the consistent presence/absence of social variations in disease across populations, we can start to tease out how much health in old age is influenced by the socioenvironmental context and how much it links to biology and genetics.

Table 2.4 presents the reported diagnosed prevalence of eight different diseases derived from the first wave of the ELSA survey in 2002. While heart disease, stroke, diabetes and cancers are evident, it is hypertension and arthritis that have the highest reported prevalence rates. The reported prevalence of diagnosed heart disease increases from 8% and 2% for men and women respectively aged 60-69 to 12% and 7% respectively for those aged 80 and over. This compares with an overall prevalence of about 37% for hypertension and 44% for arthritis. It is these two diseases that dominate the health problems reported by older people. We can contrast this pattern with the major sources of mortality described earlier in this chapter, which was dominated by circulatory diseases, respiratory diseases and cancers. Mortality data do not necessary reflect the major health problems experienced by older people nor reflect the impact that such diseases can have on daily life. The reported prevalence of key conditions is similar for the 11 countries in the initial SHARE survey (see www.share-project.org/) and that reported in ELSA and the HRS in the US (see Table 2.5). So there seems to be some evidence for the robustness of the population prevalence rates of hypertension (44%), arthritis (46%) and diabetes (8-10%).

Table 2.4: Prevalence of specific conditions by age and gender, population aged 60+, England, 2002 (%)

	60-64		65-69		70-74		75-79		80+	
	M	F	M	F	M	F	M	F	M	F
Heart attack	8.6	2.3	9.8	3.5	12.7	7.9	14.2	6.0	12.1	7.0
Hypertension	37.5	35.4	40.0	43.3	44.3	49.1	44.5	50.8	38.3	46.1
Diabetes	8.1	5.7	9.9	6.4	13.0	9.9	12.3	9.4	9.7	6.5
Lung disease	6.9	7.3	8.5	6.3	9.0	9.9	10.5	5.5	9.8	6.0
Asthma	12.8	15.3	9.7	13.8	11.3	11.4	8.5	11.0	7.0	10.6
Arthritis	26.6	36.0	26.8	40.1	30.4	45.6	32.4	47.1	38.3	48.8
Osteoporosis	1.1	7.7	2.1	8.1	1.5	11.9	2.9	10.2	1.5	11.2
Cancer	4.4	7.7	6.3	6.7	7.8	6.5	9.8	9.1	7.0	9.9

Source: Marmot et al (2003, tables 6A1 and 6A6)

Talking about a heart attack, an older female interviewed for a study about social relationships reported (see Victor et al, 2009 for details of the study):

> I had a heart attack a couple of years ago and I was taken into hospital and they put me on all these pills I got to take now, you know, but they really take the go out of you.... I get up in the morning have a breakfast and get washed and dressed as I come down and set myself in the armchair, I've had enough.... But that's not me, I'm a lively person. (Respondent 209★)

Another described the real impact that arthritis had on daily life:

> I do suffer from arthritis I go and see a specialist every six months or so. I don't have the strength that I used to have so if I want to do gardening I mustn't do too much at the time. Last August I trimmed the hedge, which is a thing I used to do regularly and then for about four days my arthritis really came back, so I thought well that's stupid, I must now stop it. (Respondent 205★)

Table 2.5: Comparison of the prevalence of specific diseases in England (2002) and Europe (2003–07), population aged 60+ (%)

	England (ELSA)	Europe (SHARE)
Hypertension	44	43
Diabetes	12	9
Arthritis	47	44
Osteoporosis	8	6

Source: Marmot et al (2003, table 6A1); Börsch-Supan et al (2005, table 1)

Both these quotations illustrate the impact of specific conditions on the daily lives of individuals: something that it is easy to forget when we concentrate on statistics of incidence and prevalence of specific conditions. However, the opposite point also holds true – individuals may underplay the consequences of some diseases. One respondent stated in response to a question about whether she had any health problems: 'No. No. I'm a diabetic, so is Lesley, but we're sensible' (respondent 102, 8, 42).

The gender differential of diseases is inconsistent. For some diagnoses, such as heart attack and diabetes, the prevalence is higher among males than females. We can explain this observation as reflecting a 'true' difference in the prevalence of the disease between men and women: an under-diagnosis of the disease in women by doctors; a lower consultation rate by women who do not consult for symptoms of heart disease; or a differential recall of the diagnosis between men and women. With these large-scale community surveys it is difficult to determine which of these explanations for the observed difference is correct (or whether it is some combination of these). There are two diagnosed diseases where women have a substantially higher reported prevalence than men – arthritis and osteoporosis. Certainly the latter diagnosis potentially reflects a 'real' biological difference between men and women, namely the loss of bone density experienced by post-menopausal women.

These more specific condition-related data illustrate a more complex pattern of gender differentials in health than did mortality and acute illnesses. This suggests that gender-based disease (and by implication health) differentials do not have a single explanation but reflect the interaction of biological, social, environmental and healthcare access factors.

Incidence of key diseases

One clear and valuable advantage of longitudinal studies is that they can provide information about changes over time: indeed, this is the whole point of longitudinal studies. They can provide information about 'new' cases of disease that are identified between sweeps of the studies; provide information about disease progression (either improvement or deterioration); and provide data about 'risk factors'. We can use data from waves 1 and 2 of the ELSA study to look at the onset of disease with increasing age. A third, 33% of those aged 65 reported the onset of a new disease in the two-year follow-up period, ranging from 28% of those aged 65-69 to 37% of those aged 80 years and over. The most commonly diagnosed 'new disease' was arthritis, with approximately 10% of participants reporting this (see Table 2.6). This is a very much larger rate of onset than for some other key chronic diseases such as diabetes, heart disease and lung disease, which are all in the order of approximately 2% over the same period. These data reinforce the point raised earlier about the importance of arthritis in understanding the health status of older people.

Table 2.6: Incidence (onset) of specific diseases by age between waves 1 and 2 of ELSA (%)

	60-74	75+
Ischemic heart disease	2.0	3.4
Diabetes	1.9	2.0
Stroke	1.4	3.0
Arthritis	9.0	11.6
Osteoporosis	2.4	4.2
Cancer	2.1	2.0
Lung disease	1.6	2.3

Source: Banks et al (2006, tables 4A5 and 4A6)

Key points

In this chapter we have seen that virtually all health problems – as measured by mortality, acute illness and exemplar conditions such as heart disease – demonstrate an age-related increase. We have shown that the types of health problems identified as the major problems of old age vary according to the data source used – mortality data highlight the importance of cancer and heart disease while morbidity data highlight the importance of arthritis.

We have found that there is an inconsistent distribution of disease by gender: mortality rates are higher for men than for women while for other measures of health there is no consistent pattern. Social class or social position more broadly, exerts a powerful influence on the experience of health in later life. Consistently, where data are available, older people from the least privileged backgrounds are less likely to reach old age, and experience worse health in old age than their more privileged contemporaries. We have very limited evidence about ethnicity but it seems reasonable to speculate that members of minority ethnic communities probably experience worse health in old age than the rest of the population. Thus, we can conclude that factors other than biology are important in influencing the pattern of disease in old age.

A key theme identifiable in the literature concerns issues of unreported (health) needs and undiagnosed disease. Williamson et al (1964) in his survey in Edinburgh drew attention to the extensive amounts of morbidity and health problems experienced by older people but they were not known to GPs and service providers more generally. This resulted in a series of studies and screening interventions to detect unmet needs among older people. Such studies largely emanated from the professional perspective – instead of asking older people about their problems researchers presented interviewees with a predetermined list of issues. However, such studies rarely asked the older people if the identified problem did actually pose problems for them in maintaining daily life. More recently, debates about ageism and age discrimination in healthcare have reignited interests in the 'unmet need' debate in that it is argued that the prevalence of ageist attitudes within a health context means that disease is less likely to be identified in older people and, once diagnosed, less effectively treated. We can review the extent to which selected key health issues may be undetected using evidence from the ELSA study. Results from validated screening questions (such as the Rose angina questionnaire, direct measurement of blood pressure and the analysis of blood samples) can be compared with self-report data of diagnosis. Potentially undiagnosed diabetes was evident for 1.5% of those aged 65 and over. Undiagnosed hypertension was estimated at 17%, with no clear patterns in terms of age and gender. It is not clear whether these levels of 'undiagnosed' disease are greater than those characteristic of younger populations and this gap in our knowledge suggests another fruitful area of research in making comparisons across generations and looking at factors such as class and ethnicity across rather than between generations.

Notes

[1] ★ in text denotes data hitherto unpublished but which informed the research in Victor et al's 2009 publication.

[2] Those who volunteer to participate in research studies are often differentiated from the general population by being motivated by a strong personal experience, having the time (and money) to participate in studies and often are in better health.

Further activities

▸ Obtain the most recent mortality data for your locality and look at the numbers of deaths by age and gender.

▸ Apply the prevalence and incidence rates for the key measures of morbidity described and calculate the number of older people in your locality with these conditions.

▸ Calculate potential levels of 'unmet' need for diabetes and hypertension for your locality.

▸ Do you think that levels of undiagnosed disease are greater among older people compared with younger people? If so, what factors might explain this difference?

Further reading

Bowling, A. (2004) Socioeconomic differentials in mortality among older people. *Epidemiology and Community Health*, 58(6), 438-40.

Bowling, A. and Grundy, E. (2009) Differentials in mortality up to 20 years after baseline interview among older people in East London and Essex. *Age and Ageing*, 38(1), 51-5.

Cann, P. and Dean, M. (2009) *Unequal ageing.* Bristol: The Policy Press.

Grundy, E. (2001) 'Health, health care and death among older adults in England and Wales: a hundred years' perspective. In Zaba, B. and Blacker, J. (eds) *Brass tacks: Essays in medical demography* (pp 270-91). London: Athlone Press.

Harper, S. (2006) *Ageing societies: Myths, challenges and opportunities.* London: Hodder Arnold.

Lloyd-Sherlock, P. (2010) *Population ageing.* Bristol: The Policy Press.

Marmot, M. (chair) (2009) *Social determinants of health.* Geneva: WHO (available at www.who.int/social_determinants/en/index.html).

Sheldon, J.H. (1948) *The social medicine of old age.* Oxford: Nuffield.

Useful websites

- *UK mortality data:* www.statistics.gov.uk/STATBASE/Product.asp?vlnk=10530
- *ELSA:* www.ifs.org.uk/elsa/
- *Living in Britain (formerly GHS):* www.statistics.gov.uk/lib2002/
- *Social Trends:* www.statistics.gov.uk/socialtrends/
- *HSE:* www.dh.gov.uk/en/Publicationsandstatistics/PublishedSurvey/ HealthSurveyForEngland/Healthsurveyresults/index.htm
- *Survey of Health, Ageing and Retirement Europe (SHARE):* www.share-project.org

THREE

Chronic disease and disability

Key points

In this chapter we consider:

- how older people define and evaluate their health status;
- the prevalence of chronic illness among the population aged 65 and over and how this varies within the population.

We should not underestimate how central health is to the experience of old age and later life, although in doing so we should not forget the importance of good health to the rest of the population. Indeed, 68% of those aged 50 years and over worry that their health will get worse as they get older and, by implication, that they may face challenges in maintaining daily activities and that their ability to live independently at home may be compromised. Health status influences, very directly, the ability of older people to retain their independence as these observations illustrate: 'I have angina which prevents me from doing lots of things – I can no longer go to town shopping'; 'if you have your health you can stay in your own house'; 'I've got impaired sight which is a great drawback and I suppose if I could see life would be a lot different. I'm not independent, that's been taken away from me' (Bowling, 2005: 131-2, 124). This resonates with the comments of one the respondents in Victor et al's (2009) study, who told of the consequences of her failing eyesight on how she spent her time and, ultimately, on the quality of her life:

> I'd like to be more active, stronger and more active, but I know I can't do so I've accepted that. But I would like a change now and again. Being able to do more and longer you see. I've got to more or less pace my time. I'd like to get really stuck in and continue with work but I can't nowadays ... I used to do a bit of painting but I couldn't settle to it now what with my eyes and not being able to ... all I want to do is sleep now. But I would have liked to go back to the days when I could sit down with a paintbrush. Just the smell of paints that I miss. But I've still got some that I managed to finish before my eyes let me down. (Victor et al, 2009: respondent 103★)

ACTIVITY 1

▶ How do the types of specific health conditions such as diabetes and arthritis described in Chapter Two enhance (or compromise) quality of life and independence in later life?

▶ How do you think older people define and understand health?

▶ How do older people themselves rate their health?

How do older people understand health?

As with many other dimensions of life, how we think about and define 'health' can be both complex and (sometimes) contradictory, are very definitely historically and culturally rooted and are strongly related to the values and expectations of specific population subgroups. Lay (that is, 'non-professional') understandings of health, as researched by medical sociologists, are very much influenced by the historical, social, cultural and temporal context. In contemporary Western societies, comparatively few people explain or understand their experiences of health and illness in religious terms – although this might have been the case several centuries ago and does still apply for some groups where the experience of especially chronic illness is seen as a manifestation of God's will. Bury (2005) reminds us that, while concerns with health and illness (and the consequent diagnostic, treatment and preventative regimes) are the focus of attention for healthcare professionals and many researchers, they are not necessarily the overriding concern of the rest of the population. Very broadly, the general population does not 'think' about health in these ways. Health forms a 'background' resource for daily life, which is, perhaps, taken for granted until – as illustrated in the comments noted earlier – things start to go wrong and daily life becomes restricted because of the limitations consequent from a health problem (and usually one of long duration). This may be especially problematic for older people where health problems may compromise quality of life and the ability to engage in social and other activities, live independently in the community and exercise autonomy and self-determination.

   Sociologists have expended considerable energy in researching a variety of different aspects of our understanding of health. These include lay definitions of health and illness, lay beliefs about illness causation, the 'interaction' of lay health beliefs and medical knowledge and variations within and between populations in terms of articulated health beliefs and knowledge. Here we provide a brief overview of the key concepts in order to contextualise our empirical data and to again make the point about the potential disjuncture between professional and lay discourses. This is not to establish one perspective as 'correct' and one as 'incorrect', but simply to point out that there may be differences in the language and meaning used to talk about health. The initial sociological work on lay health beliefs was undertaken by Herzlich (1973), who focused on the 'commonsense' and experience-based ideas about health (and illness) derived from the reports of 80 middle-aged, mostly middle-class, Parisians. Thus, when evaluating these reports we need to be mindful of the influence of class, gender and ethnicity. Perhaps the most extensive research into understanding lay health beliefs in Britain was that undertaken by Blaxter (1990). She eloquently demonstrated how understandings of health vary with age, gender, socioeconomic position and, probably, ethnicity and that health is not a single unitary concept (see Blaxter, 2004a, 2004b). Her work has provided the framework for subsequent researchers to enhance and develop. She demonstrated that lay understandings of health involve three broad conceptualisations:

- health as an absence of illness – a rather negative definition that has a resonance with the medical model and meshes with many of the health measures and indicators that feature in this book;
- functionality – health as the ability to undertake routine everyday activities, a perspective that is clearly evident in the comments of the older people whose voices are featured in this book;
- health as physical activity and/or fitness – a more positive conceptualisation of health and a rather broad-ranging notion of wellbeing.

Blaxter's work demonstrates clearly that older people are more likely than those of younger ages to define health in terms of functionality and the ability to cope with the activities and demands of daily life. This is the dominant paradigm for those aged 65 and over. Support for this is provided by Williams (1990) and more recently by Bowling (2005) whose respondents clearly saw coping and the ability to undertake 'normal' daily activities as central to their understanding of health in later life (see also Bowling and Gabriel, 2004). As a respondent from Victor et al's (2009) study noted:

> I mean I've got a dodgy knee but that's all. That is a concern I think. I think possibly I get more concerned about it working in nursing homes and seeing how the health side affects people hugely and changes their outlook on life. It quite frightens me I think looking into the future…. (Respondent 203★)

This is reinforced by the work of Netuveli et al (2006) where health factors – notably reductions in mobility, longstanding illness and ability to undertake routine activities of daily living (ADL) – significantly reduced quality of life (see also Blane et al, 2007; Netuveli and Blane, 2008).

These comments from older people link with Blaxter's (1990) ideas about health being a specific form of 'capital' (like social and material capital) ,which reflects our genetic heritage and which can be enhanced (or diminished) by our lifestyle, occupation, family circumstances and environment (Macintyre et al, 2006). Blaxter posits that older people may feel that their health reserves are depleted by the onset of the physical and mental health problems that often accompany old age (or growing older). Hence, health is conceptualised as being able to successfully complete routine tasks such as self-care or engage in social activities, events that are largely taken for granted by those aged under 60. Indeed, one element of the 'successful' ageing triangle proposed by Rowe and Kahn (1997) is the maintenance of physical/mental function (and by implication of 'ordinary' activity). In the next two sections we focus on compromised ability to undertake ADL by looking at chronic illness, ADL and notions of physical disability and impairment. This chapter largely focuses on physical health while Chapter Four focuses on psychological and emotional health.

Chronic illness in later life

ACTIVITY 2

▶   What percentage of older people (those aged 65 and over) do you think have chronic illnesses?

▶   How do levels of chronic illness vary within the older population? Which groups have the highest/lowest levels of chronic illness?

▶   What do you think are the most common types of chronic illness experienced in old age?

Chronic health problems are long term and not usually characterised by a cure and so the emphasis in therapeutic terms is on 'palliative' treatment – the management of symptoms with the aim of maximising quality of life (and autonomy and independence). Illustrative of such chronic conditions are diabetes and arthritis but heart failure, obstructive airways disease, Parkinson's disease and the after-effects of stroke are emblematic of these types of conditions.

Within the UK context, chronic diseases and their management are seen as both major public health problems and the key challenges for health policy in coming decades because of the link between these types of health problems and the use of health resources. A key source of routinely available data about the prevalence of chronic disease in the general population is the General Household Survey (GHS). This has been running since 1972 and adopts a two-stage approach to establishing the extent of chronic illness in the general population by first asking respondents whether they have a chronic illness (lasting 12 months or more) and then whether this illness or condition limits their activities of daily life (without specifying precisely what these are). Thus, we have two distinct concepts: (a) the prevalence of long-term illness and (b) the prevalence of limiting long-term illness. As with many aspects of health and social care for older people, we are equating long-term (limiting) illness with chronic illness. While these may be conceptually very close it is an assumption that we are making that they are synonymous and there is considerable scope for research in testing the veracity of this assumption. However, long-term limiting illness is clearly relevant for our population as it links closely with the ideas of older people about health being defined in terms of limited activities although, of course, it is up to participants to implicitly evaluate both 'normal' levels of activity and the degree to which their health problem does (or does not) compromise this. The GHS question noted above was also used in the 2001 UK Census and in the Health Survey for England (HSE) from 1996 onwards so there are a range of sources for the data, which enable us to examine socioeconomic variations in the extent of chronic illness and, potentially, temporal trends as well as variations between countries (see Chapter Seven).

Overall, 71% of both men and women aged 65 and over living in the community in England report that they have a longstanding illness while 42% of men and 46% of women in this age group report that they have a limiting, longstanding illness (see Table 3.1). For both longstanding and limiting longstanding illness there is a clear trend for prevalence to increase with age, which is consistent with data from the GHS and the 2001 Census (see Table 3.2). For those aged 80 and over, 70% report that they have a longstanding illness and approximately 60% that they have a limiting longstanding illness. So while there is a clear age-related trend in prevalence rates, these do not reach 100%! Indeed, the 2001 Census reports that, for those aged 90 and over, 75% report a limiting longstanding illness, which means that some 25% of nonagenarians do not report the presence of a chronic illness. However, we need to exercise some caution when interpreting these findings, especially in the upper age ranges where substantial numbers are resident in care settings and it is important to establish whether such populations are (or are not) included within the cited studies. The rates reported are for those living in the community; when we add in those older people living in institutions, prevalence rates for those in the 'oldest' age groups are increased. Additionally, these data are based on perceived restrictions on daily activity and, as we shall see later in this chapter, older people potentially 'under-report' limitations on daily activity when compared with responses to questions focusing on disability (see Gooberman-Hill et al, 2003; Melzer et al, 2004).

Table 3.1: Chronic illness by age and gender, population aged 65+, England, 2005 (%)

Age	Longstanding illness		Longstanding limiting illness		Mean number of conditions	
	M	F	M	F	M	F
65-69	67	66	36	35	1.8	1.8
70-74	70	67	43	42	1.9	1.8
75-79	72	73	42	48	1.9	2.0
80-84	75	76	45	57	1.8	1.9
85+	77	78	57	59	2.0	1.9
All 65+	71	71	42	46	1.9	1.9

Source: Craig and Mindell (2007, table 2.4)

If we accept the widespread stereotype of old age as a time of universal ill-health and disability, then we might not expect to see any variability in the distribution of chronic illness as everyone over a specified age would be so classified! Looking at Table 3.1 we can see that there is no real gender differential in the distribution of longstanding illness and no consistent relationship for longstanding limiting

Table 3.2: Comparison of prevalence rates of longstanding limiting illness, population aged 65+, England, 2005 (%)

Age	Longstanding limiting illness (%)	
	2005 Health Survey for England	2001 Census
65-69	36	39
70-74	43	45
75-79	45	54
80-84	51	61
85+	58	72

Source: Craig and Mindell (2007, table 2.4)

illness. Before midlife (aged below 45 years) there is a slight 'excess' in longstanding illness among males. The female excess in longstanding illness does not emerge until the mid-seventies age group where there is at most a modest – 5-10% – differential. This differential is certainly not as marked as that for mortality rates and this may reflect either (a) that there is very little difference in chronic health problems between men and women in later life or (b) an under-reporting of the true extent of health problems by either men or women.

The two other sociodemographic factors that we are examining within this book are socioeconomic position and ethnicity. Health status in the UK, in terms of both mortality and morbidity, is strongly differentiated in terms of socioeconomic position. The GHS only presents information on longstanding illness by socioeconomic group for those aged 65 and over as a single group. For longstanding illness there is only a limited (4%) differential for men, with 64% from professional classes reporting this compared with 68% of those from the non-professional/manual occupations. This differential is larger for women at 14%, with 71% of those from the 'non-professional' occupational groups reporting longstanding illness. This differential is 9% for the responses to the limiting longstanding illness question, with 45% of men and 49% of women from the lower part of the social hierarchy reporting limiting longstanding illness. These data support the thesis of the preservation of social class-related differentials in health status into advanced old age (see Nazroo et al, 2009) and mirror the data for mortality presented in Chapter Two.

How does longstanding illness translate into limiting longstanding illness and does this differ by socioeconomic position? Focusing on men, 36% of those with longstanding illness from professional occupations report that it is limiting compared with 45% of their 'non-professional' contemporaries. We might speculate as to whether this reflects a 'real' difference in illness or symptom severity, the presence of (more extreme) multiple pathology or differences in the availability of resources to deploy in response to the challenges posed by the chronic illness (or, indeed, some combination of these factors). This is clearly an issue that merits further research especially in terms of investigating the differentials in health status within the older population.

One key change in the nature of British society is the 'ageing' of the migrant populations from the Caribbean and South Asia (India, Pakistan and Bangladesh) who came to work in the UK in the post-war period. Here we are concerned with establishing how the health of the older population from migrant communities compares with the general population. To explore this topic rigorously requires comparable data from both the migrant communities and the general population and the most comprehensive data to investigate longstanding limiting illness from our perspective of the burden of chronic disease are those from the 2001 Census. The populations from Asian countries have the highest rates of limiting longstanding illness at around 60%, compared with around 55% of Black Caribbean groups and around 50% of the White British population (see Table 3.3). This suggests that there is a higher disease burden among older people from our minority ethnic communities. However, we need to be mindful of the caveat that these variations may reflect gendered variations in the interpretation of the question rather than a 'real' difference in longstanding illness or, indeed, some combination of the two. Again, this is another element of the 'health inequalities' debate that would benefit from further research.

The presence of clear class, ethnicity and gender differentials in the distribution of chronic illness in later life highlights the importance of sociodemographic factors in the experience of health and illness. The importance of these factors provides some support for the thesis of Rowe and Kahn (1997) who argue that differentials in health status in later life are attributable to social, environmental

Table 3.3: Longstanding limiting illness by ethnic group and gender, population aged 50+, England and Wales, 2001 (%)

Group	Longstanding limiting illness (%)		
	M	F	Total
'Other'	52	47	49
Chinese	49	44	47
Other Black	55	48	51
Black African	53	45	49
Black Caribbean	59	51	55
Other African	59	50	55
Bangladeshi	59	65	62
Pakistani	66	59	63
Indian	65	53	59
Mixed	51	47	49
Other White	51	48	49
White Irish	49	49	49
White British	53	49	51

Source: White (2002), figure 5.17

and behavioural factors rather than biology or genetics. While our evidence cannot entirely discount the contribution of biology and genetics, our data do demonstrate the continued importance of key dimensions of social structure – gender, class and ethnicity – for the experience of health in later life. However, in our analysis we have had to address each of these major dimensions of differentiation separately and independently of each other. This is clearly limited as, in the real world, individuals do not experience them separately – age, gender, class and ethnicity all interact and are played out within a socioenvironmental and biological context. Thus, we need to examine how these different axes of social differentiation intersect. Are the relationships between them additive or multiplicative and are there better (or worse) combinations of factors? Clearly, there is a rich research agenda to be addressed in disentangling this interaction in both survival to old age and then both longevity and health status in old age. Furthermore, we may also need to factor in the effect of historical time via cohort analysis. For example, are class-based inequalities in health greater now than for previous cohorts of older people? Does the range of health indicators show the same or different trends across and between cohorts and in terms of the interrelationships between gender, class and ethnicity?

What are the major causes of limiting longstanding illness?

Data from a range of sources including the GHS, the HSE and the English Longitudinal Study of Ageing (ELSA) enable us to identify the key health conditions that underpin these overall levels of chronic illness. While the rates for specific long-term conditions reported by these differing studies may show some variability, they demonstrate a very consistent 'ranking' in importance of chronic health problems in later life. Musculoskeletal conditions and heart and circulatory diseases are the major long-term conditions encapsulated within the concept of 'chronic' health problems. Table 3.4 indicates that of those with a limiting longstanding condition, the prevalence rates for these conditions dominate, being double, triple or quadruple those for other conditions such as cancer or respiratory diseases. For example, of those aged 75 and over with a longstanding illness, the major causes are musculoskeletal disease (361 per 1,000) and heart and circulatory disease (353 per 1,000) compared with the next largest health problem, which is endocrine and metabolic disorders (mostly diabetes) (132 per 1,000). The gender pattern is inconsistent. Older women demonstrate prevalence rates for musculoskeletal diseases that are approximately a third (35%) higher than men, who have higher rates of respiratory and cardiovascular disease, although the differentials are less marked at about 15% for heart disease and 20% for respiratory disease (see Table 3.4).

Do the major 'causes' of chronic illness vary by social class or ethnicity or is this pattern fairly constant across these social categories? GHS data provide some insights into this, which show consistency across the class groupings in terms of the ordering of disease categories. Of the six major sources of longstanding

Table 3.4: Chronic illnesses reported for those with longstanding limiting illness, Great Britain, 2007 (rate per 1,000)

	45-64		65-74		75+	
	M	F	M	F	M	F
Musculo-skeletal	162	201	234	308	258	384
Heart and circulation	147	110	320	239	338	277
Respiratory	48	67	94	79	115	74
Endocrine	70	84	117	105	108	118

Source: Ali et al (2009, tables 7.12 and 7.13)

health problems (musculoskeletal; heart and circulatory; respiratory; metabolic and endocrine; digestive; and nervous system disorders), five demonstrate a 'classic' socioeconomic profile for both men and women with those from the 'lowest' socioeconomic groupings reporting the highest disease prevalence rates. Heart disease (men) and nervous system disorders (women) show the reverse trends of higher rates among the most privileged. Even allowing for the issue of sample size (and subsequent potential statistical error), which should not be ignored but does need to be put into perspective, these socioeconomic differentials are not trivial and eradicating such differentials would clearly have a very positive impact on the overall population disease burden. For musculoskeletal diseases the differences by social class are 30% for men and 22% for women while for respiratory diseases the differentials are 52% and 32% respectively. Thus, while there is no difference in ordering of importance there are clear and important differences in the burden of diseases within the social classes. Thus, not only do the most privileged have lower overall levels of disability, they also have lower prevalence rates for the major chronic disease categories.

Are there differences in chronic disease prevalence by ethnicity among older people? This is a difficult question to answer. O'Loughlin et al (2006) comment in a review of studies of chronic disease, that 85% of such studies do not report ethnicity although its importance is acknowledged. The HSE (2006) confirms that, for adults from minority ethnic communities, the types of chronic conditions associated with limiting longstanding illness in the general population also hold for these groups. However, for two key conditions – heart disease and diabetes – adults from the African Caribbean population and those from Indian, Pakistani and Bangladeshi communities demonstrate elevated rates compared with the general population. The implications of this are unclear but could mean that fewer adults from these communities will reach old age or, if they do so, they will experience increased rates of disability and dependency.

Disability and activities of daily living

ACTIVITY 3

▸ How would you define disability?

▸ What percentage of older people do you think are 'disabled'?

▸ What percentage of the total disabled population is aged 65 and over?

▸ What percentage of people aged 65 and over do you think have problems with dressing, washing, walking up stairs, shopping and heavy housework such as vacuuming?

For older people, health is very much conceptualised in terms of the ability to 'function' and perform (routine) ADL, which are often taken for granted by the rest of the population. Independence, control and autonomy are central to quality of life in old age (and, indeed, other phases of the life). Almost three quarters (725), of Bowling's (2005) respondents stated that having and retaining independence was key to quality of life. 'Having my health and a reasonable standard of living. Well they both give you the freedom to do what you want. You are not dependent on anyone' (Bowling, 2005: 194). The importance of being able to complete the routine activities that underpin daily life is illustrated by the following comments: 'I think the most important thing in my life is being able to walk and do my (house) work'; 'the best thing is that I have the health enough to go about and do my own shopping' (Bowling, 2005: 196).

What is disability?

In 1980, the World Health Organization (WHO) offered a typology for thinking about the complex notions of the consequences of disease inherent in the comments expressed above. Abnormalities of the body, in terms of structure, organ or system functions, are conceptualised as impairments: disabilities reflect the consequences of impairments in terms of functional performance or ability to undertake 'normal' activities while 'handicap' refers to the disadvantage resultant from impairments or disabilities. Thus, we can view impairments as characterised by disorders at the system/organ level; disabilities are experienced at the individual level; while 'handicap' reflects the societal-level interaction of the environment and the individual. This initial classification has been revised and upgraded into the International Classification of Functioning, Disability and Health, which complements the relatively new International Classification of Diseases (ICD) version 10. However, the new disability classificatory system is not yet in widespread use. Disability questions that operationalise the concepts in the WHO typology, distinguish between limitations in terms of sight/hearing and communication, mobility (typically walking and using steps and stairs) and 'traditional' ADL (which mostly relate to personal care but also include activities such as shopping) but the ones used in the UK do not include aspects of mental wellbeing. Researchers usually distinguish between ADL, which focus on personal care needs (such as washing), and (I)ADL (instrumental activities of daily living), which focus on tasks such as shopping, cooking and housework tasks (but rarely external maintenance tasks such as gardening). Difficulties with these activities can mean that older people require help from family, friends or statutory services or technological resources to undertake these tasks (and, hence, remain at home). In extreme cases, inability to maintain these activities places older people at risk of entering long-term care.

Defining and measuring activities of daily living

There are a variety of different ways of measuring both ADL and IADL functional abilities and disability more broadly. We can observe people's abilities in 'test' or laboratory settings, we can observe people in their own home (or virtual homes using virtual reality) or we can ask about individuals' ability to perform the key activities chosen (or we could ask other people on their behalf – gather information by proxy). The approach most often used is to ask older people directly and we can see this used in a range of surveys such as the GHS, HSE and ELSA. The precise questions and response formats used are influential in determining the results generated and subtle variations in these can, in part at least, account for variability in disability prevalence rates across studies.

One very widely used UK measure is that originally developed by Townsend (1963). This looks at the ability to perform a series of nine tasks (washing all over, cutting toenails, getting on a bus, going up and down stairs, doing heavy housework, going shopping and carrying heavy bags, preparing and cooking hot meals, reaching an overhead shelf and tying a good knot in a piece of string). Respondents classify their ability on a rating scale from: 'able to undertake with no difficulty'; to 'able to undertake with some difficulty'; to 'unable to complete the task alone/unaided'. Each activity is scored with 0 (no difficulty), 1 (can do but with difficulty) or 2 (not able to do/not able to do alone) and the scores are then summed to give a total score, which ranges from 0 to 18, with higher scores indicative of poorer functioning. This is essentially a dictionary approach in which the ability of the older person to undertake a series of tasks is recorded on a checklist with the older person rating their ability and ease with which they can accomplish the tasks specified. However, only a limited range of activities are listed in the Townsend measure.

Rockwood (2005) summarises some of the broad conceptual issues that arise with these types of measures, focusing on the breadth of the domains within which we research 'impaired function'. As with many other measures, the domains included (and those excluded) within these types of measures of functional ability are crucial. The nine items included in the Townsend measure, which focus on key self-care tasks, do not include social functioning nor more contemporary ADL such as using a (mobile) telephone, a television remote control or a computer, or driving – activities that at least some members of the population would see as essential to independent living in the community. Similarly, the HSE disability measure records performance in terms of getting in/out of bed, getting in/out of a chair, dressing, washing, feeding and toileting, but again does not include social functioning. Hence, we do need to reflect on the choice of items and consider how well they do (or do not) mesh with the key issues of daily living from the perspective of older people and the problems that they face in retaining this. Additionally, we need to 'future proof' these types of measures to include new activities that might become 'essential' to maintaining an independent life in the community for future generations of older people. For example, we might question the importance of getting on/off a bus for the current generation of older people. Perhaps 40 years ago the ability to prepare a coal fire would have been important for staying at home but it is no longer relevant to the majority of the population. Both ELSA and the Survey of Health and Retirement Europe (SHARE) record broadly 'traditional' ADL (dressing, walking across a room, bathing, eating, getting in/out of bed and toileting) plus instrumental activities that include novel items such as using the telephone, managing money and medication and using a map, as well as 'traditional' activities of shopping and food preparation (but not housework?). However, the introduction of 'new items' into existing measures or the creation of updated measures does compromise our ability to track trends over time. Thus, researchers are always faced with the problem of resolving the conflicts between maintaining stability in items/measures used in surveys in order to track changes over time and the desire to ensure the currency of their work by including items of contemporary relevance (and excluding those whose relevance is no longer evident).

In this volume we are not especially concerned with the use of disability measures/(I)ADL performance in a clinical setting. However, as the work of Roehrig et al (2007) reminds us, these types of measures can have an important role in assessing populations, often in terms of screening tools, to identify the most 'vulnerable' or 'frail' (see Nowak and Hubbard, 2009; Puts et al, 2010). Working with cancer patients, Roehrig et al sought to identify the (I)ADL items that were most efficient at identifying the most vulnerable cancer patients, with the aim of reducing patient assessment burden. This is important but slightly tangential to our main interests in this volume but does demonstrate how we need to adopt a reflective and enquiring perspective towards these types of measures. They suggest that for screening purposes, clinicians should use a 'hierarchy' of six key items and that two key questions (help with shopping and meal preparation) identify 97% of all patients with compromised IADL and are sufficient to establish the most vulnerable. They propose that four key ADL – going up/down stairs, walking along a corridor, taking a bath/shower and urinary incontinence – identify 95% of those with ADL limitations. Hence, they propose that these activities are sufficient to screen and identify the most frail and vulnerable populations.

How extensive are problems with activities of daily living?

The majority of older people living in the community can undertake the broad range of both ADL and IADL without difficulty (see Table 3.5). For self-care activities such as washing and cooking, virtually 90% of individuals living in the community can accomplish these tasks without difficulty. The biggest problem experienced by older people as indicated by this range of activities is cutting toenails where some 37% have problems with this activity, while 18% are unable to do IADL of carrying heavy bags of shopping or undertaking 'heavy' housework. Mobility, as illustrated by walking 400 yards and getting/up down stairs, also presents challenges for older people living at home, with 28% experiencing difficulties with walking and 30% problems with stairs. It is important here to be able to translate these percentages into absolute numbers, which gives a more readily understood indication of the levels of 'need' represented. Thus, if 1% of the population aged 65 and over (some 8.8 million people) are unable to undertake an activity, this can translate into a large absolute number of people – 88,000 – who need help. We shall return to the issue of who provides help when it is needed in more detail in Chapter Six.

Table 3.5: Ability to undertake key activities of daily living, population aged 65+, England, 2005 (%)

Activity	Ability to complete activity (%)		
	No difficulty	Unable to complete task	Complete task only with difficulty
Walk 400 yards	72	8	20
Put arm in jacket	89	2	9
Tie shoe laces	86	5	9
Get in/out of chair	82	0	18
Manage money	98	0	2
Eat/digest food	87	0	13
Get on a bus	80	8	12
Wash all over	91	2	7
Cut own toenails	63	18	19
Do heavy housework	59	18	23
Go up/down stairs	70	4	26
Carry shopping/heavy bags	56	18	26
Prepare/cook hot meal	88	4	8
Reach overhead shelf	71	7	22
Bend down to pick up things from floor	71	4	25

Source: Craig and Mindell (2007, table 2.4)

These data contrast markedly with the care home population where a very different pattern is observed. While this is at first sight not surprising, it is always worth reminding ourselves just how dependent the care home population is. Falconer and O'Neill (2007), using data from the 2002 Irish Census, which asked about both chronic long-term illness and a broad range of disabilities, report that the prevalence of disability among the population aged 65 and over in the community was 29% compared with 85% for those resident in nursing homes. Three quarters of nursing home residents were unable to go outside and 93% had difficulties with dressing, bathing or moving about inside (this is a portmanteau question) compared with 36% in the community. To some degree, these large differentials reflect the differences in the age composition of community and nursing home populations – in the Irish study, 21% of the community sample were aged 80 and over compared with 75% of the nursing home group. However, it is a consistent finding that levels of disability are very much greater in care home populations compared with community dwelling groups – if only because disability/physical and mental health problems are a prerequisite for admission into care. If older people were not experiencing significant difficulties with these types of activities then they would not be in care but would be able to remain at home.

These global profiles of ADL obscure some important variations within the older population. Using a more restricted number of items, Table 3.6 demonstrates significant age-related trends, with the very old experiencing the most difficulties. For example, of those aged 85 and over, approximately 60% have locomotor disabilities. Personal care difficulties also increase with age, although this is illustrated mostly by the 'moderate' rather than serious category (potentially because such individuals are in care as these vulnerabilities render them unable to remain in the community). Thus, even with the 'selecting out' of the group with the most problems, difficulties with ADL-type tasks are clearly age related and, with the exception of mobility difficulties, are reported by only a minority of older people resident in the community.

Table 3.6: Prevalence of different types of disability by age and gender, population aged 65+, Great Britain, 1999 (%)

Disability type	65-74		75-84		85+	
	M	F	M	F	M	F
Locomotor/mobility	25	24	33	43	55	69
Personal care	12	12	15	18	30	32
Sight	3	5	6	9	21	20
Hearing	13	8	15	13	28	30
Communication	2	1	4	2	6	5

Source: Bajekal et al (2004, tables 3, 4 and 5)

How consistent are reported rates of difficulties with (I)ADL across very different settings? There is much to be gained in social gerontological research by developing an overtly comparative cultural perspective and thereby looking for commonalities (and differences) in the experience of ageing and later life across and between populations with very different social and cultural foundations. This is methodologically challenging as asking questions about these types of activities across differential cultural groups is problematic. However, we have to consider whether any observed differences reflect: 'true' differences in ability to perform these tasks across the groups surveyed; a methodological artefact of the populations studied; or cultural differences in the importance of these activities across the different settings. Reyes-Ortiz et al (2006) compared (I)ADL rates between Brazil and the Caribbean. The study population consisted of those aged 75 and over, and the prevalence of reported difficulties with eating (around 4.5%), toileting (around 6%) and meal preparation (around 12%) were broadly similar between the two countries but variable in terms of two indicators: shopping (where reported difficulties ranged from 6% to 25%, respectively) and bathing (ranging from 5% to 25%, respectively). This, perhaps, reinforces the more cultural specificity of perceived problems with shopping and bathing rather than tasks such as toileting and eating.

This interest in the functional capacity levels of older people stems, in part, from a desire to allocate services to those most 'in need' and to estimate current (and future) service requirements. The indices are not usually constructed to demonstrate the level of independence of older people. Rather, they concentrate on measuring dependence and the 'need' for services and consist of items that researchers and policy makers consider relevant to independent life in the community. Rarely do they reflect the views of older people as to the activities they need to undertake to successfully remain in the community or the things that are important to them (Askham, 2003). Bowling (2005) invited her participants to rank the importance of being able to undertake key ADL/ functional capacity alone. Eating, bladder control and getting up and doing things were ranked most important while tying shoelaces and putting on a jacket were least important.

Difficulties with sight and hearing

Problems with sight, hearing and communication are not usually included within (I)ADL-based conceptualisations of disability. These aspects of health in later life are often thought rather prosaic and are attributed comparatively little importance in many studies. However, they are important especially for enabling older people to participate and engage with the broader society. Respondent number 201 in Victor et al's study stated: 'I mean the only problem that I've got is a problem with hearing with the higher pitches – there is a drop-off in what I can hear. And I used to find it very difficult when I was working on committees with people who speak very quietly at the end, particularly women' (Victor et al, 2009: respondent 201★).

Table 3.6 illustrates the extent of sight, hearing and communication problems among people aged 65 and over – drawn from the HSE. Communication difficulties are, in population terms, comparatively rare, with about 2% of the population aged 65 and over reporting such problems. Problems with sight and hearing are more common, with around 20% of those aged 85 and over reporting sight problems and around 30% hearing problems. Rather than rely on a single estimate it is useful to triangulate this data with data resultant from other studies of similar populations. Data from the GHS confirm the general pattern but with higher levels of hearing problems, which might reflect a slightly different question wording. The gender pattern is not consistent: women reporting worse vision and men worse hearing. Again it is worth reiterating the high prevalence rates of these two specific sensory problems and the consequent way such problems can effectively 'cut off' older people from participating in contemporary society.

Prevalence of disability

Clearly, from the perspective of profiling the overall health status of the population, an individual item is unhelpful and somewhat misleading as the reliability/validity of individual items may be questionable. Furthermore, it seems highly likely that responses to some individual items at least may be culturally and temporally specific. Hence, these types of measures are normally aggregated into an overall score that is then translated into a series of different categories of (dis)ability or functional impairment. Bowling (2005), using the 15 IADL items, categorised the population aged 65 and over resident in the community thus: 32% of the population had no difficulties with any ADL/IADL, 33% were classed as having slight difficulties, 13% had moderate difficulties and 22% had severe difficulties. This pattern is very similar to that reported by Melzer and colleagues (Melzer et al, 2000) where 16% of their sample were classified as severely disabled and 30% as not disabled. Using a broader group of activities and factors that included sight, hearing and communication difficulties, the HSE (Bajekal et al, 2001) reported that 49% of those aged 65 and over were 'not disabled', 30% had a moderate disability and 21% were severely disabled. Hence, there is broad similarity across studies and measures in terms of the extremes of the distribution, that is, those who are not disabled (a consensus of approximately 35% of the population aged 65 and over) and those who experience severe disability where studies consistently classify approximately 20% of the population aged 65 and over. Where the variability is observed is in the intermediate categories of slight/moderate disability and this largely reflects the influence of where the boundaries between categories such as 'slight' and 'moderate' disability are drawn.

The HSE data also illustrate elegantly the simple, but often overlooked, fact that half the people with a disability – 50% – in contemporary Britain are 'old' – or at least aged 65 and over, with those aged 85 and over (1% of the total population) accounting for 7.5% of the total 'disabled' population. If we focus on the severe disability category, then those aged 65 and over account for 58% and those aged 85 years and over represent 12.5% of this group. While we have no wish to understate or denigrate the problems and issues of younger disabled people, it is a simple epidemiological 'fact' that the experience of disability is most evident among the older age groups.

If we focus on the category of severe disability then we consistently observe differentials between different social groups. Bowling (2005) reports that severe disability (as measured by her 15 ADL/IADL items) was higher among females than males (25% versus 17%) and those aged 75 and over compared with those aged under 75 (31% versus 15%). Only 3% of those with the highest socioeconomic status reported severe difficulties compared with 12% of those at the bottom of the class hierarchy and this pattern is consistent for other measures of social status, namely education, income and housing tenure. The HSE disability measure demonstrates both an age-related increase and a clear 'gender imbalance' with, from the age of 75 onwards, a clear excess of disability among females (see Table 3.7).

Table 3.7: Disability severity by age and gender, population aged 65+, Great Britain, 1999 (%)

Disability severity	65-74		75-84		85+		All 65+	
	M	F	M	F	M	F	M	F
None	66	68	57	49	28	27	83	82
Moderate	25	23	29	32	39	32	13	13
Severe	9	9	14	19	33	42	5	5

Source: Bajekal et al (2004, table 10)

Zunzunegui et al (2009) in a very different setting – large cities in Latin America and the Caribbean – sought to explain the poorer chronic health and disability outcomes demonstrated by older women as compared with men. Their analysis explored the contribution of differential exposures across the lifecourse and differential vulnerabilities to these exposures; for example, obesity and widowhood act differentially in terms of health outcomes among older men and women. However, they failed to demonstrate an explanatory link with either set of factors. This may, of course, suggest that some factors were poorly operationalised and that key factors were not measured. Their paper highlights the complexity of the explanation of gender variations in health status, which, almost certainly, involves the interplay of biological/genetic, environmental and social factors that are dynamic across the lifecourse. Again, this is another aspect of the experience of ageing and later life that benefits from the adoption of a lifecourse approach and will benefit from the analysis of longitudinal data. The existence of such differentials led Melzer et al (2000) to argue that if all older people experienced the same level of functional limitations illustrated by the most advantaged groups then there would an absolute fall in the number of older people with severe/ substantial impairment in ADL/IADL functions, despite the well-documented ageing of our population in future decades. While Melzer et al (2000) might be somewhat overstating their case, our review demonstrates that social factors, in particular class and gender (and age), clearly influence the experience of health and illness in later life and that eradicating/reducing such differentials would reduce the overall disease burden. The persistence of class-based health inequalities in later life in terms of mortality, physical health problems, chronic illness and disability indicates that patterns of morbidity in later life are not entirely explained by genetic/biological factors.

Disability and long-term illness

We have used two related concepts to examine the experience of chronic ill-health in later life, namely (limiting) longstanding illness and disability. How close are the links between these two concepts? Given the complexity of the measures of disability, what, if any, is the 'added value' of the data generated? Table 3.8 compares the prevalence of longstanding illness, limiting longstanding illness and disability derived from the HSE. For both men and women we can see that rates of chronic health problems are much higher than those of disability until the age of 80-85. This is, perhaps, not unexpected given the nature of the two sets of questions. This 'crossover' effect has been noted previously and explained thus: older people 'under-report' limiting longstanding illness as they take activity limitation to be an integral component of growing older and thus, 'downplay' these types of change while disability/ADL-type questions ask about specific and (relatively) precise activity limitations. It is also worth comparing the rates of limiting longstanding illness derived from the HSE and GHS as the HSE estimates are consistently higher. It is not clear why this is the case but might reflect the greater health emphasis in the HSE. This again indicates how different surveys can generate variable prevalence estimates of complex notions such as chronic illness or disability even when using the same questions in similar populations!

Table 3.8: Prevalence of disability and long-term limiting illness by age and gender, population aged 65+, Great Britain, 1999 (%)

	65-74		75-84		85+	
	M	F	M	F	M	F
With disability	34	32	43	51	72	73
Longstanding illness	67	67	71	76	72	79
Longstanding limiting illness	40	41	48	51	55	65

Source: Bajekal et al (2004, table 10)

We can examine the interrelationship between disability and longstanding illness more closely by looking at the proportions of those with longstanding and limiting illness in our key disability categories. Overall, of those with longstanding illness, some two thirds do not have a disability, while approximately 50% of those with limiting longstanding illness do not have a disability. However, these questions are more sensitive for those aged 65 and over where about one third have no disability but report limiting illness. So while the overlap is by no means perfect, these questions are most closely linked for the population in their seventh and eighth decades.

Disability-free/active life expectancy

In Chapter Two we looked at life expectancy and in this chapter we have looked at disability. One important development in characterising the health of populations is to use combinations of mortality and morbidity data to calculate measures of 'healthy' or 'disability-free' life expectancy. This approach has the merit of combining information about survival rates with data concerning the health status of survivors and so we can combine, in single measure, information about both quantity and quality of life experienced by the whole population or subgroups thereof. There are several measures that describe this broad concept including disability-free life expectancy, disability-adjusted life expectancy and healthy life expectancy. Despite the variation in the names of these measures, and in the detail of the methods of calculation, they all express a related, and rather fundamental, concept. How many years (or what percentage) of the expected duration of life will be healthy or free from disability, dementia or dependency?

We have already seen that Britain (and other Western societies) is well served by comprehensive and robust mortality data. However, measures of morbidity used to determine the expected likelihood of disability are rather less robust. Consequently, we need to look carefully at the data on which these measures are based before accepting their utility and arguments that healthy life expectancy has increased/decreased. Two 'self-report' measures are often used in the calculation of this measure: health rating as good (or better), termed 'healthy life expectancy' (we examine this measure in Chapter Four) or limiting long-term illness (as a proxy for disability), termed 'disability-free life expectancy'. Data for 2004 indicate that for the UK life expectancy at birth was 77 years for males and 81 years for females. Focusing on males we can see that 67.9 years (88.6%) would be classed as 'healthy' and 62.3 years (81%) as 'disability free'. Women, although having a longer life expectancy, can expect less life classified as 'healthy' (86.7%) or disability free (77.7%).

We should also note the limited nature of the definition of health and/ or disability used in the above examples, which do not include, for example, psychological wellbeing (see Pérès et al, 2008) or cognitive function, both of which can have a highly deleterious effect on quality of life, To address the issues of defining the health indicators used in these measures, Jagger and the EHEMU (2005) have been working towards developing a European Union (EU)-wide methodology for calculating healthy life years. This is an attractive proposition because, again, it will facilitate cross-national comparisons. Jagger et al (2008) note that 50 countries have estimates of healthy life expectancy but that methodological differences limit robust comparisons. As an illustration of the potential benefits, Jagger et al (2008) have calculated healthy life expectancies at birth and age 65 for 15 EU states using a disability question from the European Community Household Panel (ECHP). This analysis shows considerable variation between the member states and some inconsistencies between the genders in terms of trends in disability-free life expectancy between 1995 and 2001. Three groups of countries are identified: reducing disability (for example, Belgium and Italy; both males and females), increasing disability (the Netherlands and the UK; males) and those where there is no change (Spain and the UK; females). Given the data already presented regarding the socioeconomic and ethnic differentials in mortality and disability, it is reasonable to conclude that such gradients exist for disability-free life expectancy at both birth and age 65 and over. That these health outcomes vary with socioeconomic factors/ ethnicity and gender serves to (re)emphasise the importance of social factors in the experience of health and illness in later life.

The giants of geriatric medicine

An important, but more historically based and somewhat unfashionable, perspective on the health status of older people derives from the Beveridge Report (1944), which established the broad shape of the post-1945 welfare state in Britain to combat what were termed the 'five giants' that stood in the way of social progress: want, ignorance, disease, squalor and idleness. Borrowing from this idea, Bernard Isaacs, who held the Chair of Geriatric Medicine in Birmingham and who produced some strikingly original and accessible work (Isaacs et al, 1972), identified the 'four giants' of geriatrics as: immobility, instability, incontinence and intellectual impairment. He argued that 'They [the giants] have in common the qualities of multiple causation; chronic course; deprivation of independence; [and] no simple cure' (1972: 16). It was his proposition that most, if not all, problems experienced by older people could be traced back to these four 'geriatric giants'. Geriatric medicine has fallen out of favour as a medical speciality. It is now easy to disregard the early pioneers such as Marjorie Warren and Lionel Cosin and a series of high-profile clinical professors such as Bernard Isaacs, John Brocklehurst and Arnold Exton Smith (one of my PhD examiners!) as misguidedly colluding in the ageist marginalisation of older people from the medical mainstream while simultaneously 'medicalising' old age and later life. The four giants indentified by Isaacs may not be very fashionable in terms of healthcare priorities (for treatment, education or research), especially as they do not map directly onto the explicitly disease-focused priorities of the National Health Service (NHS) as embodied by the cancer and heart disease strategies. However, they are important to older people and their importance largely stems from the effect that these unglamorous and 'unfashionable' (compared with cancer and cardiovascular disease) health problems have on the ability of older people to live independently in the community, to function effectively and to participate within society. So in the final section of this chapter we will look at immobility, instability and incontinence – we deal with mental health in Chapter Four.

Immobility

Locomotor disability, which results in immobility, increases with age and is one of the major sources of disability among older people. Thus, 58% of those aged 65 and over cannot walk 200 yards without stopping and approximately 50% cannot manage a flight of 12 stairs (see Table 3.9). Such physical limitations can greatly reduce the size and constitution of the physical spaces that older people can use safely and effectively and limit their ability to engage with the wider social world.

Table 3.9: Prevalence of locomotor disability by age and gender, population aged 65+, England, 2005 (% reporting difficulty)

	65-74		75-84		85+	
	M	F	M	F	M	F
Walking 200m	22	17	28	36	46	65
Climbing 12 stairs	15	18	20	32	23	50

Source: Craig and Mindell (2007, table 4)

We can look into immobility in a little more detail using physical performance measures that are related to (im)mobility, such as gait (walking) speed and time to get out of a chair. Both ELSA and the 2005 HSE record gait speed and timed chair rises – both 'objective' tests of physical function that correlate well with mobility problems and functional decline. The data from these two surveys are broadly comparable but the HSE data are used here as they provide results for those aged 65 and over in 10-year age bands and have fewer 'exclusions' than the ELSA study. It is a methodologically interesting 'survey methods' question as to how to deal with those who refuse to undertake one of these physical tests, those who are unable to attempt the test or who are judged 'unsafe' to attempt a test. Should these groups be treated as 'refusers'/'non-responders', as having 'failed' the test or being unable to complete the test? The HSE adopts the last of these three stances such that those who are unable to complete a test for safety reasons are defined as 'failing' the test because exclusion of these individuals from the results would overstate the overall results. However, this is a particularly problematic issue and it would be helpful if surveys using these tests could adopt a common approach to data collection so that we can distinguish 'true' non-responders and examine reasons for non-response and adjust failure rates (if necessary).

Overall, 87% of men and 79% of women could complete a single chair stand. This test shows a strong age–related gradient, with 90% of the 65-69 age group completing the task compared with 60% of those aged 85 and over. Overall, 84% of men and 74% of women could complete five chair raises (this represents about 95% of those who completed a single raise). Again, there is a marked decrease in functional performance with age and the gender differential is especially marked above the age of 75.

The gait speed test is based on continuous recordings of the time participants take to walk at their normal speed – it is not a test of 'high performance'. Eight per cent of men and 17% of women had a gait speed that was equal to (or less) than an index speed of under half a metre per second. At this speed it would take 15 seconds to cross a single carriageway road compared with the time of 15-26 seconds allowed on pelican crossings. Some 23% of men and 39% of women aged 85 and over walk at this speed. If we add in the percentages of participants who could not complete the test then this elevates the percentage of the population that we might term as 'walking impaired' to almost half, 46% of those aged 85 and over. Undoubtedly a range of factors are implicated in generating these levels of walking impairment but this is clearly a major issue that requires further multidisciplinary research to identify effective interventions to help maintain (and enhance) the mobility of the older population.

Falls and instability

Falls, fear of falling and instability are, as identified by Isaacs (1992), one of the key challenges to health in later life. Falls, and the resultant consequences, extract a high toll for both individuals and society more broadly. From the individual's perspective, falls can result in fractures and serious injuries. They are often accompanied by more insidious psychological consequences in the resultant fear of falling, which can limit both quality of life and the ability to cope independently at home. Data from the ELSA survey (Marmot et al, 2002) indicate that 26% of men and 39% of women aged 60 and over reported that they had fallen in the previous two years. The HSE study uses a 12-month reference point and indicates that 23% of men and 29% of women reported a fall during that time (see Table 3.10). This broadly concurs with data from a variety of prevalence estimates derived from a series of community surveys that suggest that about a third of people aged 65 and over fall annually (see Dowsell et al, 1999). This estimate seems to be roughly stable in a historical context. In his 1948 survey on the health of older people in Wolverhampton, Sheldon (1948) reported that 36% had had a fall. There are also clear and well–evidenced trends illustrated in Table 3.10. The reported prevalence of falls increases with age such that some 40% of those aged 85 and over had had a fall. While it is useful to know how many older people fall within a given period, the number of falls is also relevant. Conceptually and practically we might hypothesise that multiple falls are more likely to be more problematic because of the increased likelihood of injury, loss of confidence and increased fear of

Table 3.10: Prevalence of falls in previous year by age and gender, population aged 65+, England, 2005 (%)

Number of falls	65-69		70-74		75-79		80-84		85+		All 65+	
	M	F	M	F	M	F	M	F	M	F	M	F
None	82	77	80	73	81	73	69	66	57	57	77	71
1	11	14	12	15	10	16	19	17	22	24	13	16
2+	7	9	8	12	9	11	12	17	23	19	10	13
% fallers needing treatment	23	29	21	30	25	34	27	36	18	42	23	34

Source: Craig and Mindell (2007, tables 2.1 and 2.5)

falling. About 6% of the participants in the HSE survey reported three or more falls in the previous two years and this also increased with age. We can also see that approximately one third of fallers require medical treatment (see Table 3.10) – this is why falls are so important for both individuals and the health services. Scheffer et al (2008) note that it was Murphy and Isaacs (1982) who first observed that after a fall older people develop a 'fear' of falling. This was initially thought to be as a result of the trauma of falling and it was given the title of 'post fall' syndrome. However, in their comprehensive review, Scheffer et al (2008) note that about 50% of those who expressed fear of falling had not actually experienced a fall. They note that there are a variety of estimates of fear of falling ranging from 3% to 88% but with most estimates around the 20% mark. As with falls themselves, fear of falling increases with age and is greater among males than females. Other risk factors for fear of falling include dizziness, depression and self-rated health while the relationship with gait and balance (discussed below) is ambiguous. As most studies of the fear of falling are cross-sectional in nature, the consequences of this have not been rigorously studied longitudinally. The fear of falling, as distinct from actually falling, can be every bit as debilitating and restricting as an actual fall especially in terms of reduced social activity, decreased functional independence and reduced quality of life.

The HSE and ELSA surveys provides data on gait speed (discussed earlier in this chapter) and balance, both of which are associated with falls and fear of falling, in terms of physical performance. Balance, or rather problems with balance, are a substantial risk factor for falls and many falls prevention and rehabilitation programmes address balance training as part of the intervention. There are now computer-based training and education programmes promoting the benefits of balance training (see www.balancetraining.org.uk). The balance test in the ELSA/HSE surveys consists of five elements, which increase in the challenge that they pose for individuals. The tests range from a simple 'side by side' stand where individuals stand with feet together for 10 seconds, to standing on one leg with eyes closed for 10 seconds. Again, these results must be interpreted in light of the fact that some substantial numbers did not participate in these tests – approximately 10% – thus, the prevalence rates 'overestimate' the profile. Overall,

87% of men and 78% of women aged 85 and over could complete the 'side by side' stand but only 31% of men and 19% of this age group could complete the full tandem balance.[1] There is a clear and statistically significant decrease in the ability of participants to successfully complete these balances. What is not clear is how this test performance translates into actual or risk of falling or the ability of individuals to cope independently at home.

The three measures of physical performance discussed in this chapter (gait speed, balance test and chair rise) can be combined to give an overall score. This is termed the Short Physical Performance Battery (SPPB) Test. For each of the three tests, individuals are given a score from 0 to 4, which are summed to give an index ranging from 0 to 12 with 8 or less taken as the 'cut-off' defining 'poor performance'. Table 3.11 provides data on this and confirms the general trends for the individual performance measures: a strong age-related gradient and the consistently worse performance of women as compared with men. The cumulative effect of these trends is that the physical performance of 80% of those aged 85 and over is classified as impaired. Again, however, it is not clear how this translates into the performance of daily activities and/or a threat to independent living but it certainly clarifies the physical vulnerability and frailty of those in very old age.

Table 3.11: Prevalence of physical impairment based on the Short Physical Performance Battery by age and gender, population aged 65+, England, 2005 (%)

65-69		70-74		75-79		80-84		85+		All 65+	
M	F	M	F	M	F	M	F	M	F	M	F
17	27	25	31	32	50	46	69	70	85	30	46

Source: Craig and Mindell (2007, table 5.9)

Incontinence

Sheldon (1948: 71) wrote: 'In many instances the normal control over the emptying of the bladder, on which so much social ease and comfort is dependent, becomes more difficult in the later years of life'. Thus, he neatly and elegantly both identifies an important but much-neglected health issue for older people, and illuminates the resultant negative social consequences resultant from such problems. In his survey, Sheldon (1948) reported a prevalence rate of urinary incontinence of 11%. More recently, a community-based survey by Stoddart et al (2001), using a definition of incontinence as the involuntary loss of urine, which is a social or hygiene problem (Continence Society definition), reported that 27% of those aged 65 and over were defined as being incontinent of urine. This is somewhat higher but in the same general order of magnitude as the 21% reported by the HSE (Craig and Mindell, 2007). Prevalence rates were higher among women

(31%) than men and increased with age from 20% aged 65-69 to 39% of those aged 80 years and over (Stoddart et al, 2001). The HSE produces a very similar age and gender gradient (see Table 3.12) – hence, the impact on daily life is clearly significant. Incontinence clearly has marked and profound effects on the quality of life of the sufferer. It is difficult to improve on the succinct summary of how incontinence effects quality of life described by Sheldon (1948: 73) thus: 'woman of 65 said that she was unable to walk two yards without having to pass water, and that as a result her life was a burden. She was unable to stand in queues, and could never go out in company or pay a visit to another house, unless she knew them well'. There is evidence of substantial unmet need as 48% did not do anything about the problem while approximately 28% had consulted their general practitioner (Stoddard et al, 2001) and 55% of those reporting incontinence said it affected their lives. GP consultation rates were higher among the HSE sample (50%) 30% reported that they did not do anything about their bladder problem. While there are slight differences between the responses derived from these two different sources, we can see that here is another example of an important health issue that is not being addressed in terms of GP/primary care consultation, which is indicative of significant unmet need for services. We can only speculate as to why individuals do not consult their GP but it may partly reflect expectations of such problems being part of 'normal' old age.

Table 3.12: Prevalence of bladder problems by age and gender, population aged 65+, England, 2005 (%)

65-69		70-74		75-79		80-84		85+	
M	F	M	F	M	F	M	F	M	F
16	18	20	17	23	25	25	25	31	34

Source: Craig and Mindell (2007, figure 3D)

Key points

In this chapter we have demonstrated that disability, chronic illness and problems with ADL increase with age.

There are important and consistent differentials in the extent of disability and chronic health in later life by social class. The position for gender is variable and suggests a more complex pattern of health and illness than a simple male–female differential. The link with ethnicity is not clear and is under-researched but the suggestion is that minority ethnic communities are likely to demonstrate higher levels of morbidity than the general population.

The persistence of health inequalities in later life also suggests that there is considerable benefit in policy terms to be had from the eradication of such differentials. The challenges of an ageing population would be less onerous if all experienced the good health enjoyed by the privileged few.

Alongside other more routine and accepted ways of investigating and examining the health of older people, traditional 'problem'-focused aspects of health such as falls or incontinence are important and these problems can severely compromise the independence and quality of life of older people.

Can we identify a typology of health problems in old age? Combining mortality and morbidity data we can identify three sets of health problems in later life: (a) those with both high mortality and high morbidity such as heart and circulatory disease, (b) those with high morbidity and low mortality (musculoskeletal diseases are the paradigmatic example here) and (c) those with high mortality and low morbidity (cancer). Patterns of morbidity and mortality within the population for this typology of diseases are not coterminous and this poses challenges for developing 'public health' interventions to reduce mortality and morbidity. Reducing risk factors for some major disease types such as cancer will not, necessarily, translate into reductions in morbidity in later life resultant from musculoskeletal disorders or from heart disease and stroke.

Note
[1] The full tandem balance consists of standing with the heel of one foot in front of, and touching the toes of, the other foot. Participants aged 65-69 were asked to hold this position for 30 seconds, while those aged 70 or over were asked to hold it for 10 seconds.

Further activities
▸ Calculate the numbers of older people in your locality who have (a) chronic illnesses, (b) problems with ADL, (c) falls and (d) incontinence.
▸ What factors might explain the class and gender differences seen in the prevalence of chronic illness and disability?

Further reading
Ayis, S., Gooberman-Hill, R. and Ebrahim, S. (2003) Long-standing and limiting long-standing illness in older people: associations with chronic diseases, psychosocial and environmental factors. *Age and Ageing*, 32(3), 265-72.

Ayis, S., Bowling, A., Gooberman-Hill, R. and Ebrahim, S. (2007) The effect of definitions of activities of daily living on estimates of changing ability among older people. *International Journal of Rehabilitation Research*, 30(1), 39-46.

Ayis, S., Gooberman-Hill, R., Bowling, A. and Ebrahim, S. (2006) Predicting catastrophic decline in mobility among older people. *Age and Ageing*, 35(4), 382-7.

Bowling, A., Seetai, S., Morris, R. and Ebrahim, S. (2007) Quality of life among older people with poor functioning: the influence of perceived control over life. *Age and Ageing*, 36(3), 310-5.

Ebrahim, S., Adamson, J., Ayis, S., Beswick, A. and Gooberman-Hill, R. (2008) Locomotor disability: meaning, causes and effects of interventions. *Journal of Health Services Research and Policy*, 3, 38-46.

Gooberman-Hill, R., Ayis, S. and Ebrahim, S. (2003) Understanding long-standing illness among older people. *Social Science and Medicine*, 56(12), 2555-64.

Paúl, C., Ayis, S. and Ebrahim, S. (2007) Disability and psychosocial outcomes in old age. *Journal of Aging and Health*, 19(50), 723-41.

Paúl, C., Ayis, S. and Ebrahim, S. (2006) Psychological distress, loneliness and disability in old age. *Psychological Health Medicine*, 11(2), 221-32.

Useful websites

- *Policies for healthy ageing in OECD countries:* www.olis.oecd.org/olis/2009doc. nsf/linkto/DELSA-HEA-WD-HWP%282009%291
- *WHO data on global disease burden and life expectancy:* www.who.int/topics/ life_expectancy/en/
- *Data on health status/health service use from the National Health Service Information Centre:* www.ic.nhs.uk/

FOUR

Mental health and psychological wellbeing

Key points

In this chapter we consider:

- the key elements of mental health and psychological wellbeing in later life;
- the major mental health problems of later life: anxiety, depression and dementia/cognitive impairment.

As Isaacs (1965) argued in identifying his 'giants' of geriatric medicine, 'intellectual impairment', by which he was effectively referring to dementia, poses a major challenge to health and wellbeing in later life. We extend this observation to include psychological, emotional and mental health and not just the pathological state of dementia/cognitive impairment (or other disease states including affective disorders such as anxiety and depression). Good psychological, emotional and mental health is a prerequisite for a good quality of life across the lifecourse, not just in old age. This is recognised in a range of national policy statements issued by central government in the UK and in the interest shown by researchers in profiling and ranking the attributes of a 'good life', in 'happiness studies' and in identifying the 'best' (and worst) places to live. The positive focus on mental wellbeing (rather than illness) is illustrated by standard one of the National Service Framework for Mental Health for adults published in 1999 (DH, 1999), which emphasises the importance of promoting mental wellbeing (rather then treating or preventing mental ill-health) in improving the health of the nation. However, as with the previous chapters, much of the research and evidence focuses on ill-health rather than wellness. Inevitably in this volume we can only present an overview of the key issues and domains concerned with mental health as they affect older people (for more detail, see Lee, 2006, 2007). In this chapter we focus on the broad area of mental wellbeing as it pertains to 'old age' and later life. We focus on two distinct elements: general psychological wellbeing (including expectations about health in old age) and key mental health problems in later life (including dementia/cognitive impairment and affective disorders, predominantly depression/anxiety in old age). Thus, in this chapter we offer a comprehensive overview and introduction to the mental health and wellbeing of older people, something that is often lacking when the focus is purely on mental health problems and psychological morbidity such as dementia or depression.

Psychological health and wellbeing

ACTIVITY I

▸ What do you think are the major transitions associated with later life?

▸ Are there positive transitions characteristic of growing older?

Psychological health and wellbeing are important elements of the experience of later life and impact significantly on the quality of life of individuals. While this statement is not unique to older people – it probably holds for the rest of the population – old age and later life do pose specific challenges in terms of illness and disability and stressful life events such as bereavement or the admission of family or friends into long-term care. Social roles and losses resultant from retirement and bereavement that are rare at other phases of the lifecourse and that can challenge and compromise wellbeing and quality of life are commonplace in later life. Such events may be characterised as both a crisis – a novel situation for which habitual responses are insufficient – and a transition – a turning point that has implications for an individual's ability to adapt and meet future crises. Transitions occur across the lifecourse and these result in changes for the individual, which may be either negative (there may be deleterious consequences in terms of social, physical, biological or psychological dimensions) or positive (the changes may proffer new opportunities for the individual concerned). The transitions particularly associated with growing older are often negative such as bereavement or the onset of chronic illness, although there are 'positive' transitions such as the birth of (great) grandchildren. The same transition, retirement or becoming a grandparent, may be interpreted positively (being freed from the burdens of work) or negatively (becoming a grandmother being an unwelcome external marker of personal ageing). Transitions may (or may not) be expected or unexpected, may be either welcome or unwelcome and can vary in intensity from minor to life changing. A transition such as retirement illustrates the complexity surrounding these issues. The same event such as retirement may be experienced differentially depending on the circumstances of the individual, the meaning they attach to the transition, whether the transition was anticipated, and the resources (material, social and psychological) that the individual has at their disposal to cope with the transition. However, we also know that these transitions can have an effect on the psychological health of individuals, that experiencing multiple (negative) transitions is problematic and that older people are vulnerable to experiencing multiple negative transitions and have the least material and social resources to deploy in response.

Resilience in later life

There are many aspects of the psychology of old age and later life that space does not permit us to deal with in this volume but we do just need to note some of the key psychological aspects of 'personality' that have been linked with quality of life and wellbeing in old age (and indeed other phases of the life cycle). These include coping strategies (important for responding to life transitions), self-efficacy (perceived mastery and control over life), morale, self-esteem, social comparisons and expectations of life. While we do not have space to cover all of these traits in depth it is useful to contextualise them by summarising the extent to which they are present within the general population of older people and their influence on quality of life and the maintenance of independence and autonomy. These traits are seen as forming one component of resilience in ageing. Resilience (or lack of it) becomes evident at transition points in life (Rutter, 1987). Ideas about resilience across the lifecourse represent an attempt to recalibrate research to focus on the positive (resilience) instead of the negative (vulnerability) and to identify factors that can promote and enhance resilience. Definitions of resilience are often imprecise. However, the definition of Hildon and colleagues (2008, 2009) of responding positively to adversity encapsulates the central tenets of ideas about resilience. Resilience is often conceptualised by classifying people according to their physical, cognitive (psychological) and social functioning in terms of high, medium and low function and linking these resources to key health outcomes. There are a number of debates about resilience in later life. Is resilience a 'fixed' trait – if we are resilient when we are young, will we carry this trait into old age (and vice versa)? When we are defining (and measuring) the positive response that identifies resilience, are we concerned about restoring previous functioning levels or improved functioning?

There are obvious links between the notion of 'successful' ageing and resilience. According to Rowe and Kahn (1997), 'successful agers' are those who, in comparison to their contemporaries, demonstrate no (or minimal) loss of function. They further suggest that age-associated declines are not normative and serve to deflect researchers away from investigating the external factors that generate these age-related changes. They further suggest that psychosocial factors interact in ways we do not fully comprehend to influence health and function and that they can be modified to ameliorate these age-related health declines. Baltes and Baltes (1990) highlight resilience as one of the attributes of successful ageing and they conceptualise this in their ideas about selective optimisation with compensation. They argue that this type of adaptation becomes more important in old age and later life because of the transitions noted earlier. Very briefly, this model involves three processes, which are inter-related: selection (restriction of functioning into a limited number of domains of the highest priority), optimisation (use of resources to maximise function) and compensation (strategies/resources used to compensate for reduced resources, for example using written reminders as memory aids and using technological assistance such as hearing aids). This is encapsulated by the

T-shirt slogan 'Old and treachery (or sometimes cunning) will always beat youth and talent/skill/enthusiasm!' It is argued that resilient individuals use compensation strategies particularly effectively.

While the precise composition of the complex entity of resilience is unclear, research consistently demonstrates the importance of physical functioning, psychological functioning and wellbeing. Resilient older people have high levels of physical functioning, exercise initiative and autonomy, believe they have control over their life and have high levels of life satisfaction. We have empirical evidence for the extent to which older people report self-mastery (or being in control of events). Bowling (2005) reports that 61% of those aged 65 and over who are resident in the community demonstrate high levels of self-mastery, a very positive 'enabling' characteristic, with 16% demonstrating low self-efficacy, indicating that they do not feel 'in control' of their life. It is this latter group who are going to be vulnerable when confronted with the types of negative transitions noted earlier. Also relevant to an understanding of the link between psychology and autonomy and independence are notions of positive affect (optimism) and negative affect (pessimism). Bowling (2005) suggests that 70% of older people categorise themselves as optimists by 'always looking on the bright side'; 49% expect the best and 66% are defined as optimists. Such traits are not just academic constructs but are reflected in how people live their lives and cope with life's vicissitudes, as these comments illustrate: 'I suppose I'm a bit of an optimist, in a way … I enjoy life … I think there's no point in living if your not enjoying yourself'; 'I'm an optimistic person, I look on the bright side' Bowling (2005: 151).

How do older people evaluate their health?

ACTIVITY 2

▸ What percentage of older people rate their health as excellent/good and what percentage as poor?

▸ Are older people more (or less) likely to rate their health as poor compared with younger people?

▸ What percentage of older (and younger) people expect old age to be a time of poor health?

It has been consistently demonstrated that health (and the health of those we care about) is central to quality of life across the lifecourse and satisfaction/ expectations are an important strand of 'resilience'. Bowling (2005) provides empirical survey data to support this as she reports that 62% of her respondents agreed with the statement that 'few things are more important than good health'. Lay understandings of health and the 'illness' model of health usually include an element of 'self-evaluation' that involves locating one's own health in comparison with either other people in general or those of the same age. Such measures are often referred to, not entirely positively, as a 'subjective' health rating, with connotations of a lack of rigour, and that objective measures, such as medical diagnosis or physiological measurements, are inherently more robust and credible. We posit that how individuals think about their health and their expectations of (health in) old age more generally is crucial in terms of quality of life and has been linked with a range of health and social care outcomes, including mortality (DeSalvo et al, 2006; Murata et al, 2006).

Social comparison and expectations theory underpin these self-rating types of 'health evaluation' questions. Such questions generally ask respondents to evaluate their health in the previous year (or a specified period prior to interview) as good, fair or poor in order to compare their health to other people of a similar age and to evaluate how far their current health status has lived down (or up) to expectations: an important component of, and predictor of, quality of life in later life (see Bowling et al, 2002). The heart of social comparisons and expectations theory is that those individuals whose life circumstances mesh with their aspirations and/or expectations will evaluate their life more positively than those where there is a large (negative) gap. Central to this theoretical perspective is the direction or focus of the 'reference standard' against which comparisons/expectations are being measured. Bowling (2005) postulates that vulnerable or marginalised groups – of which older people are clearly, one – make comparisons with others who are generally worse off, which enables them to feel better about themselves and their current situation. Thus, the focus is on downward comparisons. Social comparison theory has been conceptualised as a compensatory strategy to 'protect' older people from the negative effects of ageing (see Cheung and Robine, 2007). However, as Cheung and Robine (2007) observe, there are few studies that have empirically tested the idea that older people are more likely to use downward social comparisons than other age groups.

How do older people evaluate their health?

With this caveat in mind, Table 4.1 indicates that, overall, approximately 57% of men and 55% of women describe their health as very good or good; some 30% rate their health as fair and around 13% as bad or very bad. There is little obvious gender variation and the responses for men are broadly stable across the age groups.

Table 4.1: Self-reported health by age and gender, population aged 65+, England, 2005 (%)

	65-69		70-74		75-79		80-84		85+	
	M	F	M	F	M	F	M	F	M	F
Very good	22	25	19	17	19	16	16	17	24	15
Good	40	40	39	38	36	36	34	30	34	34
Fair	28	25	29	34	32	33	34	38	29	35
Bad	7	7	9	9	10	10	10	11	8	12
Very bad	4	3	4	2	4	5	6	4	6	4

Source: Craig and Mindell (2007, table 2.1)

For women, increased age brings about a change in the relative size of the good health/fair health categories but little marked change in the bad health category. Given the increased prevalence of chronic physical illness with age that we saw in Chapter Three, it is still surprising that so few older people consistently rate their health as bad/very bad. Even at the age of 85 years and over, approximately 50% rate their health as good and only around 14% rate their health as bad or very bad, although 58% report that they have a longstanding limiting illness and 46% report two or more longstanding physical illnesses (this excludes mental health and/or psychological conditions). This reflects the observation from the 2005 Health Survey for England (Craig and Mindell, 2007) that 52% of those in care homes and 56% of those in the community rate their health as very good or good and 11% of both groups rate it as poor. The 'positive' evaluation of health by older people is one manifestation of what Cheung (2002) termed the 'paradox of ageing' (or the wellbeing paradox).

However, given the profound differences in levels of chronic health and disability between the community and care home groups, the similarity of their 'health ratings' is a very intriguing observation. This illustrates the complexity of these types of evaluations, and the influence of 'health expectations' and the selection of the 'reference' framework on how individuals rate their health in old age. As Cheung and Robine (2007) note, the reference or target group against which such comparisons are made is clearly, influential in generating the empirical results. In many utilisations of these 'self-evaluation' questions, individuals are asked to compare themselves with 'most other people of the same age' (or variations of that type of wording). This task is not quite as straightforward as it sounds as our knowledge of 'most other people' is likely to be derived from stereotypical ideas about the general population, a largely undefined group. Hence, for older people the stereotypical image of the health of an older person may be highly negative. Consequently, respondents may 'distance' themselves from this image and enhance their evaluation of their own health status, what Cheung et al (2007) termed a 'contrast effect'. The same lines of argument apply to the use of these types of questions in terms of quality of life, general wellbeing or material circumstances.

It is clear that the data presented in Table 4.1 reflect a complex decision-making process that involves the choice of the normative (or reference) group, as well as how people understand and conceptualise the meaning of terms such as 'health'. The empirical evidence about the choice of the reference groups against which comparisons are made is limited but raises some interesting questions. Cheung and Robine (2007) comment that, when investigated specifically, individuals compare themselves with 'known others' rather than the general mass of people of one's own age. These authors also note the possibility that individuals may use different reference 'targets' for different comparison domains and over time. Thus, responding to the apparently simple survey-type question asking about self-rated health is underpinned by a complex and dynamic set of decision-making processes. Older people do not define 'health' in terms of the absence of symptoms or diagnosed conditions but rather in terms of their ability to discharge 'normal' roles and functions such as keeping house, undertaking 'normal' activities of daily living (ADL) and being able to engage in social relationships. For this age group, health is very much about being able to function effectively and autonomously in the community and in maintaining independence. As one of Bowling's respondents commented, 'The best thing is that I have health enough to go about and do my own shopping...' (Bowling, 2005: 196). This general comment is supported by 40% of respondents in her survey, who identified loss of independence resultant from ill-health and functional decline as one of the worst things about old age. As this respondent very appositely states, she has 'health enough'. Not perfect health or full health but health enough to cope with the requirements of everyday life. Again, understanding how older people conceptualise their health is a prerequisite for interpreting the evidence generated by these rating questions.

Within this apparently broadly stable pattern of health rating across age and gender groups, we can postulate that there may well be changes and variations within and between specific groups that are obscured by this macro-level analysis. Within an overall pattern of 'no significant change', some groups may have 'improved' (perhaps those from privileged social class groups) while others may have deteriorated or remained stable. We cannot presume that there are not intragroup differentials in both absolute health ratings (or any other health index) and relative differentials and, where we have longitudinal data, absolute/relative changes over time. Given that health ratings do not seem to exhibit significant or profound variations with either age or gender, are there variations with either class or ethnicity? Both General Household Survey (GHS) and HSE data suggest that there is an important class variation in responses to this question for older people living in the community. The HSE reports differentials of 19% for men and 13% for women between manual and non-manual classes, in the percentage rating their health as good. There is also evidence emerging that older people from the UK's key minority ethnic communities report 'worse' health ratings than the general population. For the population aged 55 and over, the majority of migrant groups, the exception are the Chinese, have a larger percentage of the population describing their health as bad/very bad when compared with the general population (see Table 4.2). Clearly, we must be cautious to not over-interpret these results because of the small sample sizes. However, some of the differentials are substantial. For the general population, 12% of women aged 55 and over rate their health as bad/very bad. This compares with 44% for the Bangladeshi population, 45% for the Pakistani population, 22% for the Indian population and 24% for the Black Caribbean population. Clearly, the magnitude of these differentials merits further research to see whether they are simply a statistical error, an artefact of the method of measurement/small sample size, reflect cultural variations in the interpretation of the question or suggest elevated levels of morbidity among these groups.

Table 4.2: Health rating by ethnic group and gender, population aged 55+, England, 2004 (%)

	Very good		Good		Fair		Bad		Very bad	
	M	F	M	F	M	F	M	F	M	F
Black Caribbean	14	12	34	23	17	40	7	20	2	6
Indian	13	14	27	31	36	33	19	16	5	7
Pakistani	6	4	28	15	33	36	18	25	16	20
Bangladeshi	8	20	15	44	23	21	33	10	20	4
Chinese	19	8	35	49	33	36	11	7	2	0
Irish	25	32	31	32	30	29	12	6	3	2
White British	24	34	38	41	26	19	8	5	4	1

Source: Sproston and Mindell (2006, table 2.2)

What do older people expect of their health?

What expectations do older people have of health in old age? According to Demakakos et al (2006), 49% of those included in the English Longitudinal Study of Ageing (ELSA) (those aged 50 years and over) agree with the statement 'old age is a time of ill-health', 27% disagree, with the remainder offering a neutral response to this statement. Responses to this statement show virtually no change with age: 51% of those aged under 60 agree that old age is a time of ill-health compared with 49% of those aged over 70. When the statement is phrased rather differently, and relates to personal expectations and worries about old age, a different set of responses emerges, revealing the very real fear that we (virtually) all have that our health will decline in old age. Overall, 68% of the ELSA sample worried that their health would get worse as they grow older but, interestingly, it is the younger age groups who expressed the most concern. Almost three quarters (72%) of those aged under 60 expressed this fear compared with 68% of those aged over 70. This indicates that the anticipated health decline is not manifest, occurs to a lesser degree than anticipated or that expectations are lowered and adapted downwards as we age. Certainly, there are some intriguing questions that we can ask about how older people understand, interpret and evaluate their own health status. These apparently conflicting results about health expectations in old age illustrate an important point about survey design relating to asking questions about general (non-specific) attitudes and individual attitudes/behaviours – the answers to these two types of questions are not always the same! So, for example, we might be generally in favour of HIV testing or abortion but would not necessarily want those tests or interventions for ourselves. Thus, when interpreting survey results it is always important to look at the actual questions that individuals were asked, especially those that report attitudes, expectations and opinions.

Another dimension of how individuals evaluate their health status relates to whether expectations of health in old age have been met. Bowling et al (2002) have demonstrated that responses to this question are an important predictor of quality of life in later life, while Victor et al (2009) have shown a link between expectation of health in old age and loneliness. Analysis of data from the national survey undertaken by Bowling (2005) shows that 31% of older people reported that their health in old age was better than they expected, 44% that it met their expectations (for better or worse) and 27% that it was worse than anticipated. It is intriguing to speculate as to how and in what ways the health of this group had failed to live up to expectations. Had they experienced a major health crisis such as a debilitating stroke or had they always been disappointed in their health across the lifecourse? Clearly, expectations of what old age (or other phases of the life cycle) might be like will have an influence on the quality of the experience and how this is evaluated by individuals. The responses to the health expectations in old age question did not demonstrate a statistically significant relationship with either gender or age and there are no data for social class or ethnicity. The failure to observe differences between groups is equally as intriguing as when we do find evidence of 'health inequalities' and raises questions about why there is an apparent uniformity of response. Brouwer and van Exel (2005) report similar data focusing on expectations of both life expectancy and quality of life. They report that their respondents seriously and significantly underestimated (potential) health-related quality of life. The degree to which such underestimation of general health status in later life reflects acceptance of negative stereotypes of old age is just one of the intriguing areas for further research as is the broader link between physical and mental status in later life and trying to get 'underneath' the statistics and examine in depth the issues of health expectations and ratings.

General psychological wellbeing

Measuring 'positive' mental health, like capturing positive physical health, is conceptually and methodologically complex, but wellbeing is clearly, an important dimension of later life. It is much easier to measure morbidity as illustrated by diagnosed disease states, symptoms or pathology than it is to capture the more nebulous concept of mental or physical wellbeing. Thus, there are fewer measures of 'positive' mental health/wellbeing than there are measures of psychological morbidity or specific mental health disease states. However, there are established generic measures of psychological health that we can use to establish a broad overview of the mental health and wellbeing of populations. One commonly used measure of psychological health is the General Health Questionnaire (GHQ), which comes in 60-, 30-, 28- and 12-item forms. The 12-item version focuses on three domains of psychological wellbeing: anxiety and depression, confidence and social function. It is widely used in research studies where a broad global summary of mental/psychological wellbeing is needed and thus, data and 'population norms' are available for a range of differing population groups (Cheung, 2002).

One fifth (20%) of those aged 65 and over demonstrate 'psychological morbidity' (Bowling, 2005). However, this means that the vast majority of older people (80%)

are in good psychological health. This conclusion is reinforced by data from the HSE where 10.5% were classified as demonstrating poor mental health (that is, had a GHQ score of 4+) (see Table 4.3). There is a clear age gradient with 9% of those aged 65-69 classed as having psychological morbidity compared with 18% of those aged 85 and over (those classed as 'psychologically well' decreased from 70% at ages 65-69 to 50% at age 85 and over). There is no clear gender relationship evident. Among Bowling's participants, 65% of those from the 'higher' managerial occupations were classed as having 'good' psychological health compared with 70% of those from routine occupations. This mirrored an education gradient – 13% of those with a university education were defined as exhibiting 'poor' psychological health compared with 23% of those without qualifications.

Table 4.3: GHQ-12 score by age and gender, population aged 65+, England, 2005 (%)

GHQ score	65-69		70-74		75-79		80-84		85+		All 65+	
	M	F	M	F	M	F	M	F	M	F	M	F
0	73	72	74	65	69	64	58	57	53	53	69	64
1-4	19	18	7	25	23	24	30	31	29	29	21	24
4+	8	9	9	11	7	12	13	13	18	18	9	12

Source: Craig and Mindell (2007, table 4.3)

Is there any relationship with ethnicity? We have only limited data. The HSE provides data for the general population and by ethnic group. This reveals that rates of psychological distress are elevated for both men and women from each key migrant group, with the exception of the Chinese group. These rates are approximately 50% higher than the general population. Thus, the percentage of the adult population with a GHQ score of 4 or more is approximately 16-20% for those from the Indian Subcontinent and African Caribbean populations compared with 11% for the general population. From this we might reasonably surmise that rates of psychological ill-health are elevated among minority ethnic older people.

How do levels of psychological morbidity for older people compare with those for younger age groups? Data from Holland reported by Hoeymans et al (2004) suggest that older people have higher rates of psychological wellbeing than younger age groups and that the levels of psychological distress reported by Bowling (2005) are robust. In Bowling's study, 75% of those aged 15-24 had no psychological problems compared with 84% of those aged 65-74 and 79% for those aged 75 and over. Bowling also presented the results for the 12 individual items. While we must be cautious as to the inferences that we can draw from individual items, her results suggest that the most frequently reported 'problematic' items for those aged 65 and over were 'concentration' (24%), the ability to 'enjoy activities' (24%) and 'strain' (21%). There is, again, a need to evaluate psychological health in old age, both within an individual lifecourse perspective and with reference to the general population of adults.

Cognition and cognitive function

Cognition very broadly refers to the mental capacity to function as a 'competent' individual within the social context. This concept describes a continuum that ranges from 'fully functioning' at one end to 'dementia' at the opposite extreme, with mild cognitive impairment (MCI), which may compromise independent living, occupying an intermediate position. Cognitive function is central to the ability of older people (and again other groups) to function as independent and autonomous adults. Clearly, learning and memory are crucial cognitive abilities as they link directly with the potential for individuals to maintain themselves in the community via the performance of key everyday and routine tasks. Such abilities are, however, also constantly being challenged. For all of us, as society becomes more complex, we require new skills to cope with the complexity, demands and developments of everyday life. We can illustrate this by noting how routine 'daily tasks' or ADL such as shopping have changed over the lifetime of today's generations of older people. Furthermore, older people, unlike most other age groups, have constantly to demonstrate and re-enforce their cognitive competence in order to maintain their independence and to 'prove' that they have not fallen prey to any of the common stereotypes concerning mental (in) capacity in old age. When a young adult loses their house keys it is 'laughed off' as a mild character defect or eccentricity whereas the same incident from an older person is deemed to be evidence of incompetence, compromised ability to cope and (potentially) cognitive decline.

Cognition and ageing

What do we know about the relationship between cognitive function and ageing? This apparently straightforward question, like so much about ageing, is more complex than might be imagined. It implies that there is a single entity that we can loosely define as 'cognitive' function, which, of course, is a gross oversimplification. Cognitive function is a multidimensional concept that consists of a range of elements such as memory and verbal function that we cannot address here. Baltes (1993) distinguishes between 'fluid' intelligence that describes basic information-processing activities such as reasoning, memory and attention, and 'crystallised' or 'pragmatic' intelligence that describes the kind of knowledge accumulated across the lifecourse as a result of education, employment and 'life experience'. Baltes argues that 'fluid' intelligence starts to decline in early adulthood, although the precise age at which this occurs is subject to considerable debate (Schaie, 1996), while 'pragmatic' intelligence remains stable until individuals are in their seventh decade. This offers some insight into the complexity of the entire area of cognition and ageing and leads us to be highly suspicious of apparently simple and unambiguous research findings that argue that cognitive function does/does not change as we age.

On selected tests of cognitive function, older people do demonstrate lower levels of performance than younger people but does this reflect a cohort, period or age effect? We need to be alert to both the nature of the tasks that are being used to measure cognitive function and the setting within which they are carried out as we must be cautious in drawing inferences from data collected from 'test' or laboratory settings with regard to an individual's ability to live independently within the community. Tests based on tasks that are more familiar to younger test participants or which involve using technology with which they are more familiar such as keyboards may distort the results by inflating the cognitive abilities of the young and downgrading those of older subjects. Devising tests that can truly record age-related or ageing-related cognitive decline is challenging.

If we accept age-related 'cognitive deficits' as 'real', this provokes a further question of whether such losses or deficits can be reversed by intervention or whether such declines are inevitable. According to Marsiske et al (1998), there is a remarkable degree of consistency across the research evidence, which indicates that performance on certain cognitive function tasks can be improved with practice, training and a variety of different interventions (Diehl et al, 2005). This is why, when preparing for exams such as the 11+ or the UK Clinical Aptitude Test (UKCAT), students are given practice at the assessment tasks as familiarity with the task improves performance. This makes interpreting 'improvements' in cognitive/psychological tasks observed in longitudinal studies complex as these may simply reflect the 'training' and experience of participants with the tests included in the studies. Current evidence indicates that ageing does not bring about inevitable and profound declines in mental ability but that the situation is highly complex and psychological changes are contextualised by factors such as class, ethnicity and the broader social context. Older people can learn and improve their intellectual functioning given the right sort of educational programmes and stimulating settings or environments. Is it any wonder that older people show declines in cognition when they are removed from the labour market and other arenas of social stimulation and left to exist in a 'twilight' world heavily influenced by the remnants of disengagement theory. We can certainly see that there is a market for products that focus on 'brain training' ranging from the University of the Third Age and traditional adult education classes to the new 'brain training' games (see www.braintraining.com.au/), the effectiveness of which remain the subject of debate (see http://news.bbc.co.uk/1/hi/health/7912379.stm). However, the growth of these products illustrates two issues: the emergence of older people as a distinctive consumer group to whom specific goods and services may be focused; and the degree to which older people fear cognitive decline and will participate in 'preventative' activities to arrest real or perceived declines in function.

There is no single clear universal pattern to describe both intellectual performance in old age and changes to this performance with age and there are enormous differences between and within individuals and the subgroups within the older population. There is an extensive research agenda to be addressed considering how factors such as gender, class and ethnicity (either individually or in combination) influence cognitive functioning in later life. It seems highly unlikely, given everything else that we know about later life, that the pattern of cognitive functioning is going to be a universal and homogeneous experience across the older population. There are further sets of research questions that also require consideration and these relate to the link between cognitive function/ change and the ability of older people to live within the community. Even when some degree of intellectual decline is observed, the influence this has on the ability of that person to exist in the community has rarely been explicitly established. This is an important but rather neglected research agenda. How do declines in, for example, performance on specific tests of verbal reasoning conducted under 'test' situations translate into the ability of an older person (or indeed a person from another age group) to reside successfully in the community and to undertake basic (and advanced) ADL? How do 'good' or 'high' levels of cognitive function promote independence and how do cognitive changes compromise this (and what interventions might promote/restore independent living?)? At what point in the 'cognitive decline' slope is the ability of the individual to live within the community and function appropriately compromised? Are these 'thresholds' that mark a step change in coping ability the same for all population subgroups? Do significant life events impact on these thresholds such as situations of change, for example dealing with challenges arising from widowhood or the onset of chronic illness? These are issues that have been much less rigorously addressed. Yet it seems self-evident that research into cognitive ability and ageing needs to be embedded and understood within the social and environmental contexts within which people live their lives.

Overall, the situation with regard to the broad psychological concept of cognitive function and its relationship with age is far from clear and almost certainly demonstrates variation within the subgroups that make up the older population. Certainly, we can be confident that the presumption of a universal, age-related and irreversible decrease in cognitive ability is a gross stereotype and an oversimplification of a very complex set of relationships and interactions. It is also very clear that there are likely to be profound differences in intellectual function between birth cohorts, reflecting differing educational opportunities and the broader social context experienced by differing groups. We can also be fairly confident that variations within the older age groups in terms of cognitive function are probably as great as those between older people and younger age groups. There is also a need for much greater research looking at: how the abstract notion of cognitive ability links with the capacity of older people to remain active and independent within the community; the identification of the key transition points at which changes in cognitive decline link with ability to remain at home independently; how changes in cognitive decline are mediated by the social and other resources available to the older person; and the development of interventions to promote and enhance cognitive function.

Mental health in later life

ACTIVITY 3

▶   What percentage of older people suffer from dementia, depression and anxiety?

▶   What percentage of older people report problems with their memory?

▶   Is depression among older people under- (or over-) diagnosed and treated?

Older people suffer from a variety of mental illnesses. While the gerontologist is keen to promote a 'positive' view of ageing and is concerned with combating the most prevalent stereotypes and misconceptions of later life, it would be foolish to argue that older people do not experience mental health problems. Indeed, it would be irresponsible to do so as it would negate the development of services and interventions to respond to these needs. Older people experience a range of mental health problems such as depression, anxiety or psychotic disorders such as schizophrenia and these may represent a continuation of a previously established pattern of health problems or be of 'late onset'. However, there is a 'special' mental health issue that is a particularly distinctive component of mental wellbeing in later life and this is 'dementia' and compromised cognitive function. It is 'dementia', as conceptualised as loss of memory such that individuals can no longer maintain independence and autonomy, that is one of the biggest fears of old age and of growing older.

Dementia

Dementia (or impaired cognitive function) is not a mental health condition that is exclusive to old age. However, it is a condition that predominantly affects older people: less than 5% of sufferers are under 65 years of age. Thus, in the rest of this section we focus on older adults. Determining the prevalence (the overall disease burden) and incidence (the number of new cases within a given reference period) of dementia/cognitive impairment is problematic given the difficulties of identifying where on the cognitive functioning continuum is the point that defines impairment, arriving at a clinical diagnosis and establishing reliable and valid methods of assessing cognitive status within the context of population health surveys.

From a clinical perspective, presenting symptoms for cognitive impairment include the touchstone marker of 'memory loss/impairment' but also problems with a whole range of other cognitive skills that can include motor functions, recognition, language, and executive planning/organisation and sequencing skills. As the previous section outlined, the key point here is that the concept of cognitive function is very much broader than just a narrow focus on 'memory' loss and dementia is a condition that manifests in compromised abilities across a range of key skills and domains. Establishing the 'true' prevalence of cognitive impairment within the population is both methodologically and conceptually challenging and we shall return to this point when examining the disease burden of cognitive impairment at the population level.

How do older people rate their memory?

Despite the complexity of the notion of cognitive function, popular discourse is focused on the index symptom or characteristic of memory loss as the key element of dementia/cognitive impairment. Several studies have empirically demonstrated the degree to which older adults fear memory loss and 'self-monitor' their own memory for signs of deterioration. Bowling (2005) invited participants to rate the probability of specific events happening to them as compared to the general population of older people. She reported that 6% thought that they had a higher chance than 'average' of experiencing memory loss and 18% a lower probability, with the vast majority of respondents (76%) evaluating their chances as the same as their contemporaries (that is, they did not rate themselves as being at 'excess risk' nor did they feel that they were especially advantaged in terms of the likelihood of cognitive decline). ELSA includes a question that invites participants to evaluate the 'health' of their memory – in a similar vein to the 'self-rated' health status questions discussed earlier – and to evaluate how their memory has changed between waves 1 (2002) and 2 (2004) of the survey – a period of approximately two years. Huppert et al (2006) reported that at baseline, 67% of people aged 50 and over rated their memory as good (or better) with 7% rating it as poor and 5% as excellent. If we look at self-rated memory by age and gender, the percentage rating their memory as excellent was stable with increased age (see Table 4.4). However, the percentage rating their memory as poor doubled across the same age range, from 8–13% for men and 4–9% for women. No obvious gender differential is evident.

Table 4.4: Self-reported memory by age and gender, population aged 65+, England, 2004/05 (%)

	65-69		70-74		75-79		80+	
	M	F	M	F	M	F	M	F
Excellent	4	2	3	3	4	2	3	2
Very good	17	20	15	21	17	19	17	19
Good	43	43	39	45	35	46	37	42
Fair	28	29	35	25	34	25	30	28
Bad	8	4	9	6	10	8	13	9

Source: Huppert et al (2006, table 8A2)

How did individuals evaluate change in their memory over the two-year follow-up between waves 1 and 2 of ELSA. Very few – 1-2% – reported improvements, two thirds reported a situation of 'no change' and one third reported that their memory had deteriorated, with no obvious age- or gender-related trends evident (Table 4.5). That one third of participants felt that their memory had deteriorated is an intriguing finding, which may, indeed, represent an accurate evaluation of their deteriorating cognitive function, or a hypercritical evaluation of small lapses from a group who are especially aware of the 'threat' represented by failing memory by participating in a survey focused on ageing.

Table 4.5: Self-reported change in memory by age and gender, population aged 65+, England, 2004/05 (%)

	65-69		70-74		75-79		80+	
	M	F	M	F	M	F	M	F
Better now	1	2	1	2	1	1	1	0
About the same	66	68	65	65	65	66	64	63
Worse now	33	30	34	33	35	33	35	37

Note: Comparison of memory changes between wave 1 (2002) and wave 2 (2004/05) of ELSA

Source: Huppert et al (2006, table 8A3)

The ELSA survey also includes three 'memory-based' tasks designed to evaluate cognitive function. These 'abstract' tasks are time orientation, prospective memory (keeping appointments, etc) and word recall tests and all three demonstrated an age-related decline when analysed cross-sectionally. However, perhaps of more interest are (a) the changes in performance over time and (b) the link with individuals' self-assessed memory/memory changes. Huppert et al (2006) reported that over the two-year follow-up 37% of those aged 50 and over demonstrated improved performance on the memory tasks; 31% showed no change; and a similar percentage demonstrated a decrease in performance. This large improvement for the group as a whole may well illustrate the 'practice' effect resultant from the repetition of tasks. This is a persistent issue in longitudinal studies whereby participants 'learn' how to do the tests. We also need to interpret these results cautiously as certain groups may be excluded because of missing data and those with the 'worst' scores in wave 1 may have died by or not participated in wave 2. If we look at these data by age and gender we can see that it is the older sample members (those aged 80 and over) who demonstrated the largest degree of cognitive decline at around 38% (compared with around 28% of those aged 65-69). The gender differential is unclear (see Table 4.6). However, we should also note that around 33% of those aged 80 and over demonstrated improved memory (as compared with around 39% of those aged 65-69). Even if this improvement was the result of 'practice effects' then it does suggest that even those in advanced old age have the capacity to learn!

Focusing on the 31% of the sample who demonstrated a decline on the 'objective' memory, there is no clear link between this and self-assessed memory change. Some 30% of those with 'objective' memory decline rated their memory

Table 4.6: Observed changes in memory by age and gender, population aged 65+, England, 2004/05 (%)

	65-69		70-74		75-79		80+	
	M	F	M	F	M	F	M	F
Improved	38	41	36	38	36	36	35	31
No change	31	33	27	31	31	30	29	29
Decline	31	26	38	31	33	34	36	40

Note: Comparison of memory performance tasks between wave 1 (2002) and wave 2 (2004/05) of ELSA.

Source: Huppert et al (2006, table 8A6)

as unchanged/improved. Thus, self-assessed memory – either positive or negative – does not reflect performance in cognitive function tests. There is a similar dissonance between self-rated health and symptoms/disability/chronic illness. The link between performance in these types of tests and ability to live independently at home remains unclear. One key aspect of these memory tests is date/time orientation. In the 'real world', older people may develop coping strategies to compensate for the problems of date/time orientation such as the use of calendars, reminders, etc. Further, more problems with date/time orientation may equally be attributed to the dislocation of older people from the highly regulated world of work and the hegemony of 'clock time' as to impaired cognitive ability.

The prevalence of dementia

However much we debate the validity of tests of cognitive function as markers of impairment and ability to cope at home independently, we cannot deny or ignore that there is a pathological state termed 'dementia' and the devastating consequences that this condition wreaks for sufferers and their families. Dementia is a chronic disease – like those physical conditions such as arthritis discussed in Chapter Three – in that it exhibits a profile of high morbidity but low mortality. In 2007 in England and Wales, there were 4,272 deaths of men attributed to dementia and 10,676 women (although the Alzheimer's Disease Society considers that the total number of deaths attributed to dementia is in the region of 60,000). From a mortality perspective, dementia does not rank very high in the 'health priority' list in comparison with the deaths attributed to heart disease, stroke, cancer, accidents or respiratory conditions. However, the development of the National Dementia Strategy in 2009 demonstrates the importance of this health problem for the individual and their family and society more generally within the context of an ageing population. We discuss this strategy further in Chapter Six where we consider the policy responses to the health and social care challenges of an ageing population.

If we look at individual studies there are a range of estimates of the prevalence of dementia within the population reflecting the ages of the population studied, the population included (community dwelling and/or including those in long-term care), the response rates for the studies (given that those who do not participate in studies are not usually 'randomly' distributed but are biased towards the extremes of the health spectrum) and the measurement tools used (there are a range of different tools that measure dementia symptoms with varying degrees of precision). Ferri et al (2005) published a consensus statement of both the prevalence and incidence of dementia globally, which suggests that the prevalence rates in Western Europe double every five years from about 1.3% of those aged 65–69 to around 33% of those aged 95 and over (see Table 4.7). This 'doubling' of prevalence rates seems to be consistently reported across population studies conducted across the developed world and dementia is demonstrably an 'age-related' disease. While we see in Table 4.7 that about a third of those in their nineties are classified as having 'dementia', it is worth noting that the vast majority of this age group do not present with this condition. Research establishing the prevalence of dementia varies markedly according to the population studied. In care settings the prevalence estimates are extremely high at 60–85% but this is unsurprising given that cognitive impairment is a major reason for entry into long-term care and is very contingent on the definition of cognitive impairment used.

Table 4.7: Consensus estimates on incidence and prevalence of dementia by age and gender, population aged 65+, Europe, 2005 (%)

Age	Prevalence		Annual incidence	
	M	F	M	F
65-69	1.0	1.5	0.2	0.2
70-74	2.4	3.1	0.2	0.3
75-79	6.5	5.1	0.6	0.5
80-84	13.3	10.2	1.4	1.8
85-89	22.2	16.7	2.8	3.4
90-94	29.6	27.5	3.9	5.4
95+	34.4	30.0	6.0	8.2

Source: Ferri et al (2005)

The prevalence of any disease reflects the interrelationship between two variables – the numbers of new cases within a given period (incidence) and the length of time that individuals survive with the condition. The consensus statement by Ferri et al (2005) suggests an age-related increase in incidence from 0.2% for those aged 65–69 (two new cases per year per 1,000 population) to (approximately) five new cases per 100 people per year for those aged 90 and over. Ferri et al (2005) suggest that the average duration of survival with dementia from diagnosis to death is approximately four years; somewhat shorter than the five to seven years reported by Jorm et al (1987). While we see a clear age-related increase in dementia prevalence (and incidence), the associations between dementia and other structural variables such as gender and class are less clear, and the link with ethnicity is largely under-researched within the UK context as it is only now becoming apparent in retirement-age older people. There is, however, evidence of racial variation in the US (see Harwood and Ownby, 2000; Sink et al, 2004).

Functional or affective disorders in later life

The study of mental (ill-)health in later life shows a not unreasonable preoccupation, given the devastating consequences of the condition for individuals, families and society, with dementia and, more broadly, cognitive impairment. This obscures a more expansive and comprehensive evaluation of the mental health of older people. The conditions included within the category of affective disorders broadly relate to disturbances of mood, especially as manifest in terms of anxiety and depression. This group of conditions can present significant problems at the individual and population level of analysis and seriously compromise the quality of life and wellbeing of older people. There are two distinctive features of affective disorders when compared with dementia. First, they are conditions for which treatment, both pharmacological and behavioural, can bring positive benefits in terms of alleviation or reduction of symptoms if not a total 'cure'. Thus, there is no doubt as to the benefit of identifying and treating those older people with these conditions. Second, for those older people who experience these conditions in later life, they may represent the continuation into old age of a pre-existing problem or may be the first manifestation of the conditions. So the disease typology and presentation is complicated because the experience can be the continuation of an experience across the lifecourse or it can be 'late onset'.

What is depression?

As with the other chronic physical conditions, disability and dementia, the definition of depression remains a challenge, irrespective of the population/group that forms the focus of the investigation. Depression is a term that is regularly used in popular discourse to describe the characteristics of individuals. We regularly describe members of our families, ourselves and our friends as 'being depressed'. Over our life we all experience periods of sadness or upset that may make us feel 'depressed' but usually such episodes are self-limiting and resolve spontaneously (or at least without medical/therapeutic intervention). How, then, do we distinguish 'normal' feelings of sadness from depression? Mann (2000) very helpfully suggests a tripartite typology of depression in later life. *Depressive symptomatology* describes the most wide-ranging and inclusive definition of depression and is characterised by individuals demonstrating one (or more) of a range of depressive symptoms including worry or sleeplessness. *Depressive syndrome* is less inclusive and more restrictive based on the number, intensity and duration of symptoms. It is at this level of intensity that Mann (2000) argues that quality of life and daily activities start to be compromised and is the threshold for treatment, although not necessarily with drugs. *Major depression* is the most extreme form of the condition and is ascertained by clinical diagnosis based on severity and duration of symptoms and treatment is almost always pharmacological. This is a very useful typology and helps us to make sense of the conflicting and often contradictory prevalence estimates of depression in older adults. However, a useful adjunct to this typology would be to differentiate between depression continued from earlier phases in the life cycle and that of 'late onset'. Depression is also on a continuum of symptoms and where the clinical case thresholds are drawn is important. Furthermore, it is not always straightforward to draw a direct link between 'disease severity' and ability to cope at home.

As with other age groups, the prevalence of depression within older age groups is contingent on the definition used and the method used to operationalise it. The two main measures used in population surveys are the Geriatric Depression Scale (GDS) and the Centre for Epidemiological Studies Depression Scale (CES-D Scale). Based on his work on 'community dwelling', Mann (2000) reports that as many as 30-40% of older people aged 65 and over in the Gospel Oak district of North London exhibit depressive symptoms, 12% exhibit depressive syndrome and 1-2% 'major depression'. However, this is a locally based survey and there is always the potential risk that the study locality may exhibit higher/lower rates because of specific characteristics of the area. What is the prevalence rate resultant from national surveys? The ELSA survey reported rates of depressive symptomatology of 27% for men aged 65 and over and 40% for women aged 65 and over, which approximates to the rates of depressive symptomatology reported by Mann. Djernes (2006), in a systematic review, broadly concurs with the findings of Mann (2000) and estimates the prevalence of major (clinical) depression at 1.6%, minor depression at 10% and depressive symptoms at 30%. The HSE, using the 10-item GDS, suggests that the prevalence of depressive symptoms is approximately 25% for those aged 65 and over and demonstrates a clear age-related gradient such that 40% of those aged 85 and over are classified as having depressive symptoms (see Table 4.8). The link with gender is, like the GHQ data, inconsistent with the gender gap most pronounced in the 70-84 age range. Lack of energy and dropping activities are the two most common depressive symptoms that may (or may not) reflect depression or a response to changes in physical health and other factors. This is a problem with these types of questions as positive responses to questions about reduced activities, or energy, may have a physical as well as a psychological origin.

What are the major 'risk factors' or triggers for depression in later life? Is depression in later life, or at least 'late onset depression', a distinct syndrome? Koenig and Blazer (1992) argue that it is a distinct clinical entity produced in response to the negative transitions accompanying later life. In terms of predictors of depression in later life at a 'population level', there are a well-established set of factors of which chronic somatic diseases and functional limitations resultant

Table 4.8: GDS (depression) score by age and gender, population aged 65+, England, 2005 (%)

GDS-10 score	65-69		70-74		75-79		80-84		85+		All 65+	
	M	F	M	F	M	F	M	F	M	F	M	F
0	42	40	37	33	31	25	18	16	10	10	33	28
1-2	39	40	45	44	48	47	50	45	50	48	45	44
3+	19	20	18	24	22	27	31	39	40	43	22	28

Source: Craig and Mindell (2007, table 2.1)

from chronic health problems are the two most important (Djernes, 2006). This reflects the observations of Harris et al (2006), who report that the predictors of depression for older people are dominated by disability and chronic health conditions. Consistently across studies, regardless of the study location, those with poor physical health are at a considerably elevated risk of experiencing depression. Indeed, Djernes (2006: 383) notes that 'It seems likely that functional impairment is of central significance to late life depression'. In the work reported by Harris et al (2006), adjusting for disability weakened the oft-reported relationship with gender and eradicated the link with age. Thus, it seems plausible to argue that it is not age per se that is linked with depression but the associated disability and chronic health problems. Djernes (2006) further observes that a whole range of 'social support' variables are also linked with depression, including loss of social contacts, widowhood, dissatisfaction with social support, social isolation and lack of social activities. Previous episodes of depression and anxiety are also important. These findings are robust in that they are supported by both cross-sectional and longitudinal data (Henderson et al, 2001; Cole and Dendukuri, 2003). Thus, if we were developing methods to screen for those at risk of depression then the key factors – decreases in functional status resultant from chronic illness – are clear and it is also clear that, as well as behavioural or pharmacological treatments, socially based interventions may also be of use.

Understanding the natural history of depression in later life is problematic as, like many physical illnesses, we do not easily know from epidemiological studies whether it is a 'first' episode of depression or a recurrence/continuation of an illness experienced earlier in the lifecourse, which, as noted above, is an important risk factor for further episodes of depression. Thus, there is a need to undertake further studies of depression using a longitudinal approach to establish the epidemiology of the disease across the lifecourse. The complexity of this task is, however, illustrated by the work of Haynie et al (2001) who looked at depression longitudinally. Haynie et al (2001) focused on the 'oldest old', and their paper illustrates the problem of, for example, sample attrition, which is selective, thereby introducing bias, the failure to complete the assessment tool (the CES-D) by some of the most vulnerable participants and also the statistical, logistic and conceptual complexity of handling data with multiple follow-up points. They show that, for those aged 80 and over followed up for four years, the vast majority of individuals (80%) were not depressed, 5% were depressed across each wave and for approximately 15% their status changed – either 'improved' (5%) or deteriorated (9%). Harris et al (2006) followed a general practice population of people aged 65 and over for two years and investigated two groups – those whose depression 'persisted' across both study waves and those with 'new onset' depression at wave 2. They reported that 8% of participants demonstrated new onset depression, that this is consistent with the range of estimates from previous studies (range 6-12%) and that pain and worsening disability were the main explanatory factors. Almost two thirds (61%) of survivors at two years who were depressed at baseline were still depressed, and this is also in line with previous estimates (range 61-63%) and associated with poor health status and limited social support. Intriguingly, the study suggested that a third of survivors demonstrated 'improved' depressive symptomatology but this was not investigated by Harris et al (2006). It remains intriguing as to what factors contributed to the improved mental health of this subgroup and it is clearly an issue worth exploring. This links to the ideas advanced by Beekman et al (2001) that there are two patterns of depression in later life – chronic and acute. We can see from epidemiological studies that older people can recover from depression, so it is a shame that this condition is both under-diagnosed and undertreated. The majority of studies of depression within the community of older people estimate that the vast majority of individuals with depression – approximately 80% – are not being treated and that only about a quarter are known to their general practitioner.

Suicide in later life

A clear and unambiguous demonstration of psychological ill-health is suicidal behaviour in terms of either (a) attempted suicide (parasuicide) and (b) 'successful' suicide or intentional self-harm. Suicide is an important public health problem and there is a national suicide prevention strategy, which includes the target of lowering suicide among older people. Mortality reports regularly publish details of deaths from intentional self-harm (suicide) for all ages. However, these statistics must be interpreted with some caution for not all cases of death by self-harm are intentional and there are most certainly cases of deliberate self-harm where the coroner is not convinced that the intent was clear. In 2007 in the UK, there were 5,377 deaths attributed to suicide, which is almost a thousand fewer than in 1991 and of which those aged 75 and over accounted for 280. In 1991, those aged 75 and over had the highest suicide rates – 23 per 100,000 population – but by 2007 this group had the lowest recorded rate at 15 per 100,000 population. Focusing on England and Wales in 2007, 3,165 deaths were attributed to intentional self-harm. Of the 2,481 males in this category, 15% were aged 65 and over and of the 684 females, 21% were aged in this age group. Thus, we can see that suicide is comparatively rare among older people (in absolute terms) and that both absolute numbers and relative rates have declined over the last 20 years. While classification of a death as suicide/intentional self-harm is problematic, it is unlikely that the observed declines in suicide in later life are simply the result of 'attribution bias' but do reflect a real decrease. Suicide demonstrates a male:female gender differential of 3:1 for those aged under 50, which narrows to 2:1 for those aged 50 and over.

Sainsbury (1961) drew attention to the link between depression, dementia and suicide. He noted that approximately 50% of suicides of those aged 60 and over were depressed (although this is difficult to establish with certainty because of the nature of suicide) and 10-20% demonstrated evidence of dementia or cognitive impairment. Improved methods of studying suicide now suggest that major depression is evident in two thirds of successful suicides among people aged 65 and over, with up to another 20% showing evidence of less severe depression (see Cattell, 2000). Severe physical illness is also now recognised as an important risk factor for suicide in later life.

Parasuicide and deliberate self-harm (the two are often conflated although they are conceptually distinct) are much rarer among older people. Welch (2001), in a systematic review of studies of parasuicide, reported that at most 15-20% of parasuicides are among those aged 60 and over. Batchelor and Napier (1953), in a study in Edinburgh, reported on a case series of attempted suicides of which 20% were aged 60 and over, with depression and psychiatric morbidity being present in the vast majority of cases. More recent work by Shah et al (2009) on the Oxford deliberate self-harm monitoring system reports that of the 1,129 cases recorded for 2007, 25 were aged 65 and over. So although parasuicide and deliberate self-harm are (fairly) rare among older people, the work by Shah et al suggest that attempted suicides by older people are increasing and that we should not be complacent in presuming that suicide and parasuicide are the province of the young.

Anxiety

At various times in our lives we all experience anxiety or worry but the symptoms are usually transient. However, there is a wide range of pathological states that are broadly categorised as 'anxiety disorders'. These range from a generic portmanteau condition – generalised anxiety disorder – to much more specific conditions such as obsessive compulsive disorder (OCD). There is some debate as to the validity (or otherwise) of terms such as generalised anxiety disorder as distinct from the more specific states such as OCD. As with depression, anxiety disorders may be differentiated into 'late onset' conditions and those where the sufferer has experienced the state of mind across the lifecourse. How many older people experience these conditions? Researchers from Canada suggest that the prevalence of probable OCD in the community is 1.5% (Grenier et al, 2009) with approximately 6% of the total population reporting symptoms of anxiety disorders (see Préville et al, 2008). This is not dissimilar to the 4% estimate derived from the review undertaken by Flint (2005) and proposed as the 'planning estimate' by Lee (2007). In addition, Lee (2007) suggests that 10-20% of those aged 65 and over have symptoms of anxiety but fail to achieve the threshold for 'clinical' diagnosis. Lee (2007) remarks on the slim evidence base concerning the impact of anxiety disorders on older people and their families, the (potential) differential experience of 'late onset' compared with 'lifelong' anxiety, basic incidence and prevalence data, the valuation of interventions to alleviate and prevent anxiety and the extent of unmet need for support, care and treatment.

Key points

In this chapter we have demonstrated that the vast majority of older people enjoy 'good' psychological health free from the pathological states noted earlier.

The most persistent and pernicious stereotype regarding old age relates to mental health, especially dementia. The 'best' evidence indicates that 3-5% of those aged 65 and over have significant dementia; the annual incidence rate is 1% with an average survival from diagnosis to death of three to five years.

While the prevalence of dementia is age-related using the criteria outlined in Chapter Two, dementia does not merit classification as an age effect because it is not evident by all older people, even at the most advanced ages.

Up to 40% of those aged 65 and over experience some form of depression (30% having depressive symptoms, 10% having mild depression and 1-2% having significant depression); 6% have symptoms of anxiety and 10-20% are regarded as having psychological ill-health.

The link between mental health and psychosocial factors is more complex than for mortality/physical morbidity. Both depression and dementia (both prevalence and incidence) show an age-related trend but this may, for depression, reflect chronic illness/disability rather than age per se.

Psychological health shows little variation with age or gender and the link between mental health and class and/or ethnicity is under-researched. There is a pressing need to focus on mental health among our minority ethnic communities as there is (virtually) no robust empirical evidence for this population. However, this represents a significant challenge for researchers as measures of mental health/psychological wellbeing are culturally specific. This is only one aspect of an extensive research agenda that is required to fill in many of the gaps in our knowledge about the natural history of mental health/mental wellbeing in later life and the key risk factors for these conditions.

We need a more robust evidence base that looks at the link between disease progression and the ability of the older person to remain living successfully at home. What are the key tipping points/transitions that render independent living no longer a viable option? Answers to these questions are required if we are to successfully develop interventions to enable older people to remain at home in the community as fully participating and engaged social actors.

Further activities
▸ Calculate the number of older people in your locality who suffer from dementia and depression.
▸ What percentage do you think are known to services?

Further reading

Baldwin, C. and Capstick, A. (2007) *Tom Kitwood on dementia.* Maidenhead: Open University Press.

Bowling, A. (2007) Gender-specific and gender-sensitive associations with psychological health and morbidity in older age: baseline findings from a British population survey of ageing. *Aging and Mental Health*, 11(3), 301-9.

Downs, M. and Bowers, B. (2008) *Excellence in dementia care: Research into practice.* Maidenhead: Open University Press.

Gilleard, C. and Higgs, P. (2008) Promoting mental health in later life. *Aging and Mental Health*, 12(3), 283-4.

Kitwood, T. (1997) *Dementia reconsidered.* Buckingham: Open University Press.

Lee, M. (2006) *Promoting mental health and well-being in later life,* London: Age Concern England.

Lee, M. (2007) *Improving services and support for older people with mental health problems.* London: Age Concern England.

Useful websites
• *Bradford Dementia Group:* www.brad.ac.uk/health/dementia/Research/
• *Dementia Services Development Centre:* http://dementia.stir.ac.uk/
• *The Cognitive Function and Ageing Study (CFAS):* www.cfas.ac.uk/
• *Dementia UK report:* www.alzheimers.org.uk/site/scripts/download_info.php?fileID=2
• *Dementia 2010 report:* www.dementia2010.org/
• *World Alzheimer Report 2009:* www.alz.co.uk/research/files/World%20Alzheimer%20Report.pdf
• *Depression in older adults:* www.rcpsych.ac.uk/mentalhealthinformation/mentalhealthproblems/depression/depressioninolderadults.aspx
• *UK Inquiry into Mental Health and Well-Being in Later Life:* www.mhilli.org

FIVE

Consumption and health

Key points

In this chapter we consider:

- the longevity of the idea of 'life extension' and the ways that we have tried to achieve this goal;
- the development of contemporary 'anti-ageing' medicine, locating this within a historical context;
- the role of the consumption of health goods in later life;
- the health-related lifestyles of older people.

One topic that is typically included in any analysis of the health of specific population subgroups is 'health-related lifestyles', examining factors such as participation in exercise, diet, smoking and alcohol (and use of drugs), issues that are addressed in this chapter. However, we also want to augment this traditional analysis with a novel and innovative examination of patterns of 'health-related' consumption and expenditure by older people as developed by the work of Jones and colleagues (Jones et al, 2008, 2009; Higgs and Jones, 2009; Higgs et al, 2009). There is increasing recognition of the 'grey market' and the development of goods and services aimed at the grey consumer (see Turner, 2009). Until recently, little has been written about the role and contribution of older people to 'consumer society' especially within the UK. Two inter-related factors probably account for this omission: the predominantly homogeneous patterns of (low) income in 'old age' and, more speculatively, the attitudes of those interested in consumer research who largely did not see older people as being engaged in 'consumer culture'. To set the context and framework for a consumption-based examination of health, it is evident from routinely available economic data that the economic position of older people in Britain has improved and levels of poverty among older people have decreased (relative to other groups). Bowling (2005) reminds us that state retirement benefits still form the major source of income for those who are formally retired from the labour market. In very broad terms, pensions from the state (50%) or previous employer (25%) make up the bulk of older people's income in Britain. Furthermore, levels of poverty in retirement have declined with about 25% of pensioner households in the bottom quintile (20%) of the income distribution – half the level recorded for the 1970s (DWP, 2009). Higgs et al (2009) have sought to contradict the stereotypical view of 'old age as a time of poverty' by noting the economic assets held by older people and, indeed, economists have expressed great academic interest in these economic assets – mostly in terms of housing stock. Higgs et al reported that those aged 50 and over own 80% of all personal assets in the UK, 60% of savings and account for 40% of consumer spending. We can conclude that current generations of older people are both better off in retirement than their predecessors and better off in comparison to some other social groups. Of course there are considerable variations within the population who are retired in terms of economic security. The very old, women and those from unskilled occupational groups and/or with interrupted working lives have the lowest levels of income in later life and demonstrate the lowest level of material resources.

The focus in research on income in later life has almost exclusively been on levels and sources of income for older people, with little consideration of what their income is spent on. Jones and colleagues (2008) have started to address this by asking questions such as 'are older people excluded or included from the consumer society?' and 'what are the consumption behaviours of older people within the context of a society where lifestyle and consumption have become important forms of social differentiation?'. Of particular interest has been the role of the baby boomer generation – those born in the immediate aftermath of the Second World War and who exemplify the 'consumer generation'. As they enter old age, will they maintain, increase or decrease levels of consumption into later life? This has formed part of a wider academic interest in the ageing of the baby boomer generation in both the UK (Evandrou and Falkingham, 2006; Quine et al, 2006; Biggs et al, 2008; Phillipson et al, 2008) and the US (Moody, 2008). The focus of this chapter is on an examination of older people's consumption of health-related goods, products and services and the development of health as a consumer good. Partly this stems from the work of Gilleard and Higgs (2000, 2005) who posit that the accepted pattern of identity in later life, made up of clearly demarcated stages between adult and late adult life, is redundant. They argue that previous certainties about life after 'retirement' have been eroded and notions of 'old age' and retirement are being replaced by consumer-based lifestyles where what we consume is more important than what we do or how old we are. One element of the consumption-based lifestyle is the active engagement with, and maintenance of, good health. Hence, in this chapter we focus on enumerating the degree to which older people engage in health-related lifestyles, in the traditional sense of health behaviours in terms of exercise, diet and smoking/alcohol consumption, and the broader issue of more consumption-based health activities that are lifestyle focused. Before the presentation of these more empirical aspects of this topic, we introduce one highly contentious but emblematic issue – the concept of anti-ageing medicine. This is an aspect of mid and later life that has provoked considerable debate in a whole range of arenas: academia, practice and policy making. It is not our intention to offer a full history of this topic but to focus on the key issues, especially as it relates to the commodification of health in later life and the development of a distinctive and identifiable concept of healthcare consumption.

Anti-ageing medicine

ACTIVITY 1

'I hate men who would prolong their lives by foods and drinks and charms of magic arts. Perverting nature's course to keep off death. They ought, when they no longer serve the land, to quit this life and clear the way for youth.' (Euripides, 500 BC, cited in Andre and Velasquez, 2010)

▸   What do you think are the implications of this statement?
▸   Should we strive to live longer, whatever the cost, or should we 'allow' those over a certain age to die?
▸   How do we reconcile the quantity or duration of life with concerns for the quality of life?

The American Academy of Anti-Aging Medicine (A4M) was established in 1992 and since this time has been actively promoting the initially medical but now more broadly based healthcare 'specialty' of anti-ageing medicine. It established the American Board of Anti-Aging Medicine (ABAAM), which offers courses and conferences on anti-ageing medicine as a distinctive healthcare specialty, and publishes the *International Journal of Anti-Aging Medicine*. Anti-ageing medicine self-declares that it operates at the boundaries of biomedicine and is seeking to 'push back' these boundaries in order to enhance our ability to overcome ageing. The A4M defines this sphere of activity thus:

> Anti-aging medicine is a medical specialty founded on the application of advanced scientific and medical technologies for the early detection, prevention, treatment, and reversal of age-related dysfunction, disorders, and diseases. It is a healthcare model promoting innovative science and research to prolong the healthy human lifespan As such, anti-aging medicine is based on principles of sound and responsible medical care that are consistent with those applied in other preventive health specialties. (see www.worldhealth.net/)

The emphasis in this definition is on promoting 'life extension' by (ultimately) reversing age-related physical and mental diseases. This is a much more expansive and ambitious goal than a simple focus on cosmetic surgery designed to make individuals 'look younger' or 'enhance' their appearance – exterior cosmetic changes that do not intervene in the ageing process. Rather, the A4M offers a much more radical goal in seeking to ultimately be able to reverse the ageing process.

Mykytyn (2008) argues that anti-ageing medicine operates within a paradigm where 'ageing' itself is the target of the therapeutic interventions and not a disease or specific pathology. This perspective differentiates anti-ageing medicine from geriatric medicine where the emphasis is predominantly on disease and pathology (with some focus on prevention, but often of a secondary nature). Essentially, the anti-ageing proponents argue that the biological decline manifested as ageing is reversible and remedial and that optimising 'body states' should be the focus of biomedicine, with benefits for both individuals and society at large. Vincent et al (2008) observe that anti-ageing has been conceptualised in a number of different ways, representing the tensions between the different areas of activity. We distinguish between the 'potions, lotions and cosmetic treatments' dimension of anti-ageing, which focuses on the outward, conspicuous, external, bodily 'signs' of ageing, and the 'scientific' biomedical dimension, which is an 'internally' focused bodily perspective (see Katz, 1996; Vincent, 2008). Binstock (2004) offers a typology that suggests that anti-ageing encompasses three distinct objectives with regard to ageing: reversal/rejuvenation, halting/stopping and slowing/retarding the ageing process. Thus, we can see that, within what may be broadly termed the 'anti-ageing enterprise', there are a diverse range of activities and competing perspectives and goals. In part the debate about this area is generated by the diversity of the activities encompassed within this term and the balance between these activities.

The 'speciality' of modern anti-ageing medicine has developed considerably in the US where the A4M claims a membership of 20,000 practitioners. The World Anti-Aging Academy of Medicine, established in the UK in 2002, is the vehicle that promotes anti-ageing medicine globally (see www.waaam.org/). There is also a British Society of Anti-Ageing Medicine and a European group with organisations across a range of member states. The Life Extension Foundation, a US-based organisation, similarly focuses on activities to promote and enhance the longevity of individuals. Hence, 'life extension'-promoting longevity, such that the 120 years attained by Jean Calment becomes a conservative norm rather than an exceptional case, is an underlying goal of the 'anti-agers'.

Anti-ageing medicine, or at least the focus on extending life and reversing/slowing ageing that it espouses, is neither new nor specific to postmodern Western societies (see Fishman et al, 2008; Turner, 2009). Turner (2009) observes the fascination with an elixir of life is itself of considerable longevity with evidence that in the third century BC there were men in China 'knowledgeable in the techniques of immortality'. Luigi Cornaro, in his book *Discourses on the temperate life* (cited in Turner, 2009), argued that the body's finite resources could be husbanded to enhance longevity by temperance, diet and exercise (Turner, 2009). In 1633, Sir William Vaughan wrote: 'to live forever ... is a thing impossible: to prolong a man's life free from violent sickness, and to keep the body in a temperate state, I veryily believe may be done' (cited in Haycock, 2008: 105). In 1622, the scientist Francis Bacon published his treatise *The history naturall and experimentall of life and death*, which had the subtitle *Of the prolonging of life* (cited in Haycock, 2008).

This interest in 'life extension' may seem strange until we understand that while early modern societies did not have the large percentage of older people that characterises contemporary society, older people were still part of the fabric of society. It is a truism that life has always been seen as preferable to death at whatever time period and society one studies. Thus, the existence of what were believed to be very old people such as Thomas Parr who died in 1635 at the age of 152 (there is a plaque marking his burial place in Westminster Abbey) offered the enticing hope to our forefathers that such longevity could become the experience of the many rather than the privilege of the few. Indeed, Parr was not the only British subject to claim advanced longevity – Henry Jenkins of Yorkshire was reported to have died in 1670 at the age of 169 and John Bayles died in 1706 at a mere 130. A local doctor, James Keill, conducted an autopsy on Bayles and sent the report for publication in the *Philosophical Transactions of the Royal Society* (Keill, 1706) and attributed his longevity to Bayle's robust cardio-pulmonary system. Keill noted that in order to understand ageing and the biological processes underpinning these examples of extreme longevity we needed to undertake more autopsies and research.

However, Thomas Parr was blind and thus, Bacon and other observers of ageing, mostly physicians and doctors, wanted longevity to be associated with good health and they sought to identify 'the rules for the preventing of the ill consequences of extreme old age' (Keill, cited in Haycock, 2008: 15). Bacon's rationale for wanting to prolong human life was that he saw it as a means to extend and enhance human achievements. His argument was expressed in terms of how much we achieve with regard to the arts and sciences in our (currently) short lifespan and how much more we could achieve with greater longevity. Haycock (2008) observes that the foundation for Bacon's argument that life could be extended was biblical in origin. He argued that the book of Genesis indicated that, had not Adam and Eve succumbed to temptation, we would all have enjoyed the fruits of eternal life in perfect health. Bacon's preoccupations mirror, to a large degree, those of contemporary 'anti-agers', in the desire to understand the causes of ageing and how to intervene to slow (or even reverse) the process. Thus, we can see that many of the concerns of contemporary anti-ageing medicine resonate with debates and interests of earlier historical periods and as such represent a continuation of an almost universal human desire to extend life.

Mykytyn (2010) observes that the activities of the professional associations concerned with establishing anti-ageing, especially A4M, have focused on sponsoring national and international conferences, establishing journals, developing an educational portfolio and funding research. This represents a classic strategy for establishing the credentials and professional credibility of a field of academic enterprise, legitimising the area of activity and 'professionalising' the expertise of practitioners. This concern with legitimacy has been a preoccupation of anti-ageing and its antecedent practitioners and enthusiasts since the time of Bacon and earlier. It is therefore not a new concern, rather it is a 'modern' manifestation of the process whereby areas of scientific endeavour and professional practice establish their credentials as 'legitimate' experts. This suite of activities clearly demonstrates how anti-ageing medicine has sought to establish itself, in the US at least, as a credible medical (and broader healthcare) speciality on a par with psychiatry and cardiology, with the issues of public trust, credibility and accountability that follow from such a status. However, the speciality of 'anti-ageing' is not among the 130 specialities recognised by American Board of Medical Specialties (ABMS) nor are its treatments, therapies and interventions covered by health insurance. Anti-ageing medicine/life extension is not concerned solely with understanding the causes of ageing but, as the mission statement from A4M observes, with developing interventions to halt ageing and, by inference, in selling and promoting those interventions. However, while in the US, insurance companies may not fund expenditure on these treatments (nor the National Health Service [NHS] include such treatments within its portfolio), 'customers' are free to purchase such treatments and services from their own resources. So, websites such as Anti-Aging (www.anti-aging.org/) in the US offer extensive ranges of 'treatments' and products and provide a search facility so that consumers/customers can find the clinic/provider nearest to them.

At first sight, the definition of anti-ageing medicine provided by A4M seems largely unproblematic and uncontentious. It is hard to disagree with the underlying objectives of reducing the global and individual burden of disease and ill-health and promoting and/or enhancing quality of life for older people. In many ways it mirrors many of the aims and objectives of biologists, technologists, gerontologists and geriatricians/physicians working in 'mainstream' science and care settings. Indeed, a key plank of the strategy for the British NHS is focused on (age-related) chronic diseases and the prevention, treatment and management of such conditions. Fishman et al (2008) notes that the goals and mission of anti-ageing medicine largely mirror those of America's National Institute on Aging where a key research goal is to develop interventions and therapies to reduce and/or delay age-related degeneration and ill-health. The term 'anti-ageing medicine' is not as unproblematic as the definition noted earlier might imply (Mykytyn, 2006a). Indeed, it is a highly contested term that is characterised by a range of interpretations and meaning. There is no consensus on what constitutes the core and essential components of anti-ageing medicine, what they should be and what areas of activity constitute the more peripheral domains. Anti-ageing can mean a range of different things to differing audiences, ranging from scientists and clinicians, through researchers to consumers. The consumer group highlights one of the key components of the debate about anti-ageing medicine, namely the avowedly commercial aspect that promotes a variety of goods, services and interventions to consumers especially those in the US.

One of the major critiques of anti-ageing is, as Wick (2002: 1138) notes, 'its clear-cut commerciality'. There is an extensive market for anti-ageing products in the US with three product categories: appearance focused (both pharmacological and surgical), drugs/supplements focusing on age-related diseases and technologically based services, worth at least $72 billion in 2009 (Fishman et al, 2008). This is a significant underestimate of the broader anti-ageing market as it excludes exercise/ physical therapy type goods and services and other purchases such as vitamins, 'health foods' and supplements. However, again, as indicated in the section on promoting longevity, the development and marketing of goods, services and interventions to prevent, delay or overcome the ageing process and its deleterious consequences are not new. Alchemy in particular was associated with the search for the philosopher's stone, one element of which was the elixir of life, which could restore health by curing diseases and prolonging life (possibly indefinitely). For example, Qin Shi Hung, a Chinese Emperor in the third century BC, took medicines to achieve immortality, in 1667 Roger Bacon recommended medicines made from snakes to restore the body while in 1658 George Starkey promoted the benefits of an elixir made from the oil of evergreen trees (see Haycock, 2008, for a very detailed history of human endeavours to live longer and delay/stop the ageing process). Such products are not so dissimilar from our use of 'super foods' such as watercress or calorific restriction to promote healthy ageing or longevity. Indeed, virtually every person achieving the age of 100 is asked to identify what is the cause of their longevity. In many ways, the concerns and activities of the anti-agers mirror those of the general population who are interested in the secrets of achieving a long and healthy life.

The proponents of anti-ageing medicine see their endeavours as the logical extension of current interests in preventative health into old age and later life by focusing on the early detection, prevention and treatment and ultimately the reversal of age-related diseases for the extension of life. Central to the concept of anti-ageing is that biological/biomedical interventions can target and reverse the ageing process. Hence, the focus is on the biological rather than the socioenvironmental understanding of ageing. Protagonists of this approach see themselves as revolutionaries: challenging and extending the frontiers of science and medicine by implementing a paradigm shift in how we think about ageing, disease and longevity. They argue that biomedical researchers have been following the 'wrong' research agenda by focusing on the complications of ageing such as diabetes, dementia or heart failure rather than identifying and changing the process of ageing: the ultimate preventive medicine (see Mykytyn, 2008, 2010). They characterise the biomedical gerontological establishment as essentially defeatist in their stance on the 'war on ageing' with their emphasis on the identification and palliation/mediation of disease rather than the fundamental causes of ageing and seeking ways to reverse them. If we accept at face value the premise of anti-ageing medicine then it is difficult to understand all the controversy that this topic has provoked.

The fundamental premise of the anti-ageing endeavour is the notion of 'ageing as decline', in biological, social and sociological domains. This is illustrated by the comments of the proponents of anti-ageing interviewed by Mykytyn (2008, 2010). They all saw ageing as an enemy to be fought, a war to be won and as a process and experience that is entirely negative, with no acceptance of any positive dimensions of the ageing process. For many gerontologists, notably those from a social science background, this return to the 'ageing as inevitable decline' discourse represents a highly retrograde step as does the notion that biology is the only process fundamental to shaping the ageing experience. For social gerontologists in particular, the individualised perspective of anti-ageing discourse and the denial of the importance of socioenvironmental factors are especially problematic. While recognising the importance of the debates within the biomedical context, Vincent et al (2008) observe that it is important not to let this obscure the social, environmental and cultural aspects of debates surrounding anti-ageing (Vincent, 2003b, 2006, 2008; Turner, 2009).

Anti-ageing medicine is not without its critics and we can identify three key strands to the critique. There is a strongly rooted ideological opposition based on the disputation of the promotion of non 'evidence-based' therapies/interventions to what are conceptualised as 'gullible populations'. The 'ageing as decline' premise on which anti-ageing is based is disputed as are academic, practice and discipline boundaries. For example, where does 'legitimate' biomedicine and biogerontology research end and 'anti-ageing' medicine start? This represents a 'classic' example of boundary work – legitimate scientists distancing, differentiating or demarcating themselves from what they perceive to be pseudo science (Fishman et al, 2008). In terms of healthcare practice, where is the point at which legitimate therapies, based on a sound evidence base, end and 'quackery' begin? There are many reasons why such boundary work is engaged in but one key factor is to sustain academic authority, legitimacy and power.

In 2002, Olshansky et al published a position paper in the *Journal of Gerontology*, endorsed by 51 scientists in the field of ageing, both biological and psychosocial, in which they questioned the legitimacy and fundamental premise of anti-ageing. They stated:

> no currently marketed intervention has yet been proved to slow, stop or reverse human aging.... The entrepreneurs, physicians and other healthcare practitioners who make these claims are taking advantage of consumers who cannot easily distinguish between the hype and reality of interventions designed to influence the aging process and age-related diseases. (Olshansky et al, 2002b: 92).

They also published a version of this paper for a 'popular' audience in *Scientific American* (Olshansky et al, 2002a), had the article translated into a range of languages and published in a range of international journals. Furthermore, the American Association of Retired Persons (AARP) had the *Scientific American* story as a lead article. Olshansky and colleagues see anti-ageing medicine as a contemporary manifestation of the 'fountain of youth' concept. They characterise anti-ageing medicine as a close relative, or direct descent, of the ancient search for divine potions, elixirs and magical cures that can promote longevity, eradicate the ageing process and promote eternal youth. Vincent (2003a, 2003b) summarises their position as that anti-ageing medicine, in its current form, is dangerous because at best it may not work or at worst it may be harmful. Furthermore, they argue that, while science cannot modify the ageing process at present, it may be able to do so in the future. They also note that currently science can and does improve health in old age by developing treatments and interventions for the key age-related diseases.

The response by the anti-ageing lobby to the position articulated by Olshansky et al is that it represents the essentially 'conservative gerontological establishment' who are not prepared to confront new realities or change the way that they think about ageing. The 'anti-agers' offer a discourse that challenges the established and traditional academic and clinical/practice perspectives on the study of ageing, especially (but not exclusively) the biomedical perspectives with their perceived emphasis on decline, disease and pathology. Thus, they represent themselves as revolutionaries stifled by the innate and overt conservatism of established academics, practitioners and policy makers who have a vested interest in maintaining the status quo of the 'aging enterprise' (Estes et al, 2003). Binstock, from the US perspective, locates this debate within a broader historical context, notably the struggle of gerontology (and geriatric medicine as a speciality of healthcare practice) to establish itself as a legitimate area of academic activity. It now wishes to ensure that there is 'due distance' from what it characterises as the pseudoscience underpinning anti-ageing medicine (Binstock et al, 2003; Post and Binstock, 2004). 'Legitimate' scientists do not wish to see their own research and, importantly, research funding status lost because of a perceived link to anti-ageing medicine. However, maintaining this distance is highly problematic for 'established' scientists who wish to address issues of longevity and health in old age, questions that are also of interest to anti-ageing researchers. One suggestion is to differentiate the 'legitimate' sphere of activity from the less rigorous approach of anti-ageing by the development of a distinct vocabulary that differentiates the two areas of activity and enables judgements to be made about the legitimacy (or otherwise) of research, treatments and interventions. One proposal is for the creation of the speciality of longevity science, which would focus on robust research into the means to extend healthy life. We should not underestimate the importance of this debate as to the differentiation of 'legitimate' academic research in the field of ageing and, what Mykytyn (2008) terms the 'suspect'. The debate is particularly sensitive given the long struggle of medical and social care specialities, focusing on the needs of older people, and academic research, which focuses on gerontology, to obtain recognition from practitioners and scientists (as well as funding bodies).

Moody (2002) suggests that questioning whether anti-ageing or life-extending technologies and interventions 'work' and subjecting their claims to rigorous scientific and transparent analysis and scrutiny is only one of three important questions that should be posed about anti-ageing. He proposes we ask two further critical (in the sense of reflective) questions: could anti-ageing work (now or at some time in the future) and should anti-ageing interventions work? This latter question, according to Vincent (2003a, 2003b), is perhaps the most important question, in that it is concerned with the moral values and principles underlying 'life extension'. Here Vincent (2003a, 2003b) is positing the 'age-old' premise – just because we can do something it does not necessarily follow that we should! He characterises the debates about anti-ageing in terms of the crisis that it presents for gerontology. He argues that the focus on longevity (and immortality) denies old age as a valued (and final) part of the lifecourse and consigns old age and older people (a phase of life that could last four decades) to a state of redundancy and social worthlessness (see also Gullette, 2004).

Vincent et al (2008) open up some further and broader aspects of the anti-ageing debate that they argue still need to be addressed. They emphasise that the construction of old age as a uniquely biological problem with, therefore, a biological solution results in the neglect of sociocultural/socioenvironmental issues. They argue that we need to explore in much more detail the cultural construction of ageing embedded in, and advanced by, anti-aging protagonists. We also need to examine the perspectives of older people themselves on the anti-ageing debate and, from a policy/service perspective, determine where (if at all) anti-ageing interventions are located within the health and social welfare infrastructures of contemporary Western societies. These authors suggest that we need to develop a more rounded debate as regards anti-ageing and to focus on complex and difficult underlying questions including:

- questions related to existential issues regarding the purpose of life and questions such as 'is life always preferable to death?';
- questions related to societies' institutionalised ageism and the central debate about the value of old age within society (or should we seek to abolish old age at the earliest possible opportunity?);
- questions related to the biological nature of ageing: is ageing a single biological process (or several related and integrated processes)? Should ageing be considered a disease and, if so, what are the consequences of this?
- questions related to issues of personal behaviour, especially in terms of lifestyle. What and how much should we eat, how much should we exercise? Is alcohol good (or bad) for us, in what quantities and at what phases of the lifecourse? Will 'mainstream' preventive activities delay ageing and, but not unique to this domain, how much (if at all) should we 'require' or compel individuals to regulate their behaviours to conform to the structures of a 'healthy' lifestyle?

As these questions illustrate, to date we have only just started to address the complexities that are wrapped up in the anti-ageing enterprise.

Gullible fools or informed consumers?

ACTIVITY 2

▶ Visit your local chemist, pharmacy or health food store or look in women's (and increasingly men's) magazines and see how many products are aimed at older people and at improving their health and appearance. What kinds of images of old age do such products and advertisements represent?

As the book by Haycock (2008) very elegantly describes, there has always been a 'market' for interventions (pills, potions and more invasive procedures) that purchasers hope will enable them to achieve immortality. However, such preoccupations have predominantly been the province of privileged groups within a given society. Up until recently (and it remains the case in less developed parts of the world) the concern of most individuals was survival beyond infancy and childhood rather than immortality. There is comparatively little research examining the views of older people, and the wider population more generally, about the use of anti-ageing products/services and the broader philosophical and social implications of these activities. Little debate has been generated around concepts such as 'life extension' (Lucke and Hall, 2006), nor has great attention been paid to the consumers of such interventions (Cardona, 2008) or providers/researchers (Underwood et al, 2009a, 2009b). These deficits in our evidence base are reflective of the focus of the 'anti-ageing war', which has largely centred on professional discourses around legitimacy and credibility or in modelling the boundaries and possibilities of longevity (albeit for those fortunate enough to be born into the developed world).

We are all familiar with the 'health promotion' campaigns run and endorsed by national governments that exhort us to lead a 'healthy' lifestyle. The emphasis in such campaigns, which can be targeted at the general population or specific subgroups such as young adults, is predominantly on manipulating lifestyle/behaviour to reduce established risk factors for specific diseases, most notably cancer and cardiovascular diseases, or the reduction of states such as obesity that are linked to negative health outcomes. There are also campaigns aimed more specifically at older people that focus on vague but broadly positive objectives such as healthy ageing and successful ageing – what precisely is meant by these terms is usually unclear. The notion of empowered third-age consumers with the economic power to purchase and create new lifestyles is comparatively recent. Cardona (2007) notes, in her study of users of anti-ageing interventions in Australia, that the rationale for such use was expressed in terms of the desire to avoid the 'negative' consequences of ageing in terms of both appearance and physical/mental function. These participants universally expressed entirely negative descriptions of old age and were keen to avoid what they articulated as the negative consequences. As one of the participants noted: 'What I am doing now is about "healthy ageing" … using anti-aging [products], eating the right food, exercising and doing everything I can to remain healthy for as long as I can (female aged 49)' (Cardona, 2007: 223). This desire to avert the perceived negative physical and mental consequences of ageing seems to be a key dimension of the decision to use anti-ageing interventions. However, this quotation also highlights the paradox of the anti-ageing enterprise. The observance of a good diet and partaking of regular exercise are mainstream activities advocated by every government in the Western world as a means of improving the health of populations. The participants' goal of remaining as healthy as possible for as long as possible is also resonant with those espoused by governments for their populations. Hence, on this limited evidence the motives of those using anti-ageing interventions are fairly mainstream. It is, perhaps, only when focusing on appearance-based objectives that such service users deviate from the mainstream policy.

There is even less empirical data examining general (and specialist views) as to the ultimate goal of anti-ageing activities, namely life extension (Underwood et al, 2007). From a professional perspective, Underwood et al (2009a, 2009b) illustrate the diversity of opinion about the goal of life extension. For their participants – 14 researchers in the field of ageing – the positive goal of life extension was mediated by concerns about quality of life. Would life extension just be consigning individuals to extra years of poor health? Issues of social justice and equity were also important. Would these 'benefits' only be available to those with the ability to pay? Lucke and Hall (2005) use the existence of the market for anti-ageing goods and services as an indirect indication that the general population are interested in issues of longevity extension both personally and at a more global level. However, it is something of a leap of imagination to draw the inference that the purchase of multivitamins, super foods or other interventions indicates broad support for the goal of life extension. De Grey (2008) observes this paradox between the consumption of goods and services linked to anti-ageing and bioethicists'/researchers' (all professionals') presumption that the 'public' will not be interested in pursuing life extension (a conclusion arrived at without the benefit of empirical evidence). This could be constructed as a rather patronising and disparaging attitude that implies that professional knowledge takes precedence and that 'professionals know best'. We would argue that the population at large will be interested in debating and discussing life extension for the same reasons that some individuals use anti-ageing interventions, namely the perceived negative aspects of ageing – disability, dementia, frailty and the fear of death/dying. Claims that people would either exchange longevity for quality of life or desire both a longer and healthier life remain untested. However, the work of Winter et al (2003) indicates how nuanced and complex such debates can be. They reported that older frail respondents were more likely to support life extension with disabilities and had less concern for quality of life than did their healthy counterparts. Thus, as with other ethical-medical debates, the views and opinions (and personal choices) expressed by individuals are moulded by circumstances and change in response to these. The views of Winter et al's respondents resonate with the adage attributed to Maurice Chevalier: 'Old age isn't so bad when you consider the alternative.' There is clearly a considerable interest in anti-ageing in terms of the ideology of life extension that it espouses and the challenges that this raises for the gerontological establishment and society more generally. Turner (2009) is of the opinion that much of what he terms the 'gimmickry' of life extension will become commonplace in the next half century. This may be an overly optimistic reading of the anti-ageing debate. However, what does seem certain is that this is an approach towards ageing and later life that needs to be taken seriously and used to raise a more robust and inclusive debate about the nature of ageing and later life.

Is health a consumption good?

Debates around financial and material circumstances within the UK have predominantly focused on income, especially in developing comparisons between the incomes of older people relative to other groups within the population, and on income differentials within the older population. However, income is only one prism for examining the material circumstances of older people, as we can also look at expenditure from both economic and sociological perspectives. Gilleard and Higgs (2000, 2005) and Jones et al (2008, 2009) have argued that 'consumption' is an important source of identity in postmodern society but this perspective has only recently been advanced as a potential source of identity in later life, although it is self-evidently the case that older people consume goods and services. We restrict our focus to a consideration of 'health' as a consumption good with specific reference to older people and later life. Clearly, this is a qualitatively different approach from reviewing access of older people (or indeed, any other group) to 'traditional' consumption items such as videos or televisions, items that convey a myriad of social messages about the purchaser, including identity, aesthetics and sense of self (see Higgs and Gilleard, 2000, 2004; Jones et al, 2008). Consumption, especially as a marker of identity, is not limited solely to the types of tangible goods as in the previous example but is also concerned with services (both tangible and intangible – for example 'anti-ageing creams'), leisure pursuits and more generic 'lifestyle' purchases such as food items, cultural goods and services and technological products. Gould and Gould (2001) have argued that both healthcare and the less concrete concept of 'health' can be conceptualised as consumption goods, which requires us to consider a range of different components, including the provision (and consumption) of healthcare-related goods and services (examined in Chapter Six), the experience and distribution of 'health' within and between populations of older people (examined in Chapters Two, Three and Four) and the development of health-related lifestyles addressed in this chapter.

Conceptualising health as a consumption good is not unproblematic, especially given the wide-ranging approaches to the definition of health, especially within the context of a socialised NHS where access to health represents a citizenship right rather than a market purchase (see Victor, 2008). It is, perhaps, more obvious to see health as a consumption good within the context of societies such as the US, where health exists within a highly marketised framework whereby individuals often have to decide how much healthcare to purchase. Choices range from purchasing it via out-of-pocket expenditure, a health insurance plan or to select one's employment based on the health insurance benefits offered. (How the reforms to the US healthcare system are implemented following the policy changes championed by President Obama remains the subject of heated debate. We await the outcome with interest.) However, we would argue that, since the introduction of a range of different types of 'internal markets' within the NHS, patient choice, and by implication ideas about consumption, have become a consistent theme of health and social policy in Britain and that we have developed (or are still developing) an increasingly individualised pattern of consumption of health and healthcare (Gilleard and Higgs, 1998).

A healthcare market?

The use of healthcare services varies with age across the population, with individuals in older age groups being more likely to use health services than those in the younger age groups. Older people are therefore the largest single 'consumer' group for the services provided by the NHS (see Chapter Six). However, in this chapter we are thinking about 'health-related' goods and services – such as health foods, over-the-counter medications, cosmetic surgery, gym memberships or the use of private medical services – which might be indicative of a specific healthcare market, the emergence of an overtly anti-ageing market and/or the types of goods and services used to establish identity as an 'active' ager rather than utilisation of state-provided healthcare. Within the UK there has always existed a 'private' healthcare sector alongside the NHS. Propper and Green (2001) and Propper et al (2001) using data from the British Household Panel survey, estimate that about a fifth (20%) of the population use private healthcare, mostly optical (13%), dental (11%) and physiotherapy (5%) services, with only 1% reporting the use of private inpatient care (see also Propper, 2002). The private healthcare market is focused on optical and dental services, dimensions of healthcare where NHS provision is sparse and the consumption of private sector services is, perhaps, more out of necessity than 'true choice' or an identity-establishing practice. Consequently, it is not clear whether this type of expenditure truly represents a marker of health consumption as argued above.

Our focus here is on trying to look for evidence of an emerging market for healthcare goods and services among older people as evidence of health being constructed as a consumption-based concept and of health consumption being used as an indication of identity. One potential way of starting to investigate this issue is via the analysis of consumption patterns as manifest by how people spend their income: this is a novel analytical strategy as the bulk of the work in the UK has focused on sources of income in later life rather than on how older people spend their money. This lack of interest in the analysis of expenditure patterns is not entirely explicable, as data on expenditure patterns among the population have been collected in Britain since 1953 through what was originally termed the Family Expenditure Survey and, from the perspective of research concerned with older people, remains a largely neglected dataset. This survey has undergone a number of changes of both name and areas of income/expenditure recorded. The data provide a meta-level overview of how the 'consumer society' has emerged during the last five decades of the 20th century with the inclusion of an increasing array of consumption goods ranging from 'white goods', through personal entertainment items to food items and lifestyle purchases (for example, gym memberships). The survey has always included questions on a variety of health-related purchases and expenditure, although these have been characterised by subtle (or not so subtle) changes in definition over time, the inclusion of new items and exclusion of others. Until 2001/02, health services such as medicines, prescriptions and spectacles, and medical, dental, optical and nursing fees, were classified as 'personal' services, a category that also included toiletries and soap, cosmetics, beauty treatment and leather and jewellery goods. Non-NHS expenditure on spectacles was recorded under the optical and photographic expenditure category. The survey has, however, always distinguished between expenditure on private goods and services – such as spectacles – and contributions towards NHS services such as prescription charges.

At a macro level, we can chart the development and diffusion of consumer goods (see Jones et al, 2008) in the health field as evidenced by the inclusion of contact lenses (1994), prescription sun glasses (1992) and medical insurance (1979). Since 2001/02, an overall category of 'health' expenditures has been created. However, 'health-related consumption' is not limited to goods and services with an overt and specific health function; goods can have 'health effects' or be linked to health. Self and Zealy (2007) distinguish between health-related expenditures that have a positive impact on health (or at least that is the intention) (medication, health foods and glasses) and those with a negative outcome (smoking and alcohol consumption and 'unhealthy' eating). They estimate that in 2005, households in the UK spent £125 billion on positive, direct health-related expenditures while £28 billion was spent on goods with a proven 'negative' health outcome, notably tobacco and alcoholic drinks.

In 2007, the 'average' expenditure per household on 'health-related' goods and services was £5.70 per week out of a total spend of £459.00 (1%) and this percentage was constant across the income distribution deciles (ONS, 2010). We can look at 'pensioner' households in more detail by distinguishing between size of household (single person versus couples) and degree of dependence on the state for their income. However, this analysis reveals no substantial deviation from the overall norm, with all of these household permutations spending about 1% of total expenditure on explicitly health-related products. Have health-related expenditure patterns changed over time? Is there evidence of the emergence of a health goods/services market and the development of consumption patterns that support notions of a health-related consumption-based healthcare lifestyle? Analysis of data from the inception of the Family Expenditure Survey in 1953 enables us to trace the development of health spending. Victor (2005) estimates that before the creation of the NHS, direct health service purchases accounted for about 1.4% of average incomes with, very obviously, large variations around this. In 1953/54, pensioner households spent about 0.5% of income on health purchases compared with 1% in 2007. Within the very important limitations of our data we see that both absolute and relative expenditure on health-related goods are currently only a small component of older people's budgets and show little increase over time. These data suggest that, at a population level, there is little overt evidence of the emergence of a significant healthcare market in the UK nor of older people spending a significant fraction of their income on healthcare (although that is not to negate the possibility that there are subgroups of older people for whom this may be the case).

One important part of the debate about the development of consumption as a form of identity and about health as a consumption good is the purchase of discrete and identifiable goods and services that define a 'health' lifestyle. Examples of such purchases include cosmetic surgery, dietary supplements, vitamins, health supplements and leisure activities such as gym membership and the apparel/equipment required for participation. Most of these components of expenditure cannot be readily identified from our routine expenditure data sources. There is some evidence from these data that even those well into 'retirement' are using their income to participate in leisure-based activities, some of which will be linked to health via activities such as golf club memberships and gym-related activities. However, from routinely available datasets there is no evidence of a widespread developing healthcare market by older people, either in health consumption activities or expenditure. Nonetheless, we can conclude that older people in contemporary Britain are spending their income in very different ways from their counterparts in 1953/54 where there was virtually no expenditure on 'non-essential' goods or services.

Personal healthcare expenditure: international perspectives

Thus far we have looked at expenditure on health-related goods and services by older people in the UK. This has been an inherently limited analysis given the paucity of the data but serves to highlight an embryonic area of research and, as has been argued elsewhere, is one with considerable potential for providing novel and challenging insights into the nature and experience of old age. Even given the very limited nature of the available data, it is possible to identify the development of expenditure patterns and consumption that hint at health-related lifestyles and activities and the use of disposable income to overtly (or perhaps indirectly) engage in lifestyles that promote 'healthy' ageing. We have focused here on those who are currently categorised as 'older'. However, it is clear that those who will be entering into old age in the next two decades may present a rather different profile in terms of expenditure patterns in later life. It may be the ageing 'baby boomers' who more strongly present evidence of a consumption-based perspective on health and identity in later life. As with most other aspects of life in contemporary Britain, there is evidence suggesting variations or structurally based inequalities in expenditure in these areas among older groups with clear differentials in terms of age, gender and (probably) social class and there are considerable research opportunities for considering the relationships between measures of social location, gender and age-based differentials in these types of expenditure. However, our analysis of health-related expenditure is located within the context of the provision of the majority of health services to the population via the NHS, which is still largely a comprehensive healthcare service, ranging from acute hospital care and primary medical care services (although less so for optical and dental care) to continuing care (although again less universalist in coverage here), which is funded out of general taxation and (mostly) free at the point of use. This inevitably means that older people in Britain, unlike many of their European and North American contemporaries, do not have to have a detailed knowledge of healthcare costs and/or rules of eligibility before accessing services or a deep level of engagement with the healthcare market. Furthermore, the onset of chronic illness or disability in old age for older people in the UK does not presage the same financial consequences as those experienced by older people in the US. For older people in the US, a co-payment of $10 or $20 may be required for a consultation with a doctor (2007 data). This clearly has to be factored into the consultation decision alongside the symptoms/healthcare problem the older person wishes to discuss. Older people in Britain can consult their general practitioner without recourse to financial consideration of either the consultation itself or any consequent treatment outcomes.

How does health consumption figure as a component of the expenditure of older people in other countries? This is a challenge to examine rigorously and systematically as each country has different systems for organising and providing healthcare and a range of 'payment' options and requirements. However, data from the Health and Retirement Survey for the US and its European equivalent – the SHARE survey – do enable at least a preliminary examination of this topic. The 2005 US Consumer Expenditure Survey (2005), the equivalent to the UK's Family Expenditure Survey, reveals that those aged 65 and over spend 13% of their annual income on out-of-pocket healthcare expenses (this rises to 15.6% for those aged 75 and over) and excludes any insurance premiums. Of this, 3.7% of annual income is spent on drugs and 3% on medical services (www.bls.gov/cex/2005/share/age.pdf). This is an overall figure and clearly varies across the population. For those in the bottom quintile of the income distribution, direct healthcare-related payments may account for approximately 25-30% of their expenditure. Health and Retirement Survey data indicate that direct 'out-of-pocket' health expenditure increased from $1450 per annum for those aged 55-64 to $2,200 for those aged 85 and over (Karp, 2007). These are almost certainly underestimates as they do not include nursing home care and other health-related activities. UK data is problematic and almost certainly an underestimate but Family Expenditure Survey data suggest that older people in Britain are spending well under £200 a year on direct healthcare – even given the problems of classifying expenditures this is several orders of magnitude different from their US counterparts, although both of these analyses exclude long-term care in either communal or community settings.

The contrast between the UK and US is illustrated by the examination of health expenditure in the year before death, the most 'expensive' phase of life in terms of healthcare costs. Karp (2007) reports longitudinal Health and Retirement Survey data that estimates that for the average couple, health expenditure was approximately 15% of income five years before the death of a spouse; 25% of income three years before death and 50% in the final year of life.

We anticipate that this area of research will grow as social gerontologists (and sociologists of later life) focus on how older people spend their money; not as an alternative to but in conjunction with studies of income and wealth in later life. We also anticipate the research potential for examining consumption patterns over the lifecycle. How do patterns change over time? What elements of consumption are retained in later life and what new consumption patterns emerge and what aspects decline? For example, we would argue that gym membership and participation in health and exercise based activities represent a very different form of 'health consumption' from gardening; although the latter is clearly important as a form of exercise it is not necessarily a consciously lifestyle-creating, identity-forming or health-promoting activity.

Healthy lifestyles?

ACTIVITY 3

▸ What would you define as 'active' ageing?

▸ How would you encourage older people to adopt 'healthier' lifestyles?

Promoting healthy and/or active ageing – these terms are used interchangeably or together – is a key policy objective for most Western societies and globally. The World Health Organization (WHO) sees active ageing, which it champions, as a broader concept than healthy ageing because it includes ideas not simply about optimising health and access to healthcare in old age but also notions of social engagement and participation and safety and security. Thus, the goal of active ageing is to maximise quality of life in old age (and as people age) by promoting and enhancing safety and security, social participation and engagement and health. Thus, active ageing focuses on enabling individuals and populations to achieve their potential in terms of physical, social, and mental wellbeing across the lifecourse. The 2005 WHO statement on active ageing (see http://whqlibdoc.who.int/hq/2002/WHO_NMH_NPH_02.8.pdf) is underpinned by the definition of health championed by the WHO, which emphasises optimising the dimensions of physical, mental and social wellbeing as a means to the maintenance of autonomy and independence for older people. Healthy ageing describes the portfolio of activities and behaviours undertaken by individuals to reduce the risk of illness, disability and disease and promote and enhance physical, emotional and mental health. Thus, healthy ageing has a narrower focus than active ageing as there is not a concern with social participation or the need for safety and security. Included within the 'healthy ageing' remit are 'traditional' lifestyle health–promotion activities such as exercise/activity promotion, diet and alcohol consumption plus preventative screening activities (such as mammography or the management of hypertension). In this section we focus on the three 'lifestyle' aspects of healthy ageing – exercise, diet and smoking/drinking –which form the 'traditional' content of debates about 'healthy' lifestyles and the core of policy initiatives and interventions to promote 'healthy' ageing. While each aspect of lifestyle is dealt with individually there are clearly links between these domains of life as individuals demonstrate an integrated suite of 'lifestyle behaviours'.

Exercise and physical activity

Exercise and physical activity across the lifecourse is important in psychological, social and physiological terms. In psychological terms, participation in exercise and physical activity can provide a source of identity, support and enhance self-esteem and feelings of self-worth and promote mental wellbeing, potentially, helping to ward off specific mental health problems such as depression. In terms of social domains, participation in exercise promotes social inclusion and engagement by enhancing and supporting opportunities for social interaction. There is now a copious and robust body of evidence demonstrating the very positive health benefits of physical activity, which can help prevent disease, reduce disability and improve quality of life and a sense of wellbeing (see Galloway and Jokl, 2000; Dugan, 2007; Harris et al, 2009). More specifically, Powell (2005) argues that the promotion of physical activity can be a means by which to prevent (and treat) diseases of old age. Indeed, Dominguez et al (2009) suggests that exercise (and a balanced diet) are the only two interventions that have a proven 'anti-ageing' benefit in terms of preventing age-related diseases. While these authors may somewhat overstate their case, there are a number of age-related physiological changes, such as decrease in muscle mass, decrease in maximum heart rate and decrease in VO2max (that is, the maximum amount of oxygen that an individual can utilise during intense exercise), which continued physical activity can, at the worst, slow the rate of decline, and, at best, reverse such changes. Conversely, it is well established that physical inactivity is extremely detrimental to older people's health (and indeed, other population subgroups). There are a range of negative health effects linked with physical inactivity, which include increasing overall mortality, increasing the risk of over 20 physical and mental health problems (including cardiovascular disease, diabetes, obesity, osteoporosis, musculoskeletal problems, several cancers, depression and dementia), increasing falls risk, reducing function and independence, and reducing quality of life and emotional wellbeing (Chief Medical Officer, 2004). There seem to be no negative aspects to the promotion of exercise in later life (or, indeed, other ages) although for serious exercisers there is the issue of injuries and for older people the specific problem of falls.

How much physical activity should older adults (aim) to undertake? There is no specific guidance that relates exclusively to older people. The UK government advises that older adults, like the general population, should aim to undertake activity of moderate intensity (that is, levels of activity sufficient to result in increases in breathing, heart rate and temperature) for 30 minutes (or more) on at least five days a week. It is not deemed necessary to complete the 30 minutes in a single session and may be broken up into 10-minute 'bursts'. The importance of exercise in later life is evidenced by a range of national policies that all stress the importance of helping older adults to maintain and/or increase their levels of physical activity (DH, 2005b, 2006).

This raises the question of how active older people are. How many individuals achieve these target activity levels? Accurate measurement of physical activity is methodologically complex. As with many other areas of research and policy we need to define the concept that we wish to measure and distinguish between physical activity (any form of bodily movement) and exercise (specific activity that is planned and structured and undertaken with the goal of improving physical fitness or performance). Both exercise as in participating in 'fitness-improving' activities, such as attending an exercise class or activity, walking the dog or gardening, can enable individuals to achieve the activity targets. If we shift the focus for achieving the targets to increasing activity then we can embed achieving this within the framework of daily life. We can emphasise the 'health benefits' of gardening and walking and include every domain of life including leisure but also domestic tasks and activities of daily living.

Measuring and recording these concepts are challenging. The dimensions of activity that we require to measure are: frequency, intensity, time (these help us to monitor achievement of the national activity guidance thresholds) and type of activity. There are a range of ways of assessing activity levels at the population and individual level. The most popular (and cost-effective) is via specifically designed questionnaires such as the Global Physical Activity Questionnaire (GPAQ) or, in portmanteau surveys, 'self-report' questions that require individuals to recall the amount, type and intensity of activity undertaken within a specific reference period. Data from the Health Survey for England provide an overview of the levels of activity across the population and limited data about trends over time based on self-report questions.

Overall, in 2008, 39% of adult males and 2% of adult females achieved the recommended activity levels; this represents an increase from 1997 when 32% and 21% respectively achieved the targets. For the population aged 65 and over, only a minority achieved these targets, approximately 15% of males and 9% of females with a further 28% and 23% respectively reporting some activity. Levels of activity decrease with age (see Table 5.1). Encouragingly, Table 5.1 suggests

Table 5.1: Trends in the achievement of physical activity recommendations by age and gender, population aged 65+, England, 1997-2008 (%)

	65-74		75+	
	M	F	M	F
1997	12	8	7	5
1998	14	9	6	3
2003	17	13	8	3
2004	18	14	8	4
2006	21	16	9	4
2008 – self-report	21	18	9	6
2008 – accelerometer study	9	6	5	2

Source: Craig et al (2009, tables 2.6 and table 3.12)

that there was an increase in the percentage of those aged 65 and over achieving the target activity levels (although from a very low base) in the period analysed.

However, it is at least plausible to argue that these types of questions, which focus on activity, are consistently mis-answered by older people who may not construe the types of activity that they do such as walking, gardening or household-based activities as 'physical activity', leading to this segment of the population consistently under-reporting activity levels. The availability of relatively cheap motion sensors such as pedometers and accelerometers, which can monitor levels of activity, means that population surveys can now use more 'objective' methods of collecting activity data rather than relying on self-report. These are especially useful in surveys of older people given that they record the most frequent form of physical activity undertaken by older people, which is walking (see Harris et al, 2009). However, preliminary research studies using accelerometers with older people are not encouraging in terms of the achievement of target exercise levels by this segment of the population. Recent work measuring activity levels using accelerometers reported that only 2.5% of those aged 65 and over (Harris et al, 2008) and 1.8% of those aged 70 and over (Davis and Fox, 2007) actually achieved the target activity levels. The 2008 Health Survey for England included an accelerometer study and produced results in line with these previous studies, with around 7% of those 65-74 and around 3% of those aged 75 and over achieving the guidelines (see Table 5.1). While the accelerometers used in these studies did not record a small number of activities such as swimming or cycling, it is highly unlikely that inclusion of these would have increased these levels in any meaningful way. Thus, we are forced to conclude that activity levels among older people are extremely low, that 'self-report' based studies overestimate activity levels and that there is a considerable public health challenge to be embraced in order to increase activity in later life.

The other element of recording physical activity and exercise is to record the types of activities that older people undertake. One important source of information about the types of physical exercise and activities (rather than overall activity levels) is provided by the General Household Survey, which investigated participation in a range of physical activities. This demonstrated that walking was the most popular form of physical activity with 35% of men aged 65 and over reporting that they had done this in the four weeks prior to interview and 25% of women (Rickards et al, 2004). Indeed, regular walking is specifically promoted for older people as it is an activity with a very low risk of any resultant harm. However, for walking to achieve the activity targets it needs to be undertaken at a brisk pace of three miles per hour (Ainsworth et al, 2000). It is unclear from our self-report data as to how many of the 25–35% of older people who report walking do it at a sufficiently vigorous pace for it to meet the targets. However, the work of Harris et al (2008) suggests that this will not be a very large number. Health Survey for England data reinforce the importance of walking as a form of physical activity, with about 15% overall reporting partaking in 'brisk' walking in the month before interview (see Table 5.2). Similar proportions engage in sports and exercise but we can see that the over-75 age group is much less active than its younger contemporaries.

Table 5.2: Participation in a range of activities in the four weeks prior to interview by age and gender, population aged 65+, England, 1997-2008 (%)

	65-74		75+	
	M	F	M	F
Heavy housework	46	54	34	30
Gardening/DIY	33	13	20	5
Brisk walking	23	20	10	7
Sport and exercise	27	28	14	13

Source: Craig et al (2009, tables 2.6 and table 2.7)

Is there any evidence of participation in the types of exercise most obviously linked to ideas about consumption such as gym membership and other types of activity? Unfortunately, the General Household Survey does not record this specific variable. In the four weeks prior to interview between 5% and 6% of those aged 60 and over had been swimming and a similar percentage to a keep fit class (attending a gym was not included in the list of potential activities) and this is roughly stable from 1996/97, so again there is no substantial evidence of a more consumption-based health focus emerging. However, this is not to say that such a trend will not emerge with the ageing of the 'baby boom' generation.

There is a small subgroup of highly active older people who participate and volunteer in sports and fitness. This is clearly a minority lifestyle but nevertheless is of interest despite being largely ignored by researchers despite the existence of (relatively) large numbers of 'older' participants in mass participation sporting events. For example, at the 2008 London marathon there were 529 finishers aged 65 and over and there are significant levels of participation in Veterans/Masters competitions across a range of sports within Britain and internationally. Those who participate in Masters or Veterans sporting events constitute an interesting if small subgroup of the older population. Can they tell us anything about ageing in general, physical decline, the health benefits of physical activity or how to engage others in activity? There is an extensive literature, from a largely sports science perspective, examining the physiological aspects of 'Master' athletes. The focus is on issues such as muscle mass and aspects of physical fitness such as lung function and the accumulated evidence demonstrates that physiological changes can be arrested and reversed. However, there is a rich and largely unexploited research agenda looking at the extent of older people's participation in leisure and sporting-related activities and their motivations. Does this represent a manifestation of a continuation of an established lifestyle, a way of resisting or denying old age or the ultimate manifestation of active ageing? What do older people see as the benefits arising from participation in sporting activity? There is also a need to develop a more qualitative approach to complement the predominance of quantitative, physiology-based research.

In addition, we should critically evaluate the research and ideology underpinning the evidence and policy initiatives promoting activity and exercise in later life. Tulle (2008b) offers an interesting and stimulating critique of sports science and reconstructs it as part of the anti-ageing enterprise. Focusing on falls prevention for which exercise interventions are promoted, she argues that the evidence base for such activities is not uncontested. In particular, she argues that the evidence base is limited in terms of the nature, intensity and duration of exercise-based interventions for specific conditions such as sarcopenia and falls. Some physicians and sports scientists liken such interventions to prescriptions with all the implications of the accuracy and efficacy of the intervention that this metaphor implies. Tulle (2008b) argues that this is a fallacious metaphor. She believes we are unclear as to the dosage, intensity and composition of such interventions and the nature of the 'health gain', which may range from specific physiological indicators to improvements in functional capacity or the ability to live at home independently. Tulle (2008b) argues that we should focus on exercise/activity across the lifecourse as a means of promoting what she defines as 'physical competency' and that we should look at the wider socioenvironmental context, which contextualises opportunities for exercise, and investigate the degree to which these can be manipulated to enhance greater physical engagement. However, it should not preclude us from also developing exercise-based interventions for use in specific circumstances (for example, falls prevention) but that we should be realistic about the limits of our knowledge.

Diet and obesity

Manipulation of diet is one of the most persistently proposed ways of 'achieving' longevity. Turner (2009) notes that both Lessius and Cornaro published books in the late 15th/early 16th centuries that advocated 'dietary control' as a means of promoting a long (and healthy) life, as did George Cheyne in 1773. Perhaps the most extreme form of dietetics and longevity is the notion of calorific restriction. In 1934, two US researchers – Mary Crowell and Clive McCay – reported that laboratory rats fed a severely reduced calorie diet, while maintaining vital nutrient levels, had lifespans of up to twice as long as expected. These findings were developed by Anderson et al (2009) who reported that mice fed restricted diets demonstrated a longer lifespan, 'youthful' appearance, higher activity levels and delayed onset of age-related diseases compared with 'normal' experimental mice. The link between calorific restriction and healthy ageing as measured by a range of biomarkers is well established in animal models such as rats, mice, fruit flies, worms and, more recently, primates. However, it remains unclear as to whether calorific restriction in adults demonstrates a positive influence on a range of 'ageing' biomarkers or extends lifespan (see Heilbronn and Ravussin 2005) and, indeed, as these authors point out, conducting trials to test these hypotheses is both methodologically complex and ethically fraught. However, calorific restriction, a diet with a calorie intake 20-40% below 'accepted norms', remains one of the most widely promulgated paths to extending life but, as yet, the science does not support the proposition. One anti-ageing website for Europe (http://antiaging-europe.com/) promotes a range of therapies and interventions. At the time of writing, fasting and calorific restriction was the key therapy offered and the following diseases were identified as being cured or prevented by this intervention:

- asthma
- cardiovascular diseases
- cholecystitis and gout
- chronic fatigue syndrome
- cognitive decline
- diabetes
- diseases of the digestive system
- epilepsy
- glomerulonephritis
- hypertension
- infections
- infertility
- low immunity
- memory loss
- neurodegenerative disorders
- obesity
- obstructive sleep apnoea (OSA)
- psoriasis
- psychiatric disorders
- rheumatoid arthritis
- skin disorders
- spinal column diseases
- thrombophlebitis
- tumours

There are less restrictive strictures and policy guidance as to what constitutes an optimal diet in terms of both calorific intake and composition (nutritional and micronutrient composition) of diet adjusted for different population subgroups (for example, young children and pregnant women). *Food matters* (Cabinet Office, 2008: 10) reporting on the diet and nutritional status of the general population (including children) notes that 'for our health, most of us do not need to eat more, but we do need to eat a better or more varied diet'. The population of the UK has yet to achieve key dietary targets specified by the Department of Health in terms of the consumption of index foods indicative of a 'healthy' diet, including fruit and vegetables, saturated fats, sugars, fibre, oily fish and salt. Approximately one third (30%) of adults achieve the target dietary guidance of five or more portions of fruit and vegetables per day; the average intake of fruit and vegetables is 2.8 portions (estimated portion size of 80g) per day. Saturated fats account for 13% of energy intake compared with the recommended 11%; salt intake is 43% higher than the target level (8.6 grammes/day compared with the target of 6 grammes/day); fibre intake is 73% of target levels and consumption of oily fish is 30% of the target level. There are also a plethora of micronutrients where the population are not reaching the Lower Reference Nutrient Intake (LRNI), including calcium, iron, magnesium, vitamin A and riboflavin.

As with exercise, diet is one of the few interventions that might be categorised as promoting 'healthy ageing'. Diet, in terms of both quantity and types of food consumed, is linked with a range of negative health outcomes including specific conditions such as cardiovascular diseases and cancer and obesity (which itself is linked with a range of poor health outcomes in terms of mortality and diseases such as diabetes). However, in parallel with exercise, the scientific measurement of diet is extremely complex and very challenging to deliver in population surveys. There are a range of different approaches from highly intensive recording of diet via the weighing of food consumed through 'food diaries' to the consumption of key types of food indicative of dietary status. Typically, studies such as the Health Survey for England or English Longitudinal Study of Ageing, as they are 'portmanteau surveys', explore consumption of what might be termed 'index foods' such as the five portions of fruit and vegetables a day. Older adults are more likely to report achieving the 'five a day' target than younger people, although two thirds of the population still do not achieve this target. Older people were less likely than other age groups to be aware of the 'five a day' policy but, like the rest of the population, feel that they ate a healthy diet.

It is also challenging to evaluate the effect of specific diets on both the chances of reaching 'old age' in optimal health and maintaining a 'healthy old age'. Interest has been expressed in a range of diet types for promoting health – perhaps the most well known is the 'Mediterranean' type diet (see Battino and Ferreiro, 2004, for a review).

One manifestation of poor diet, in terms of overconsumption of calories, is obesity. While there is a concern about mal/undernutrition of older people in specific settings such as hospitals and care homes, there is a much greater prevalence of being overweight rather than underweight among contemporary populations of older people in Britain (and other Western societies) (see Chapman, 2008). Table 5.3 shows that two commonly used indicators of obesity – Body Mass Index and waist circumference – demonstrate high levels of obesity among British older people. Overall, in 2007, 2% of those aged 75 and over were underweight, 29% were classified as demonstrating weight within the 'normal' range, 44% were overweight and 24% were obese. These levels are similar to those observed in the US and Australia (see Chapman, 2008). Some caution is required in interpreting

Table 5.3: Obesity by age and gender, population aged 65+, England, 2005 (%)

	65-69		70-74		75-79		80-84		85+	
	M	F	M	F	M	F	M	F	M	F
Body Mass Index (BMI)										
Underweight	I	I	I	0	I	2	2	3	I	3
Desirable	22	24	25	33	28	32	34	42	48	42
Overweight	47	41	47	36	50	37	47	36	41	36
Obese	29	30	27	29	21	28	16	19	10	19
Morbidly obese	I	3	0	0	0	I	I	0	0	0
Waist circumference										
% with waist circumference over 102cm (male) and 88cm (female)	48	61	47	57	49	59	40	60	36	48

Note: BMI classification: 18.5 or less = underweight, 18.5-25 = desirable, 25-30 = overweight, 30-40 = obese, 40+ = morbidly obese.

Source: Craig and Mindell (2007, tables 4.2 and 4.5)

these trends. Age-related body compositional changes such as decrease in body length and the loss of lean body mass may result in the overestimation of both Body Mass Index and waist circumference. However, other measures for evaluating obesity among older adults at a population level (Villareal et al, 2005) have not yet been validated. Even with the methodological caveats noted earlier, which may result in some overestimation of obesity levels, the increase in levels of obesity observed among older people (and the rest of the population) is not a measurement artefact and this represents a 'real' issue, which has an impact on functional health and morbidity (Lang et al, 2008; Salihu et al, 2009), although there does not seem to be an increase in mortality (see Janssen, 2007; Janssen and Mark, 2007; Janssen and Bacon, 2008).

Alcohol and tobacco consumption

The final element of lifestyle to be discussed in this chapter relates to the use of alcohol and tobacco. The health message for smoking is straightforward. Tobacco consumption is associated with poor health outcomes in terms of both mortality and morbidity and there is no 'safe' level of consumption. The focus of interventions is on giving up smoking. The situation for alcohol consumption is less clear cut, with the health agencies promoting levels of consumption – in terms of units per week – indicative of 'safe' levels of consumption. Alcohol consumption at a range of levels has been associated with good and bad health outcomes and thus, there is a much less clear 'health promotion' message to be conveyed.

In terms of alcohol in England in 2007, 68% of men and 30% of women aged 65 and over consumed alcohol, with 30% of men and 12% of women consuming alcohol on five days a week (NHS Information Centre, 2009a). These prevalence levels have remained static for the last decade. In terms of hazardous drinking (as defined by responses to the Alcohol Use Disorders Identification Test), approximately 11% of men and 6% of women aged 65 and over were so defined, with well under 1% classed as harmful drinkers (NHS Information Centre, 2009a). To put these responses into context, 27% of men are classified as being hazardous drinkers and 6% as harmful while for women the respective prevalences are 14% and 2% (NHS Information Centre, 2009a). Thus, at a population level, 'problem' drinking is not one of the major problems of old age, although we do need to note that there are a minority of heavy drinkers within the population.

In terms of smoking, the general population prevalence has decreased from 52% in 1948 (65% of males and 41% of females) to 22% in 2006 (23% of males and 21% of females) (NHS Information Centre, 2009b). For those aged 60 and over, 28% were classed as smokers in 1990 (34% of males and 24% of females) compared with 12% for both in 2006. Older people are less likely to smoke than the rest of the population – smokers are less likely to reach old age and those who do may give up smoking for health reasons. The gender difference in smoking that previously used to characterise older people has now disappeared and smoking and hazardous drinking are negative health behaviours of roughly the same order of magnitude but much less common than overweight or obesity.

Key points

Anti-ageing medicine represents a contemporary version of the enduring human preoccupation with 'living longer' as well as raising ethical and moral debates about extending life.

In terms of lifestyle, overweight/obesity and lack of exercise are problems of much larger magnitude among contemporary older people than hazardous drinking or smoking.

Obesity may have an important impact on the health of the population in general and for expectation of life for future cohorts of older people. High levels of obesity among younger age groups in the US may result in a decrease in life expectancy of two to five years because of the increase in mortality resultant from obesity at younger ages (Olshansky, 2005).

We should not become complacent about continuing increases in life expectancy – as the potential impact of obesity and AIDS demonstrates, there is nothing inevitable or universal about increased life expectancy. Second, health behaviours such as obesity do influence health outcomes at the population level.

Behaviours such as smoking, exercise and diet can influence our probability of surviving to old age and our levels of morbidity and quality of life in old age and changes in behaviour can have an impact on the experiences of future cohorts of older people.

We need to study these factors at two levels: the population and the individual. In particular, we need to consider how, for example, issues such as diet and exercise are embedded within the routine and rhythm of daily life and are interwoven into the socioenvironmental context within which individuals live their lives. Many aspects of our daily life such as the food we eat or the activities we engage in are not well studied or understood, especially in later life. Activities such as shopping and food preparation are 'taken for granted' parts of daily life that are rarely exposed until challenged by disruptions that may result from changes in our physical and social world, such as the onset of chronic disabling illness or bereavement. This transition can disrupt habituated patterns of daily life. Bereavement – and the radically altered social environment that can result from this – can disrupt the food choice and eating patterns of older people.

Further activities

▸ What does the term 'health promotion' mean to you?

▸ Is it worth trying to improve the health of older people?

▸ What types of health promotion activities are aimed at older people in your locality?

▸ There are three main levels on which we can approach 'health promotion' activities: the individual, groups and at the community/population level. Can you think of an example from each of these levels of engagement that relates to older people? Which approach is most widely used and which is likely to be most successful?

Further reading

Bowling, A. (2008) Enhancing later life: how older people perceive active ageing? *Aging and Mental Health*, 12(3), 293–301.

Bowling, A. (2009) Perceptions of active ageing in Britain: divergences between minority ethnic and whole population samples. *Age and Ageing*, 38(6), 703–10.

leontowitsch, M., Higgs, P., Stevenson, F. and Jones, I.R. (2010) Taking care of yourself in later life: a qualitiative study into the use of non-prescription medicine by people aged 60+. *Health*, 14(1), 1–19.

Jones, I.R., Higgs, P. and Ekerdt, D.J. (eds) (2009) *Consumption and generational change*. New Brunswick, NJ and London: Transaction Press.

Jones, I.R., Hyde, M., Victor, C., Wiggins, D., Gilleard, C. and Higgs, P. (2008) *Ageing in a consumer society: From passive to active consumption in Britain*. Bristol: The Policy Press.

Useful websites

Note: the following are examples of anti-ageing websites and are presented as examples. Appearance in the list does not represent an endorsement of their activities.

- *Anti-ageing website:* www.worldhealth.net/
- *World Anti-Ageing Academy of Medicine:* www.waaam.org/
- *Los Gatos Longevity Institute:* www.antiaging.com/

SIX

Responding to needs: provision and utilisation of services

Key points

In this chapter we consider the responses developed to the needs of ageing individuals and ageing societies by examining:

- the development of services for older people;
- recent policy developments in terms of older people;
- the utilisation of services by older people;
- the relationship between statutory, voluntary and family care in meeting the needs of older people.

In this chapter we look at the broad topic of health and social care provision developed, directly or indirectly, to respond to the needs and problems identified in Chapters Two to Five. We examine the issues of services designed for and/ or used by older people but also contextualise this by looking at the role and contribution of the family in the provision of care for older people. If we consider the history of social and healthcare provision in Britain, it is only within the last century (approximately) that older people have been distinguished as a separate and distinct group with a set of specific needs for care. The identification of 'aged paupers' and the development of a system of pensions was the initial step in the differentiation of older people as a distinct care population: prior to that they were simply part of the broad mass of 'the poor' and were seen as being the responsibility of 'the family' (see Means and Smith, 1998). With the development of the post-war British welfare state, older people have had access to a wide range of health and social welfare services, most of which are generic in nature rather than being designed specifically with the needs (and wants?) of older people in mind. We need to differentiate between generic services designed to cater for the needs of all users (for example, primary care or general medicine) and specialist services targeted at specific conditions (for example, HIV) or client groups (for example, paediatrics). The relative merits of these two models of care remain an issue of debate and are a recurrent theme underlying the provision and development of health social care services within Britain. For older people this debate is manifest in terms of whether older people are best served by the generic services that cater for all adults or by 'age-based' services that provide specialist care to people above a threshold age. Advocates of the generic model propose that services should be able to cater for all needs, no matter how complex. Proponents of the 'specialist' care model argue that neglect, poor care and suboptimal outcomes are a consequence of 'mainstream' services not being able to cope with the complexity of an older person's needs. Marginalisation and stigmatisation from 'the mainstream' are advanced as the 'down side' of the specialist care model. Without high-quality evaluation data comparing outcomes for users treated via these two care models, we cannot with any certainty identify the 'best' model of care in either the social or the healthcare domain.

Comparatively few of the health and social care services that are used by older people were designed specifically to meet their needs. Older people utilise the generic provision encompassed within the broad structure of the welfare state, and within a framework based on professionally defined needs and services. The model of care provision has been one where the focus is on fitting people to existing services rather than evaluating and assessing the needs of (older) people and then tailoring solutions to meet these. This approach is exemplified by the now almost extinct mobile meals and home help services. Mobile meals services developed from the need to provide food to those whose houses had been destroyed in the Second World War while the home help service originated as a way of supporting new mothers. While these services, or at least their successors, are still extensively used by older people, how appropriate are they as a response to the identified needs, especially those around personal and house care needs identified in Chapter Three? How successful have these types of services been in achieving the wider policy objective of maintaining older people in the community?

Unlike in the US, there are no specific social welfare Acts in the UK concerned specifically with older people, although with devolution we have seen the creation of ministers with responsibility for old age within the devolved administrations in Wales, Scotland and Northern Ireland. The UK does not have the equivalent of the Older Americans Act nor does it have an Administration on Aging, which forms part of the US Department of Health and Human Services. Estes (1979) offered a critique of the array of organisations, professionals and volunteers involved in the development and delivery of special programmes and projects for older people in the US, which she termed the 'aging enterprise'. Estes argued that such activities have a 'vested interest' in the maintenance of the 'separateness' of older people and in perpetuating stereotypes of their dependence in order to justify their existence. This is a useful perspective to bear in mind when evaluating the development of policies and services for older people. However, we can also argue that such formalised structures serve to ensure the visibility of older people within the formalised structures of government.

Key issues in the structure and organisation of care for older people

ACTIVITY 1

▶ Are there specific types of care needs presented by older people that should always be met by state/professional services?

▶ Are there some that should always be the responsibility of the family?

▶ How would you organise a care system that could recognise this division?

We cannot in this volume provide a comprehensive review of British social policy either in general or as it pertains to older people. Interested readers are referred to the following texts for a more detailed exposition and analysis of these subjects: Victor (1997, 2007); Means and Smith (1998); Means et al (2008). Here we focus on identifying the key issues as they relate to the health aspects of later life and the compromised independence that chronic health problems can bring in their wake. The state response to the perceived problems of old age and older people may be categorised and conceptualised in several different ways, reflecting wider debates concerned with how best to organise effective service delivery to those 'in need'. There are, in essence, three key issues concerning health and social care provision for older people: the identification and classification of care needs; the categorisation of who provides care; and the location of care provision. While for the sake of clarity we deal with each of these dimensions of the debate separately here, they are clearly interlinked and these interrelationships vary over time (see Phillips, 2007).

Defining and meeting care needs

A key distinction within the British welfare policy and provision framework relates to the nature of the need presented by the older person as this determines the responding agency, which then has implications for types of services/support provided and any resultant financial contribution. A crucial distinction is drawn between needs to be met by health services and those characterised as falling within the domain of social care agencies. The post-1945 British welfare state was predicated on the presumption that we can differentiate those with 'social care' needs from those with 'healthcare' needs and, perhaps, that individuals would not present with a complexity of needs that might require the intervention of several agencies at the same time. The current system is still premised on the differentiation of health services (designed to cater for those with health problems) and social care services (designed to deal with those who have non-health problems such as personal or home care needs). This structural division has had a marked influence on the development and delivery of services for older people and is at the heart of many of the debates, reorganisations and policies that have characterised the history of the 'welfare state' over the last 60 years.

This dichotomy between health and social care needs has been problematic from the inception of the welfare state. Older people who often present with a pattern of complex needs have found this dichotomy especially challenging as it has meant that the responsibility for care provision becomes contested by different agencies and varies over time (see Means and Smith, 1998; Phillips, 2007). While the 'contested' nature of care provision for older people is not unique to Britain, it is much more obvious because of the bipartite nature of the welfare system. What is the nature of the 'boundary' that is drawn between health and social care? How is this framed in terms of both policy and the reality of practice? Does the nature of the boundary vary across and between client groups? Twigg (1997, 2000a, 2000b) argues that there is not a single simple static boundary between the health and social care domains. Rather, she suggests that this is a dynamic entity, varying over time and in response to changes in structural factors such as the nature of the care need identified, the characteristics of the presenting client, the potential responsible agency and issues of payment. Thus, we can see the response to chronic conditions and disability increasingly being recast as the province of social care services because the emphasis is on care rather than cure (which is the province of medicine). It is the redefinition of health needs as the province of social care, played out in terms of long-term care, that so concerns Ebrahim (2002). He argues passionately that older people are being disadvantaged by the complicity of the medical profession in this process, especially in terms of the withdrawal of medicine from long-term care provision. As well as the structural health–social care boundary, we can observe 'intra-domain' care boundary issues with the debates about the relationship between primary and secondary care and the increasing emphasis in medicine on acute hospital-based care (real medicine) while the focus of national policy is on the management of chronic diseases. These debates about the relative remit of the health and social care agencies are not of interest simply to academics and commentators on social policy. They have real implications for both practitioners and recipients of care/those with care needs and their families.

One key dimension of the distinction between health and social care provision is that it can promote discontinuities in care. One key problematic interface is around discharge from hospital back to the community (or long-term care) where the health and social care agencies have to work together to ensure 'seamless' care and the smooth transfer of the responsibility for care provision between agencies. We return to this issue of 'delayed hospital discharge' later in the chapter. There is an extensive literature examining the issues surrounding the integration of health and social care to ensure that older people experience seamless care (see Means et al, 2008; Phillips, 2007). Here we are concerned with illuminating the underlying factors that contribute to effective 'joint working'. Health and social care services and professionals are characterised by differential knowledge bases (biomedical versus the social sciences), accountability frameworks, educational and training frameworks and therapeutic objectives (cure versus care). These dimensions of difference are brought into sharp distinction around index conditions such as dementia, key interfaces within the care system such as hospital discharge and specific care needs such as those for personal care. Twigg, in a series of incisive publications (Twigg, 1997, 2000b), highlights these problems by dissecting the issues with respect to responding to the needs of older people who need a bath. As Phillips (2007: 126) observes, 'personal care is not straightforward. It lies on the fault line of community care that divides the two territories of health and social care yet there is no single definition of the boundary'.

Twigg (1997, 2000b) raises another dimension of the health–social care boundary, which relates to the ideological perspectives on the nature of health and social care and the relative (perceived) merits of public versus private responsibilities. Analysis of a range of different forms of welfare provision suggests that medical care (and medical need) is almost universally recognised as an element of care provision that merits special consideration. Under many forms of welfare provision, medical care is provided free or with users having to pay only a modest contribution. Even in the US, where healthcare may be construed as closest to a consumption good, there are aspects of the system that demonstrate the special status of medical need such as the Medicare programme for older people. We may contrast this with social care, which has no such 'special' status for either expressed needs or practitioners (and their knowledge). Furthermore, responding to social care needs can sometimes be perceived as part of 'normal' social relationships. Typically, tasks involved in social care such as house care, preparing meals and helping with activities of daily living (ADLs) such as bathing are often seen as those synonymous with 'normal family life' or the types of tasks where we might be expected to pay for help. Indeed, across the range of forms of social welfare provision, social care is often represented as an area of private personal responsibility in contrast to the more collective responsibility ascribed to medical care, especially within Western Europe.

In the UK, the provision of social care has always been characterised by the presumption that the individual should contribute towards their care if they have the 'means', although the size of the contribution may be variable. Thus, there is a distinction between health and social care provision based not just about how needs are defined and met, but also how they are paid for. Healthcare services in Britain are provided free at the point of consumption and funded largely out of general taxation and are conceptualised as a national-level service (although devolution has introduced some variability between England, Wales and Scotland). The National Health Service (NHS) is based on an ideological commitment to social and spatial equity of access to and quality of care, with clinical need the criterion for access to care. Older people should have equal access to services as any other age group and the services they receive should be comparable with those provided to other age groups. Furthermore, access and quality should be the same irrespective of which part of the country an older person lives in. In contrast, social care within Britain is provided within an organisational and conceptual framework designed to respond to 'local needs'. Variation in both levels and types of services was positively encouraged; it was not felt appropriate that social care provision should be uniform. Needs that are defined as falling within the remit of 'social care' may require users to pay. Local authorities are free to determine levels of payment resulting in the 'postcode' payment lottery. This perceived inequity in how older people with apparently similar needs could be responded to between both different parts of the country and different components of the social welfare system illustrates how such 'demarcation' disputes can have a profound impact on the experience of care. The recent Green Paper on social care, advocating a national social care system, is one very recent response to these perceived inequities (Victor, 2009, 2010b).

Who provides care?

Who provides the care is another of the key debates in the area of care provision for older people. We have already introduced this issue within the framework of the health–social care boundary. Here we develop this further by examining the distinction between care that is provided by the 'formal' sector, which embraces the state, the private sector and voluntary agencies, and 'informal' providers who are largely drawn from the family and broader kinship and social networks. Formal care may be succinctly characterised as that provided by those who are paid, highly organised and subject to training (including continuing professional development), regulation, accreditation and monitoring. To be deemed competent to provide care the workforce may (or may not) be required to complete a rigorous process of training supplemented by formalised continuous professional development and, increasingly, reaccreditation. With formal care providers there are criteria for entry into the workforce and, once engaged, providers are subject to public and professional scrutiny and accountability. This may be contrasted with 'informal care', which is 'unpaid', unregulated, unmonitored and provided by a 'workforce' that is recruited because of filial or social obligations and responsibilities rather than being professionally trained and, as such, may be described as 'unprofessional'.

The balance of 'care responsibilities' between public and family provision of care to older people is dynamic. Contemporary social policy places the responsibility on the family to be the main provider of care, with the state occupying a residual position providing care 'in the last resort'. However, the nature of the relationship between these two sectors is unclear. Policy makers and academics have yet to decide whether 'formal' care, provided by paid professionals, complements (that is, enhances family-based care), parallels or duplicates care (but may not fill identified gaps), substitutes or replaces family care (on the presumption that families will withdraw care if formal services are available) or 'competes' with the care provided by the family (Ward-Griffin and Marshall, 2003). Another perspective conceptualises family carers as fulfilling a range of roles, including: as 'unpaid' resources providing support that would otherwise have to be provided by the state; as co-workers supporting a shared care plan that involves formal support; as co-clients with 'needs' of their own; or as superseded carers (that is, no longer seen as contributing to the provision of care). These typologies derive from the perspective of the professional worker – not from either the carers or those receiving care – and are framed within the context of a dichotomy between the care sources. However, we would argue that this framework ignores the similarities between the types of tasks undertaken by the different sectors. Thus, both formal and informal care workers are engaged in providing support with ADLs. Ignored also are domestic workers who do not fit neatly into this typology (for example, Pilipino maids providing care to older Singaporeans) and the location of these caring tasks within the domestic rather than 'professional' space. Martin-Matthews and Phillips (2008) have drawn attention to the importance of the domestic setting for developing our understanding of the formal–informal care boundary. Domestic or 'private' spaces are increasingly becoming the foci of 'formal' care provision with the consequent blurring of professional and private or personal spaces (see Martin-Matthews, 2004; Mahmood and Martin-Matthews, 2008; Martin-Matthews and Sims-Gould, 2008). We consider this latter aspect in the next section where we examine the geography of care.

Where is care provided?

A key but often neglected aspect of care provision is, as we introduced earlier, the location where care is provided. This is what Phillips (2007) terms 'the geography of care'. We need to distinguish between two important terms here. 'Space' is characterised as a 'neutral', abstract concept while 'place' is space that has been transformed by the actions of humans and which is ascribed with sociocultural meaning (see Peace et al, 2005a, 2005b; Smith, 2009). There are two broad dimensions to the geography of care: the location of care and the effect that distance and proximity have on the delivery and experience of care. Here we focus on the location within which care is provided as this has been a particularly important aspect of the debates about care provision for older people (and others with long-term care needs). There are, essentially, three broad spaces within which care is located: in institutions such as hospitals or care homes, in the community or in the home. Each of these is depicted and presented in varying ways within the policies and debates about the provision of care for older people.

Concern about the location of care has been the most important, influential and enduring aspect of the debate about care for older people in post-war Britain. A dichotomy has been drawn between care provided in institutional or group settings and care provided in the community, preferably in the recipient's own home. Caring for older people within an institutional or group setting has a long historical pedigree, which can be traced back to at least the 3rd and 4th centuries (see Means and Smith, 1998; Victor, 2005). The pre-war workhouses where older people, and others with long-term care needs because of frailty or poverty, were housed in harsh conditions to deter 'scroungers' personified all the negative images that were associated with institutional care. With the creation of the post-war welfare state, the NHS took over responsibility for long-stay wards from the workhouses/public hospitals and local authorities provided residential accommodation (the so-called 'part three homes'). Two key streams of academic and empirical research served to identify the very negative effects that institutional care settings could have on the quality of life of older people. Goffman (1961), in his book *Asylums*, articulated the notion of the 'total institution'. This was characterised by an inhuman, depersonalising and all-pervasive timetabled regime devised for the 'benefit' or convenience of staff and which rarely meshed with the needs and wishes of individual residents. This theoretical proposition was supported by the empirical research of Townsend (1962), who in his book *The last refuge*, drew attention to the poor standards of care and a quality of life for residents, who experienced poor-quality environments, poor facilities, a highly regimented and distinctly unpersonalised regime, with no clear therapeutic goals or objectives. Combined with a series of damning reports documenting systematic and sustained abuse in British long-stay hospitals, such as Ely in Cardiff, this created a powerful image that institutional care was inherently a 'bad thing'. Such care settings were seen as being inevitably characterised by lack of autonomy and dignity and depicted as 'bad' spaces to experience and provide care.

We may contrast this picture of institutional care with the 'good' care space of the community and individuals' own homes. Community-based care is depicted as having all the positive attributes so evidently lacking in the institutional setting – autonomy, independence, dignity and choice. Initially, community care was to be provided in settings such as day hospitals but increasingly care is provided in a familiar and comforting location – the family home – by care staff not organised around the rigid timetables characteristic of institutional living. The advantages of community-based care solutions have been consistently advocated over the last 50 years. A common theme in the debate about community-based care solutions is around the 'prevention' of hospital admission, hospital readmission or admission to nursing/residential homes: outcomes specified and deemed negative by policy makers rather than older people or their families. Thus, a consistent feature of much policy development in this area is the avoidance of externally defined negative outcomes rather than more positively framed objectives. We might speculate that a frail older person might be (more) positively disposed to entering residential care where they would not have to struggle to look after themselves in terms of ADLs and where meals and laundry are taken care of.

The switch in emphasis of the location of care provision from public to private spaces is not unproblematic. However, it is an area of policy analysis and empirical research that is only just starting to develop. Victor (2005) has argued that care in an individual's own home may reproduce many of the negative attributes associated with care in group settings, a state Phillips (2007) describes as 'forced independence'. As we now know, abuse of older people can occur in the domestic setting, perpetrated by family and carers, as well as group environments (see Manthorpe et al, 2007a; Biggs et al, 2009). Current policy developments are creating a change in the status of 'the home' as it becomes a place where 'professional' care is delivered and a place of work for a range of care workers (see Martin-Matthews and Phillips, 2008; Martin-Matthews and Sims-Gould, 2008). One of the unacknowledged challenges of this shift in the location of care is that both health and social care workers are often 'working' in physical environments that were never designed with the provision of care in mind. Looking at care solutions through the lens of place and space reveals a new range of important research questions with important policy implications (see Phillips, 2007). For example, by focusing care within the domestic sphere, are we contaminating and eroding the positive feelings older people and carers have about an important and highly personal space? This is only one example of the types of questions that we need to pose if we are truly to rigorously evaluate the impact of community-based care solutions.

National strategies for health and social care services for older people

ACTIVITY 2

▸ Look at the National Service Framework for Older People (for either England or Wales) or the National Dementia Strategy.

▸ What factors may have been responsible for the development of these strategies?

Although the NHS is a national service with a commitment to a vision of equal access to services of equal quality for all subjects, the reality is that the NHS is characterised by wide variations in access to care, quality of care and care outcomes. The existence of inequalities in health outcomes both socially and spatially within the UK is well documented (see the Black Report: Black, 1980) but during the New Labour administrations of the late 1990s attention was directed at variations in the quality of care provided by the NHS. One policy response to these variations has been to establish a more 'open' information system whereby information on mortality rates and other 'quality of care' outcomes data are published: thus, we can all review the performance of our local hospitals. Via the creation of a series of evidence-based National Service Frameworks (NSF) for specific conditions such as dementia or population groups such as older people, the NHS in England is attempting to address variations in the quality of care, promote 'evidence-based' healthcare and establish a broad framework in terms of both types and levels of service provision. The NSF for Older People in England was published in 2001 by the Department of Health (available at www.dh.gov. uk/en/Publicationsandstatistics/Publications/PublicationsPolicyAndGuidance/ DH_4003066). Philp (2002a, 2002b) describes the process of developing the NSF and the establishment of the eight key standards, which combine (fairly) uncontentious targets for improvements in the management of several significant health problems of later life, namely stroke, depression, dementia and falls (but no mention of arthritis); the creation of new services (for example, intermediate care); with system-wide attitudinal changes in how older people are perceived and treated within the healthcare system (the focus on age discrimination) (see Table 6.1). Follow-up documents relating to the NSF focusing on implementation include *Better health in old age* (Philp, 2004) and *A new ambition for old age: Next steps in implementing the National Service Framework for Older People* (Philp, 2006). The NSF for Older People in Wales was published in 2006 (www.wales.nhs.uk/ sites3/documents/439/NSFforOlderPeopleInWalesEnglish.pdf) and includes 10 targets, eight of which are broadly similar to those for England, but also includes a commitment to addressing dependency and improving medicines management (see Table 6.1).

Table 6.1: Standards in the English and Welsh National Service Frameworks for Older People

England	Wales
NHS services will be provided, regardless of age, on the basis of clinical need alone. Social care services will not use age in their eligibility criteria or policies, to restrict access to available services.	Health and social care services are provided regardless of age on the basis of clinical and social need. Age is not used in eligibility criteria or policies to restrict access to and receipt of available services.
NHS and social care services treat older people as individuals and enable them to make choices about their own care. This is achieved through the single assessment process, integrated commissioning arrangements and integrated provision of services, including community equipment and continence services.	Health and social care services treat people as individuals and enable them to make choices about their own care. This is achieved through the unified assessment process, integrated commissioning arrangements, the integrated provision of services and appropriate personal and professional behaviour of staff.
Older people will have access to a new range of intermediate care services at home or in designated care settings, to promote their independence by providing enhanced services from the NHS and councils to prevent unnecessary hospital admission and effective rehabilitation services to enable early discharge from hospital and to prevent premature or unnecessary admission to long-term residential care.	The physical and emotional health and wellbeing of people aged over 50 is promoted through strong partnerships, with the aim of extending healthy life expectancy and quality of life.
Older people's care in hospital is delivered through appropriate specialist care and by hospital staff who have the right set of skills to meet their needs.	A range of enabling, community-based services is available to intervene promptly and effectively when older people's independence is threatened by health or social care needs, with the aim of challenging dependency and maximising wellbeing and autonomy.

England	Wales
The NHS will take action to prevent strokes, working in partnership with other agencies where appropriate.	Intermediate care is established as a mainstream, integrated system of health and social care which: • enables older people to maintain their health, independence and home life; • promptly identifies and responds to older people's health and social care needs, helping to avoid crisis management and unnecessary hospital or care home admission; • enables timely discharge or transfer from acute hospital settings to more appropriate care settings, which promote effective rehabilitation and a return to independence.
The NHS, working in partnership with councils, takes action to prevent falls and reduce resultant fractures or other injuries in their populations of older people.	When admission to hospital is necessary for older people, the care they receive is coordinated, efficient and effective in meeting their clinical and non-clinical needs.
Older people who have mental health problems have access to integrated mental health services, provided by the NHS and councils to ensure effective diagnosis, treatment and support, for them and for their carers.	The NHS, working in partnership with other agencies where appropriate, take action to prevent strokes, and to ensure that those who do suffer a stroke have access to diagnostic services, are treated appropriately by a specialist stroke service, and subsequently, with their carers, participate in a multidisciplinary programme of secondary prevention and rehabilitation and appropriate longer-term care.
The health and wellbeing of older people is promoted through a coordinated programme of action led by the NHS with support from councils.	The NHS, working in partnership with local authorities and other stakeholders, takes action to prevent falls, osteoporosis, fractures and other resulting injuries, and to maintain well being in their populations of older people. Older people who have fallen receive effective treatment and rehabilitation and, with their carers, receive advice on prevention through integration of falls and fracture services.
	Older people who have a high risk of developing mental health problems and others with related diagnosis have access to primary prevention and integrated services to ensure timely and appropriate assessment, diagnosis, treatment and support for them and their carers.
	Older people are enabled to gain maximum benefit from medication to maintain or increase their quality and duration of life.

The creation of the English NSF provoked a lively debate about the appropriate care of older people. Supporters such as Philp (2002a, 2002b) argued that this presented new opportunities to transform services for older people (for the better). Grimley Evans and Tallis, (2001) expressed concern about the framing of objectives in terms of preventing hospital admissions. They feared that intermediate care beds were simply a reincarnation of the 'warehousing' care locations into which older people were discharged from acute beds in the hope that they would go away. Grimley Evans and Tallis (2001) feared that intermediate care was (another) way of marginalising older people, while Ebrahim (2001) expressed concern over the evidence base used to justify the investment in intermediate care.

How effective has the NSF been in transforming older people's services in England? While the NSF is imbued within a framework of targets and monitoring, these are predominantly focused on implementation rather than measuring outcomes. The standards/milestones focus on processes and planning. The strongest numerical (and therefore measurable) milestone relates to intermediate care where the goal was to establish, by March 2004, a minimum of 5,000 intermediate care beds and 1,700 non-residential intermediate care places compared with the baseline of 1999/2000. By this target date there would also be a minimum of 150,000 people receiving rehabilitation and supportive discharge and 70,000 receiving intermediate care, which 'prevented' unnecessary hospital admission. There was an evaluation of the implementation of intermediate care with ambiguous results (see http://cat.csip.org.uk/index.cfm?pid=194). Manthorpe and colleagues (Manthorpe et al, 2007b) undertook a mixed methods evaluation of the NSF and reported a very mixed picture in terms of how the NSF was perceived and understood by older people; the lack of specific operational targets (except for intermediate care); and the lack of additional funding. They argued that the NSF was conceptualised as a system-wide 'redesign' but one that was taking place alongside other changes, thereby rendering it impossible to evaluate the NSF in isolation from the myriad of other changes happening simultaneously (Harwood, 2007).

Although there was a standard on dementia within both the English and Welsh NSFs, the issue of dementia and dementia care has gained momentum as a policy issue since their publication, culminating in the Department of Health publishing a National Dementia Strategy in 2009 (available at www.dh.gov.uk/en/SocialCare/Deliveringadultsocialcare/Olderpeople/NationalDementiaStrategy/DH_083362). This has three key elements: improving awareness of dementia; earlier diagnosis and intervention; and improving the quality of services with a string of initiatives designed to achieve these key objectives. This is a five-year strategy and it remains to be seen how effective it proves to be although it is an important landmark in recognising the importance of dementia, which the government estimates afflicts approximately 500,000 people in England and 750,000 in the UK.

In terms of social care, there are a range of key policies that provide the context for the provision of care for older people but few are explicitly focused on older people in the way that the health-related dementia strategy and NSF are. Social care policies tend to be generic – applying to all care groups and specific age groups, usually (but not always) differentiating adults and children. The key social care policy objective for older people is to maintain older people independently in the community – most recently articulated in the Green Paper on the future of social care for adults (Victor, 2009, 2010b). The key areas of tension that the Green Paper seeks to address are the criteria of eligibility for care, access to care and assessment of care needs (see Victor, 2009). These are the three areas of the social care system where there have been the most substantial shifts in the last three decades and where the 'postcode' lottery is most evident. Following the 1990 NHS and Community Care Act, services are being 'targeted' at those with multiple and complex rather than single needs. The variability between geographical areas in the treatment of older people with apparently similar needs prompted the publication of *Fair access to care services* (DH, 2002). However, the durability of this issue has resulted in the 2009 Green Paper proposing the creation of a national (in this case English) social care service to address variability in service provision and charging, especially for long-term care. Three national policy options are proposed, two of which explicitly include some element of state support for social care. Specifically excluded are both 'fully funded' state care (excluded as too expensive) and making individuals entirely responsible for their social care arrangements (excluded because too many would not be able to afford such care). In two of the proposals the state would provide a contribution of a quarter to a third of social care costs, either with individuals taking out an insurance at a cost of £20-25,000 to cover themselves against the remaining costs or individuals paying with help for those on a low income. The third option is a compulsory insurance against the need for social care.

It remains to be seen which of the options, if any, will form the basis of the future fabric of the welfare state in the UK. How to provide a robust system of social care has drawn the attention of politicians, such that all the major parties prior to the 2010 general election were proposing changes to the current system: by creating an insurance system at age 65 to cover all long-term care (Conservative Party); free home care for the most dependent (Labour Party); and creating an independent commission to reach a concensus on social care (Liberal Democrats). Following the general election, whether such policies will be implemented remains to be seen. Despite the commitment to older people articulated by the Prime Minister, David Cameron, on his accession speech in Downing Street, a parlous financial situation faces the new coalition government.

Need for and use of health and social care services

ACTIVITY 3: What percentage of those aged 65 and over do you think receive the following services:

▶ inpatient hospital care;

▶ consultation with their general practitioner (GP) annually;

▶ residential/nursing care;

▶ home care;

▶ home nursing.

Having established the broad policy context for health and social care provision, we next examine the provision, need for and utilisation of health and social care services by older people. In reviewing data on service use by older people we differentiate three specific domains of care: health services, social care services and long-term care. Determining who does, and does not, 'need' services in order to live independently at home is problematic. In particular, it is problematic in terms of translating the prevalence of specific medical conditions, such as stroke or depression, into a need for care. Thus, we utilise a perspective that focuses on dependency as defined in terms of problems with ADLs. Table 6.2 suggests that there are approximately half a million people who experience two (or more) difficulties with ADLs and 918,000 who have difficulties with instrumental ADLs (standard house care type activities). The number of individuals classified as falling annually (nearly two million) or who are incontinent (1.7 million) is high, with approximately 560,460 people with dementia in England and Wales with a further 280,230 new cases annually. Dementia, however, has a disproportionate impact on capacity for independent living. The 2003 World Health Report *Global burden*

Table 6.2: Levels of dependency and health problems, population aged 65+, England, 2007

Domain	Estimated prevalence (%)	Estimated numbers
Difficulties with IADL[1] activities	11	918,000
Difficulties with one ADL[2]	5	393,000
Difficulties with 2+ ADL	7	582,000
Cognitive impairment	5	393,000
Depression	14	1,143,660
Fallen in last year	25	1,965,000
Urinary incontinence	21	1,715,490

Note: [1]IADL = instrumental activities of daily living. [2]ADL = activities of daily living.

Source: Craig and Mindell (2007)

of disease (WHO, 2008) estimates suggest that dementia contributed 11.2% of all years lived with disability among people aged 60 and over; more than stroke (9.5%), musculoskeletal disorders (8.9%), cardiovascular disease (5.0%) and all forms of cancer (2.3%). However, mapping these needs on to the services utilisation data is problematic especially as individuals may utilise personal resources – both material and/or social – to respond to these needs and not have recourse to the state. There may also be significant unmet needs for care whereby individuals with a need for care do not access services for whatever reason.

Use of health services

There are two perspectives on the use of services by older people: establishing the percentage of utilisation accounted for by older people – this enables us to consider what proportion of the service is accounted for by older people – and determining the percentage of all older people in a given population with specific needs, such as help with bathing and receiving health and social care services.

Everyone in the UK is registered with a GP who forms part of the primary care team, which includes nursing and a range of preventive and therapeutic services. It is the GP who, as well as treating conditions, acts as the gatekeeper for accessing specialist health services provided in secondary care and often for referrals to social care services. Age-specific consultation rates for 2006 demonstrate a classic J-shaped distribution, being approximately 6.6 consultations per year for those aged under five, decreasing to approximately three to four per year for the 5–55 age groups and then increasing with age to approximately 12 consultations per year for those aged 85 and over (NHS Information Centre, 2009d). The NHS Information Centre reports a rising trend of overall consultation rates in primary care from 3.9 consultations per person per year in 1997 to 5.4 in 2007 (NHS Information Centre, 2009d). Have consultation rates for older people changed over this period? There is little difference in consultations between males and females for those aged 65 and over; consultations have increased by about three per year for the 65–74 group to about 10 per year, and doubled for the over-eighty-fives, from six to 12 consultations per year. The differential in numbers of consultations between the under-fives and the over-eighties has increased over this time period. In 1995, the numbers of consultation for these two groups were roughly equal but by 2006 the average number of consultations per year was six for those aged five and under and 12 for those aged 80 and over. People aged 65 and over account for approximately 30% of all consultations: an increase on the 23% recorded for 1995 (NHS Information Centre, 2009d). Thus, older people are a very significant segment of the total workload of primary care. Interpreting these trends is challenging – do increased consultation rates for older people reflect increased demands, an increase in both relative and absolute terms of the numbers of older people, a more 'proactive' approach towards the care of older people or the extension of primary care services via the development of additional services such as medicine reviews or flu vaccinations?

What percentage of older people consult their GP? Data from the 2007 General Household Survey (GHS) report that 19% of people aged 65 and over consulted their GP in the 14 days prior to interview. For the 65-74 age group, this percentage increased from 14% in 1972 to 19% in 2007 and the average number of consultations annually rose from four to seven. For the 75 and over age group, the percentage consulting has been static at 19% with seven consultations a year on average. Data from the GHS give a lower number of consultations per year than NHS Information Centre data. This reflects methodological differences: the GHS is based on self-report and only 'counts' GP contacts while the NHSIC data are based on computerised practice records of consultation. Almost all GP contacts (90%) take place at the surgery with 3% recorded as 'home visits', although for those aged 85 and over, 12% of all contacts are home visits. Indeed, it is only the very old who are now likely to receive care from their GP at home. What contact do older people have with other members of the primary healthcare team? The GHS data show that 12% of those aged 65 and over consulted a practice nurse in the 14 days before interview but what we do not know is whether these are the same people who consulted their GP. Annual contacts are five per annum and this has remained stable since 2000. So we can conclude that older people are significant users of primary healthcare services and that rates of contact, at least for GP services, are increasing but there are no significant gender differentials, and class and ethnicity differentials are uncertain.

Older people are the largest single client group for the services offered by the acute hospital sector. However, this does not indicate what percentage of older people utilise hospital services. Annually approximately 15% of those aged 65 and over are admitted as an inpatient and about 10% as a day patient. While inpatient treatment rates have increased by about 3% over the last three decades – day-patient utilisation has tripled, reflecting the expansion of this treatment modality.

In England, details of hospital activity data are presented as finished consultant episodes (FCEs); a discrete episode of care that takes place under the management of a specific consultant. This measure does not easily equate to either individuals treated or hospital stays but it is the basic unit of analysis for NHS hospital data. In 2007/08, there were 15,359,062 FCEs in England: a 20% increase on 2000/01. Individuals aged 65-74 accounted for 14.2%; those aged 75-84 accounted for 14.3% and those aged 85 and over accounted for 7.3%: a grand total of 35.8%, which represents an increase of 1.5% over the situation in 2000/01 but is virtually the same as the 34% reported for 1969 (Victor, 1997). Of course there are other ways of looking at hospital use that include related features such as length of stay and bed days used by each age group. In terms of bed days, those aged 65 and over occupy about 50% of all bed days and this is because average length of stay for this group is longer than the six-day national average.

Utilisation of healthcare is not simply a function of admission but also relates to the length of stay of individuals in hospital. The development of intermediate care beds heralded in the NSF illustrates that policy makers are concerned with admission to hospital (is the admission appropriate and/or necessary or are there other ways of responding to the presenting problem); the length (duration) of stay in hospital recorded by older people; and the vexed issue of delayed hospital discharge. Since the inception of the NHS, concerns by policy makers at all levels have been consistently expressed about the 'blocking' of acute hospital beds by older people. Essentially this describes a group of patients who, while deemed 'medically' fit for discharge from hospital, remain there because the required support and services are not available in the community (or there is a delay in establishing these arrangements). These used to be termed 'bed blockers'. While the terminology may no longer be deemed politically correct, this group of patients, not all of whom are older people, do serve to highlight the reality of the health–social care boundary, a key transition point at which services need to be integrated and working together across professional and administrative boundaries (see Glasby et al, 2006). As Phillips (2007) observes, care is a holistic concept that does not always mesh well with artificial divides in responsibilities for the assessment and provision of care that is characteristic of our health and social care system. However, as the studies by Lin et al (2006) and Leung and Fan (2010) illustrate, this is not a problem unique to the UK but is a feature of a range of different healthcare systems. Vetter (2003) reviewed a range of studies looking at delayed discharge. He focused on the range of measures used to classify 'delayed' discharges or 'inappropriate' stays in hospital. He noted that most of the tools used to measure inappropriate admission and/or delayed discharge have poor scientific underpinning. He suggested that the problem is not the inappropriateness of the patient but the inappropriateness of service responses and noted the very limited evidence base as to the most effective ways to manage this 'problem'.

In England, one solution to the 'problem' of delayed discharge has been the implementation of the 2003 Community Care (Delayed Discharges Act). This Act was, as McCoy et al (2007) argue, based on the premise that many delays around discharge were 'caused' by social services departments (SSDs) being slow and/ or unable (or unwilling) to provide the required post-discharge care packages expeditiously (Godden et al, 2009). Under this Act, hospitals can charge SSDs a daily fee if they fail to provide the required care package although McCoy et al (2007) report that only 14% of hospitals are exercising this option. Has this policy had an effect on delayed discharges? This is difficult to assess robustly given constraints on available data. In 2005/06, the number of delayed discharge days per month was 66,000: a substantial fall from 180,000 in 1998 (McCoy et al, 2007). In terms of patient numbers, there has been a decline from approximately 7,000 patients classed as 'delayed' in the second quarter of 2001/02 to a fairly stable 2,000 per quarter from 2004 onwards such that delayed discharges now account for 1.4% of total bed days. Was the premise that it was SSDs that were 'responsible' for delayed discharges correct? McCoy et al (2007) suggest that in 2002/04, 40% of delays were attributed to SSD factors and 56% to the NHS (the remainder attributed to a combination of factors); by 2005/06 the situation had changed to 27% of delays attributable to SSDs and 68% to the NHS. Families are also important in the discharge process and the data presented by McCoy et al (2007) enable us to estimate how much of the delay in discharging people from hospital is attributable to families/patient factors such as delays in choosing a care home or disputing the assessment. Approximately 16% of 'delayed bed days' are attributable to family/patient factors almost exclusively linked to issues around the provision of long-term NHS care. On this evidence, McCoy et al (2007) suggest that the initial proposition was probably simplistic and fallacious and that there is (probably) only limited scope for further reductions in delays in discharging older people from hospital (Smith et al, 2007; Godden et al, 2009).

The other side of the debate about delayed discharges relates to 'inappropriate admissions' and emergency readmissions. McCoy et al (2007) observe that the contemporary acute hospital sector in Britain is characterised by an aggressive treatment regime with short lengths of stay resulting in patients being discharged from hospital care in greater numbers than ever before. Admissions increased by 10% during the period 2001/02 (7.5 million per annum) to 2004/05 (8.2 per million per annum). Patients are being discharged earlier in the recovery cycle as evidenced by a 12% reduction in average length of stay over the same period (8.1 days to 7.1 days). We could interpret this as a demonstration of a more efficient use of acute beds. However, we might be cautious in drawing this conclusion, at least in all cases, as there are concerns about the robustness and quality of post-discharge care. One suggestion that post-discharge care is suboptimal is a trend for increasing emergency hospital readmissions, that is, those occurring within 28 days or less following discharge from a previous stay in hospital (not necessarily with the same diagnosis) (excluding mental health, cancer and obstetric cases). Emergency readmissions have increased from 7.7% of admissions in 1998 to 10.3% in 2006: an increase observable across all age groups. Thus, for those aged 16-75, readmissions increased by 7% to 9% while for the group aged 75 and over this increased by 4% over this period to 14% (DH, 2009). Readmission rates increase with age. In the year 2005-06, readmission rates were 10.6% for the 65-74 age group, 13% for those aged 75-84 and 15.7% for those aged 85 and over (DH, 2009). Do these levels of readmission reflect 'poor-quality care' across the system or specific clinical areas? It is plausible that a proportion of emergency readmissions do reflect suboptimal care and/or inadequate or non-robust post-discharge care. However, it is not clear what percentage of readmissions could be so characterised, from which clinical areas or which population groups. It is also possible that for many chronic conditions an episodic pattern of hospital admissions may reflect the natural history of the condition. As chronic conditions account for a greater percentage of the nation's health problems then increased readmission rates may be one manifestation of this trend. Does the trend for readmission rates to increase with age reflect the poorer care given to older people or the greater complexity of their care needs?

The creation of intermediate care beds under standard 8 of the NSF is intended to prevent admission of older people to acute hospitals; a policy objective that

Grimley Evans and Tallis (2001) found problematic. They argued that the focus policy of preventing inappropriate admissions of older people is ageist, contentious and problematic. The key issue here is determining how 'inappropriate' admissions are defined and measured. A study from Italy suggested that 10% of admissions to hospital were 'inappropriate' and that inappropriate admissions were associated with younger patients (Bianco et al, 2006; Hammond et al, 2009a, 2009b). Luthy et al (2007) provide an interesting perspective on the debate about appropriateness. They used an 'objective' structured tool and patient perspectives to determine both appropriateness of admission and duration of stay in a designed care of the elderly unit in Switzerland. The majority of patients (88%) evaluated their admission as 'appropriate' compared with only 35% defined as such by the AEP (appropriateness evaluation protocol). Thus, we need to adopt a sceptical perspective when terms such as 'inappropriate' are used with regard to admissions or the use of inpatient beds and consider how such constructs are defined and measured and from whose perspective is the admission or hospital stay deemed inappropriate. From patient, family and carer perspectives, hospital admission may be highly appropriate.

The final component of the debate about hospital admissions is linked to the management of patients with long-term conditions, of whom the vast majority are older people. National data indicate that 5% of those admitted to hospital account for 42% of inpatient bed days, 15% of people with three or more problems account for 30% of bed days, 10% of inpatients account for 55% of bed days and 5% account for 40% of bed days (DH, 2005c). These groups of users are pejoratively referred to as 'frequent flyers' or, less colloquially, as very high intensity users and are the focus of a range of policy interventions designed to promote 'better' care at home in order to prevent some of these admissions. To put this into perspective, it is estimated that a typical primary care trust (PCT) will have approximately 825 very high intensity users and an average-sized general practice will have 25. Hillingdon PCT in West London (which covers the campus of Brunel University) estimates that only 25% of these patients will be known to the district nursing service and a third to social services. Thus, the majority of this group are not explicitly known to service providers. Not all of this population group are older people: Hillingdon PCT observes that 12% of 'high intensity users' are aged under 17, 58% are aged 40-64 and 30% are aged 65 and over.

The challenge of managing long-term conditions is a major issue for health systems across the developed world. In the UK, the Department of Health published its NSF for Long Term Neurological Conditions in 2005 (DH, 2005c). This uses a threefold typology of need for the management of long-term conditions. Those in category 1, some 70-80% of those with these conditions, can manage at home with support, category 2 patients are seen as being 'at high risk' while category 3 identifies the highly complex patients with multiple conditions. One service development initiative developed specifically to respond to the challenges of managing those with long-term conditions are community matrons. Murphy (2004) summarises the creation of this new breed of case-managing clinician whose role is to identify appropriate patients, undertake an assessment of their needs, and then work with the primary care team to try and prevent deterioration of their condition and, very importantly, unplanned (unscheduled or emergency) hospital admissions. Indeed, the goal of creating 3,000 community matron posts across England is to reduce unplanned admissions by 10-20%: the level of reductions reported in studies from the US (Kane and Huck, 2000, Kane et al, 2001, 2003). By the target date, less than half (1,348) had actually been appointed and there remains confusion about the role and distinctions (if any) between community matrons and case managers. The EVERCARE study in England reported many positive aspects of the new community matron role including the benefits of having a 'dedicated' case manager, but with no obvious reductions in admissions although they were very popular with patients (Bowler, 2006; Gravelle et al, 2007). We could argue that focusing on category 3 clients is inevitably not going to offer benefits in terms of modifying admissions because this population is too frail to reverse the course of their long-term condition. Rather, it could be that community matrons would be most effective if they focused on the level 2 'high-risk' group of patients. As yet the evidence base on the management of patients with long-term conditions remains slim but is one that we need to develop if we are to create a service framework and infrastructure that is (more) appropriate to the needs of this population than the 20th-century acute hospital.

Community nursing service data are, like hospital-based data described earlier, not collected in a way that makes it easy to assess aspects of utilisation. This is not sinister for such routine data are collected for the management of staff and monitoring of specified targets, not for use by academics with specific research questions to answer. District nursing services record 'first contacts', which does not easily translate into total workload or enable us to estimate what percentage of older people receive such services. For 2003/04, 68% of first contacts for district nursing were aged 65 and over: this represents an 11% increase since 1988/89. This increase is largely accounted for by the population aged 85 and over. This group accounted for 12% of the district nurses' contacts in 1988/89 compared with 21% in 2003/04. In terms of overall utilisation levels, Victor (2005) reports that only a minority of older people (8%) receive care from district nurses although it is focused among two vulnerable groups: the very old (aged 85 and over) where 19% are receiving district nursing care and those living alone of whom 8% are receiving this care. However, we can see that such services are received by only a minority of older people.

Use of social care services

Traditionally, SSDs assessed individuals for home care/home support services and also provided these services and there was virtually no involvement of the private sector (although voluntary services were involved as care providers). However, there is now a much more complex set of organisational arrangements. One of the features of the contemporary pattern of social care delivery has been the emergence of a 'mixed economy of care' involving public, private and voluntary agencies. As initially conceived, the welfare state, as exemplified by the home help/mobile meals services, was characterised by provision by statutory services (although the voluntary agencies have always had a role). Since the early 1980s there has been a recalibration of the model underpinning the provision of social care, in particular the creation of 'welfare markets'. As both home care (and long-term care) illustrate, the 'state' (in the guise of local authority SSDs) has largely withdrawn from direct service provision such that in 2008, 81% of domiciliary home care support (as measured by hours of service provision) was provided by the independent sector compared with 52% in 1999 and 2% in 1992 (Wanless, 2006). Services for adults (as Phillips, 2007, observes, this situation is not as clear in childcare services) are now largely provided by the private sector under contract to public agencies. Within the arena of social care for adults there is now a separation of assessment for services from provision of care. Private providers are used on the assumption that the creation of a market and the involvement of competition will result in higher-quality levels of provision than the situation where the state is a monopoly provider. This development of a social care market with a plethora of providers does raise important issues of regulation, accreditation and accountability, especially in the domiciliary arena where regulation is much more challenging than in group or collective settings. As with long-term care, domiciliary care provision has been reconceptualised as a 'commodity' or consumption good rather than as a 'public good' (see Player and Pollock, 2001; Pollock et al, 2001).

Who receives 'state' home care support? In September 2008, an estimated 340,600 individuals (328,600 households) received 4.1 million hours of care. The overall number of care hours has been increasing and the number of recipients decreasing: the number of hours of contact per week has increased by 22% since 2004 to 12.4 (however, this only represents a little over two hours per day, five days per week) while the number of households receiving care has decreased by 8% (NHS Information Centre, 2009c). Care is being increasingly provided (or targeted) at a smaller number of users, suggesting the development of a model of more intensive support, again as with other services, focusing on those most 'in need'. In 2008, 32% of households were defined as 'high intensity users' receiving at least six visits and 10 hours of care per week; in 1999, such households accounted for only 16% of users. How much of the home care service is accounted for by older people? Almost three quarters (72%) of home care expenditure is accounted for by those aged 65 and over (a slight decline from the 77% in 2003/04) and 73% of the high intensity users group. Thus, older people form the largest client group for this type of community-based care and support.

Establishing what proportion of older people receives home care services is problematic as the most recent data are derived from the 2001 GHS. Victor (2005) reports that 5% were receiving a social service/publicly funded home care service (although they may have been making a financial contribution) and a further 13% had a 'private' home help – so at the maximum 18% of those aged 65 and over are receiving some care support. How does this mesh with the need for support?

Victor (2005) suggests that there is a focus on those who (probably) have the greatest needs: those aged 85 and over and those living alone. Overall, 24% of those living alone were receiving/using home care (17% from the private sector) and 46% of those aged 85 and over (28% from the private sector) with 3% and 7% respectively receiving mobile meals services. However, this does not include any 'private' arrangements and there has been little expansion in the proportion of people receiving such services since the 1980s (although there is an absolute increase because of the increase in numbers of those aged 85 and over).

How does this utilisation of service reflect need? Are we effectively responding to all of those who need care and support to remain living independently within the community? Do we have the correct mix between 'low-intensity' preventive-type services and high-intensity services in order to facilitate older people to live in the community for as long as they wish? While SSDs spend about 25% of their budget on 'social care' services for older people – either as commissioners or providers – only a minority of older people receive care. Wanless (2006) estimates that approximately 6% of those aged 65 and over received either one or some combination of home care, day care and meal services or 9% if privately organised and funded home care is included. These levels of formal support within the community are well below those reported for many other countries, including Denmark (25%), Canada (17%) or Norway (13%) but are similar to the rates for France (6%) and Belgium (5%) (Wanless, 2006). One way of evaluating the link between met and unmet need is to compare the proportion of those requiring help with an ADL to those who receive help and where this help originates from. Victor (2005) reports that of those who need help with domestic tasks some 4% receive this via the state and a further (14%) via 'private' arrangements. Of course this does not indicate how many need help but do not receive it.

Wanless (2006) examined this relationship from another more economic perspective by looking at horizontal and vertical efficiency in home care provision. Horizontal efficiency relates to the 'coverage' of care – how many of those with a defined need for care actually receive care – while vertical efficiency relates to the percentage of all services targeted at a specific needs category. Wanless (2006) devised three 'needs' categories: those with personal care needs but with some informal care support, those unable to undertake practical care tasks and those with either practical or personal care needs but without any informal support. In 1981, about 35% of each of these groups received some care services compared with 20% in 2001. And these groups account for 60-80% of allocated home care services. This serves to reinforce the overall conclusion that only a minority of older people are having their needs met from 'state' resources. It is unclear whether there are any significant gender, class or ethnicity variations in service utilisation. It seems likely that some groups are able to meet their care needs from private resources (the more affluent) while we might speculate that those from minority ethnic communities have problems accessing services. However, these are both areas where there is scope for considerably more research.

The role of families in caring for older people

ACTIVITY 4

▶ If you needed care because of frailty or disability would you prefer to receive this from (a) a health/social care professional or (b) your family?

▶ Do you think that state care should be provided free to frail older people or should this be paid for privately?

Wanless (2006) reported that 62% of adults would, if they needed care due to old age or disability, prefer to receive this in their own home with support from family and friends (56% reported the same care location preference but that they would prefer to receive care from state/trained care workers) with only 14% opting to move in with their children. Informal or family-based care is vital to the support of older people within the community. The term 'informal care' is care provided to those who are sick and/or disabled or older in a non-professional capacity and which flows from the web of social relationships and networks within which an older person is enmeshed. Such care is rarely 'informal' in terms of organisation and commitment in that it places high demands on the part of those who provide it. There are numerous data summarising the nature and extent of informal-based care provision in the UK. Victor (2005) reports that 13% of adults are self-defined as informal carers (11% of males and 14% of females); 22% of carers provide more than 20 hours of care per week (so almost double the levels of average home care provided via the state); one third of carers are looking after someone in their household; 26% of carers provide 'personal' care; 35% provide physical help; and 65% are classed as 'sole' carers, that is, they are providing this help and support without any other recourse.

What is the contribution of 'informal' carers? Clearly it is difficult for informal carers to substitute for some technical healthcare-related tasks. Victor (2005) notes that of those who need help for cutting toenails, 79% is provided by 'formal' services. However, when we examine help with the (I)ADL tasks that are essential to living at home, then the role of the informal sector is paramount. For domestic tasks such as shopping, cooking and house care, 90% of help provided comes from the informal sector (predominantly family) and 70% for personal care. Thus, family and informal care is not marginal to older people living at home but quite clearly both essential and central to their ability to remain living within the community. Given this centrality it is crucial to think about how robust these arrangements are. Who are the main providers of informal care? Typically it is spouses (both male and female) and daughters (in law) who are main care providers. It is daughters who are largely the providers of intergenerational care, with spouses providing intra (or cross-generational care). Will there be fewer 'carers' available to future generations of older people because of changes in family size and partnerships and/ or will future generations be less (or more) willing to continue to be carers? Thus, there are many uncertainties with regard to the likely pattern of care provision in the future but, if history repeats itself (a significant assumption), then it is likely that the family will continue to provide the bulk of care for older people as they have in the past (see Sheldon, 1948).

ACTIVITY 5

▸ What do you think the rewards of being a family carer are? What might be the burden or costs of caring for individuals?

▸ Transition to long-term care – for either oneself or a spouse/partner – is a major 'life event'. What factors do you think might make such a transition more (or less) successful?

▸ How do you think you would feel if you had to enter care? Would you see this as a positive choice?

The provision and use of long-term care

There are a minority of older people who present significant care needs, often but not exclusively because of cognitive impairment, and who are unable to remain living independently in the community. Within the UK, long-term care is approximately divided between residential care for those who, although frail, require care and support, and nursing homes (the successor to hospital-based 'long-term care' wards) for those with health needs, reflecting the duality of policy responses noted earlier. Issues around access and payment for long-term care and the boundaries between acute and long-term care and social and healthcare underpin many of the debates concerning social welfare reform within the UK.

Overall, some 5% of the population aged 65 and over live in long-term care. This level approximates to that reported for many other developed countries such as France (7%), Australia (6%), Belgium (6%) and the US (4%) (Wanless, 2006) and has remained approximately stable over the course of the last century (but of course this represents a substantial increase in absolute numbers because of demographic change) (Victor, 1997). The long-term care sector illustrates another aspect of the withdrawal of the 'state' from direct provision noted with reference to domiciliary care. As late as 1980, some 80% of long-term care provision was in the public sector compared with approximately 10% in 2001 (Victor, 2005). This reflects the direct effect of government policy to increase the role of the private sector in care provision in the belief that this will improve standards and the focus of social care agencies on facilitating, commissioning and strategic service development rather than actual care delivery.

How many long-stay places are available to older people? The last Department of Health census data are for 2001 when there were 341,200 residential home places in England provided in 24,100 homes and 186,800 registered beds in 5,700 nursing homes and private hospitals, offering 142,500 places for older people in nursing homes and 236,700 in residential homes; a total of 379,200 places. Expenditure on long-term care is substantial. Social services expenditure on long-term care represents approximately 50% of the total; 25–30% of those in care homes are 'self-funded' while an additional 20% receive additional non-state 'top-up' funding. Thus, virtually half of those in care are funding themselves in full or part. Hence, the growing significance of long-term care funding as a political issue given the size of the fees involved.

Who lives in long-term care and why do they go into care? The demographic profile of those in care is well established, with a predominance women (75%), a mean age of 85 years and high levels of severe disability (91% in nursing homes, 70% in residential homes and 5% in the community) (Victor, 2005), which illustrates high levels of vertical equity. However, it is unwise to draw the inference that the long-term care sector caters for all of those with significant care needs. Horizontal equity is low for those with cognitive impairment where 88% live in the community (21% living alone without an informal carer) and those with ADL limitations only where 75% live in the community. However, it is higher for those with combined dependency where 85% are in care homes (Wanless, 2006). Wanless (2006) reports that, in the event of disability or dependency in old age, approximately 5% of adults would want to reside in long-term care. This clearly is an unpopular care choice! Thus, most admissions to residential or nursing homes are 'unplanned' and usually occur at a time of crisis (often hospital admission) and in response to significant healthcare/social care needs (see Wanless, 2006).

Key points

Who provides care, where is care to be provided and who pays for care are the issues at the heart of debates about care provision as illustrated by the reports by Wanless (2006) and the Green Paper on social care (Burnham, 2009).

Formal care is being increasingly focused on the most 'in need' at the expense of lower levels of help to less dependent individuals (but which may prevent or delay increases in levels of dependency).

Formal support is received only by a minority of older people and the family remains the centrepiece of care and support for those with chronic long-term care needs.

Further activities

▸ Using data from the 2001 Census, find out how many 'informal' carers there are in your area. How many do you think are in contact with services?

▸ How many older people in your locality might be without any form of care?

Further reading

Evans, J.G. (1997) Geriatric medicine: a brief history. *British Medical Journal*, 315: 1075-7.

Isaacs, B. (1965) *An introduction to geriatrics*. London: Balliere, Tindall and Cassell.

Powel, C. (2007) Whither geriatrics? Do we need another Marjory Warren? *Age and Ageing*, 36(6): 607-61.

Warren, M.W. (1943) Care of the chronic sick: a case for treating chronic sick in blocks in a general hospital. *British Medical Journal*, 12, 822-3.

Warren, M.W. (1946) Care of the chronic aged sick. *The Lancet*, I, 841-3.

Useful websites

- *Ageism in health and social care:* www.cpa.org.uk/reviews
- *Informal care over time:* www.york.ac.uk/inst/spru/pubs/rworks/aug2001.pdf
- *Prevalence of informal care:* www.statistics.gov.uk/cci/nugget.asp?id=925
- *Series of publications on informal care by LSE research group:* www.lse.ac.uk/collections/PSSRU/researchAndProjects/informalCare.htm
- *Personal Social Services Research Unit:* www.pssru.ac.uk/
- *Carers UK:* www.carersuk.org/Home

SEVEN

Health in the future?

Key points

In this final chapter we consider:

- what the health of older people will be like in the future;
- the globalisation of population ageing.

Examining the health status of older people demonstrates that there are powerful social inequalities in terms of the experience of health, both chronic and acute, in later life. Socioeconomic position, gender and, probably, increasingly ethnicity exert a powerful influence on the distribution of health and illness within the older population. This serves to illustrate the importance of social factors in influencing the experience of health in later life. Indeed, Melzer et al (2000) suggest that we could reduce overall levels of disability by eradicating current class- (and gender- and ethnicity-based) inequalities. In this final chapter we consider the health status (and 'service' and support needs) of future generations of older people. The 'ageing' of the population poses (potentially) significant challenges to national governments in terms of providing health and social care services to an increasingly absolute and relative number of older people if current levels of morbidity (and inequities) are maintained. Even if levels of chronic illness, both physical and mental, and disability levels remain unchanged, the increase in the number of older people (especially those aged 85 and over who are most likely to experience these problems) will result in an absolute increase in the number of individuals suffering from these conditions. Clearly, it is not possible to know, with any certainty, what will happen in the future as the erroneous predictions of population trends illustrate. However, in this chapter we consider the main propositions as to future patterns of morbidity and consider the available empirical evidence to support these respective propositions.

The rectangularisation of mortality

There has been a profound change in the distribution of mortality across the lifecourse, with deaths being increasingly squeezed (or compressed) into the later phases of life. Thus, for the UK in 2007, 15% of deaths occurred before the age of 65. This pattern, which is observable across a range of developed countries, is termed the 'rectangularisation of mortality' and is associated with the work of

Fries (1980). There are two distinct aspects to the rectangularisation of mortality proposition. First, in terms of mortality, Fries (1980) proposed that under 'ideal conditions' two thirds of 'natural deaths' (that is, ageing-related deaths rather than those as a result of infection or pathology) would occur between the ages of 81–89 and 95% in the 77–93 age range. In this 'ideal world', virtually no one would die before the age of 70 nor reach the landmark age of 100 years and 10% of people would die at the modal age of 85.

Second, Fries proposed that the distribution of age-related deaths would become increasingly focused into the more advanced years. This proposition represents a development of the work by Lexis in 1878 (see Robine and Michel, 2007), who distinguished between three distinct 'types' of mortality each characterised by specific distributions in terms of age: mortality in infancy, age-related mortality and premature adult mortality. As the diseases of childhood and early adulthood are conquered via social improvements such as improved housing, decreases in poverty, improved nutrition and the development of medical and public health based interventions, we are left with a society and mortality profile dominated by 'age-related' deaths. We can see this trend clearly demonstrated in the UK. The US has moved from a situation where mortality was 'equally' distributed between childhood, adulthood and old age to one where death is almost exclusively concentrated into the 65 and over age group. In his original exposition of the theory of rectangularisation of mortality, Fries proposed a fixed expectation of life at birth of 85 years (with a standard deviation of four years, that is, a range of 81–89 years).

How accurate has this hypothesis proved to be? Robine and Michel (2007) report that in Japan the modal age of death of 85 years has been achieved, accounting for about 5% of all deaths, but that the standard deviation is very much wider than the four years proposed by Fries. Put simply, this means that more people are reaching advanced old age than was initially proposed by Fries (1980) and that deaths are less concentrated around the modal age than he proposed. The modal age of death is a key demographic and social indicator in that it defines the age that the 'largest' number of people within a given population will achieve, that is, the 'average' (in the sense of the most frequently achieved) lifespan. Robine et al (2007) argue that the pattern now displayed by Japan is for a modal age at death for women of 90 years, compared with approximately 78 years in 1950, but with no change in the overall shape of the distribution (that is, the same percentage of individuals dying at the modal age and no reduction of the standard deviation). Mortality has 'shifted' further to the right, that is, it is focused more into advanced 'old age' but there is no evidence of the further change in the shape of the distribution curve predicted by Fries (1980). Robine et al (2008) describe this trend as 'the shifting mortality scenario'. This is defined as a steady increase in the modal duration of life or age at death (depending on which way one wishes to interpret it), accompanied by a modest decrease in the standard deviation of age at death but not (yet) to the rather narrow age range of four years as proposed by Fries (1980).

Canudas-Romo (2008) highlights the attraction of using modal age at death, rather than life expectancy at birth, as a way of summarising the number of years we can expect to live for countries characterised by low infant and overall mortality rates. He notes that for the Netherlands in 2000, life expectancy at birth was 78 years compared with a modal age of death of 84 years. For England and Wales, the modal age of death increased from 70 years in 1900 (when life expectancy was around 48 years) to 85 in 2000 (when life expectancy was around 78–80 years). We can see that the substantial decline in mortality in infancy, childhood and early adulthood has resulted in the modal age at death and life expectancy at birth moving closer together.

Future patterns of mortality in later life

In Chapter Two we examined overall trends in mortality and noted the reductions in both overall and infant mortality rates. We can see in Table 7.1 that there have also been profound reductions in late-life mortality in England and Wales. Since 1950, mortality rates have declined by approximately 50% for the 65-74 age group, 55% for those aged 75-84 and 70% for those aged 85 and over. Such trends are not unique to Britain but are also evident across Europe, North America, Australasia, Scandinavia and Japan. Indeed, Oeppen and Vaupel (2002) comment that it is, in the developed world, reductions in late-life mortality that are now driving population ageing (combined, of course, with low fertility rates). What factors have contributed to these overall declines in late-life mortality? The precise pattern of causation is unclear but includes factors related to healthcare, including access to (better) healthcare for older people, improved medical treatments and interventions and improved 'post–event' health and social care. In addition, there have been general 'public health' improvements in terms of preventive care, improved nutrition and so on, as well as, perhaps, an improved health status of older people in terms of wellbeing compared to previous cohorts of older people.

Table 7.1: Changes in late life mortality by age and gender, England and Wales, 1841-2008

Year	65-74		75-84		85+	
	M	F	M	F	M	F
1841–45	65.5	59.1	143.7	131.8	305.1	288.6
1981	50.3	26.0	116.4	74.6	243.2	196.6
1990	39.5	22.4	94.3	58.9	187.8	156.7
2008	22.0	14.2	61.4	44.2	162.3	146.8

Sources: Victor (1997, table 6.7) and ONS (2009, table 6.1)

Clearly, key future policy questions include 'will these mortality rates continue to decline (at the same or changed rates)', 'how much lower can these mortality rates go?' and 'is there a "floor" below which mortality rates in later life cannot go?' As the very low rates of infant mortality recorded in Singapore and the Nordic countries illustrate, we do not yet seem to have reached a base (or floor) beyond which it is impossible to go below. It remains a matter of lively debate as to the existence of a floor below which late-life (or indeed infant) mortality rates cannot go, however much we try. To date, while the rates of decrease in late-life mortality may be slowing, they do not seem to be demonstrating a plateau (yet) and the latest UK population projections are based on continuing improvements in mortality rates based on the continuation of the 1% decrease in overall mortality per decade recorded during the 20th century.

One way of examining how much potential there is for UK late-life mortality rates to decrease further is by comparing rates here with those recorded in other countries. Table 7.2 compares mortality rates for the UK with those recorded in Japan, the country which records the lowest rates of late-life mortality, France and China. If we take those aged 65-69 then mortality rates in Japan are half those recorded in the UK (10 per 1,000 compared with 15 per 1,000). This significant differential is not just confined to the 'young' old. For those aged 85 and over, mortality rates in Japan are two thirds those reported for the UK (118 per 1,000 versus 174 per 1,000). We can also see that late-life mortality rates in the UK are approximately 20% higher than our near neighbour France. Taken overall, these data would seem to suggest that there is considerable scope for reducing late-life mortality rates for future generations of older people.

Table 7.2: Late life mortality: a comparison of the UK, Japan, France and China by age and gender, 2006

	UK		Japan		France		China	
	M	F	M	F	M	F	M	F
65-69	21.3	13.8	15.0	6.4	18.1	7.8	15.4	6.9
70-74	32.8	21.9	24.9	10.8	28.7	12.8	26.8	13.1
75-79	51.9	34.9	43.0	19.5	45.9	23.5	44.1	23.8
80-84	82.7	58.8	70.6	37.0	78.9	46.1	76.0	43.3
85+	149.1	132.6	151.6	105.4	n/a	n/a	129.1	98.3

Source: UN (2008, table 20)

Compression of morbidity

The theory of compression of morbidity, proposed by James Fries in 1980 and developed in later papers (see Fries, 1980, 1990, 2002, 2003), links the rectangularisation of the survival curve (that is, the concentration of deaths into the later phases of life described previously) with a hypothesis about the distribution of morbidity within the population. Following his propositions about the compression of mortality into the later phases of life, Fries (1980) argued that morbidity would also be 'compressed'. As with death, the modal age of onset of morbidity would be postponed from, for example, 55 years to 65 years (see Fries, 2003) and there would be a similar narrow standard deviation of chronological ages for 'disability onset'. If we assume a 'fixed' life expectancy of 85, then the number of years spent as 'disabled' or with a compromised health status would be reduced if morbidity was 'compressed'. His reasoning was based on the presumption that the factors contributing to the observed declines in mortality seen in developed countries would also bring about decreases in morbidity. So the logic of this argument is that, although more people will be surviving into old age, they will be 'fitter' because of the delayed onset of morbidity closer to the 'fixed' expectation of life, with a consequent reduction of the time individuals spent as 'disabled' and a reduction in overall disease burden. The key assumption underpinning this part of the Fries hypothesis is that reductions in mortality will bring about reductions in morbidity because: (a) mortality and morbidity are characterised by a similar set of risk factors; (b) reductions in risk factors for mortality will bring about reductions in morbidity; and (c) the onset of morbidity will move inexorably closer to the fixed expectation of life of 85 years.

Clearly, this is a very important hypothesis because, if correct, then the 'ageing' of the world's population need not inevitably bring about any great challenge to the provision of health and social care services resultant from increases in absolute numbers of older people and the 'ageing' of the older population. However, there are a number of areas of debate with regard to this general proposition. The conceptualisation of morbidity is predominantly in terms of chronic long-term physical illness and disability rather than mental ill-health such as dementia. The exclusion of mental health — especially dementia — from the general theory is clearly problematic as dementia is a major source of morbidity within the general population (see Chapter Five). Furthermore, the definition of 'morbidity onset' is problematic. Unlike death, which is a clearly identifiable and unambiguous 'end point', determining the onset of significant morbidity/disability is much more problematic and subject to variation over time and between countries. The presumption of a 'fixed' average life expectancy is an important assumption central to the work of Fries (1980) that needs critical evaluation, especially given that life expectancy at birth for women in Japan was achieving this target in 2003!

Survival of the unfittest?

This essentially optimistic view of the health implications of population ageing has not found universal acceptance, for the reasons noted above, and there are counter-propositions and explanations for the observed declines in mortality. Gruenberg (1977) argues that the reduction in mortality seen in most developed countries such as the halving of crude mortality is rare in the UK (see Chapter Two for definition and detailed analysis) is not due to a decrease in the 'risk factor profile' for specific diseases such as a decrease in smoking or improved diet. Rather, it reflects reductions in case fatality rates: as a result of therapeutic improvements (medical, surgical or rehabilitative), individuals are not dying from key disabling conditions such as heart attack and stroke. It is further argued that therapeutic developments such as 'clot busting' drugs for stroke patients have not been translated into changes in the age of onset of disability/chronic illness or the incidence/prevalence of these diseases: the sole impact of these interventions has been to prevent death. Thus, the logical conclusion of this counter-proposition is that as a result of decreased death rates we will see an increase in morbidity as more people will survive into old age with poorer health and disability resulting from 'not dying' from their stroke! Again this hypothesis focuses on physical health problems rather than mental health problems, which have generally low mortality rates and where the benefit of therapeutic interventions remains hotly contested. This is a scenario dubbed 'the survival of the unfittest' or as termed by Olshansky et al (1985) the 'expansion of morbidity hypothesis'. This also rests on an assumption of a fixed maximum average life expectancy of 85 years and with the distribution of death continually moving towards the highest age groups (Olshansky et al, 1990) resulting in an increase in the numbers of the oldest old, with a consequent increase in the number of people with (multiple) chronic diseases within the population and the obvious negative implications for population ageing and the need for care.

Trends in health status over time: expansion or compression of morbidity?

These are two important hypotheses about the future patterns of morbidity demonstrated by our ageing population. What evidence is there to support either (or both) of these propositions? This question is not straightforward to answer. In order to evaluate the debates concerning the compression/expansion of morbidity we need data describing long-terms trends in morbidity in order to be able to establish changes (or otherwise) over time. This is problematic for three reasons. First, we need the availability of long-term data to determine whether trends towards expansion/compression are emerging. These data need to include both accurate numerators, the number of people with disability/chronic health problems, and numerators; the total population or population 'at risk' (in our case, people aged 65 and over). While we have the latter, numerator data are problematic. Second, we need the conceptualisation, operationalisation, measurement and analysis of morbidity to be stable and consistent over time. Again, this requirement is less problematic when examining long-term trends in mortality – death is a fairly unambiguous outcome although there can be less completeness of data collection in the recording of deaths, especially cause of death, the classification of which can vary over time. However, when dealing with morbidity these requirements are problematic. Crimmins (2004) offers a variety of different health measures, including risk factors, functional loss, disability, specific diseases/conditions and impairments, and self-reported health, all of which could be legitimately used to examine the compression/expansion of morbidity hypotheses as they all represent different aspects of health and illness. The number of different indicators that could be used to measure and report long-term trends in health also reminds us that, when we are examining the veracity of expansion/compression of morbidity hypotheses, we need to be specific as to the measure of morbidity/disability used. When evaluating the compression of morbidity hypothesis the emphasis has been on on examining trends in limiting long-term illness (a fairly generic measure of chronic illness) and/or disability (as conceptualised in terms of functional limitation). Indeed, the debates have largely, but not exclusively, focused on the types of measures discussed in Chapter Three. Third, as we have argued throughout this book, trends in the health experience of older people have much more 'weight' if they are manifest across a range of differing countries. Thus, ideally, to come to any conclusions about the merits of these propositions about health in old age we would require evidence from a range of countries (preferably with differing healthcare systems so that we can factor out access to healthcare issues).

Robine et al (2008, 2009) observe that the different measures of health outcome noted earlier demonstrate different and contradictory trends. Crimmins (2004), using data from the US, suggests that while mortality and disability rates are declining, indicating improved health, self-reported health ratings have decreased, suggesting 'worse' health, as have rates of diagnosed illnesses, while other health indices have demonstrated no consistent trends (Crimmins, 2004). Robine et al (2009) point to the paradox represented by these trends, especially the apparent contradiction of increased diagnosed illness and decreased disability. They suggest that older people are demonstrating higher rates of diagnosed illness because (a) this population is more aware of the difference between disease and disability and have higher expectations of their own health; (b) they are more likely and able to consult a doctor than previous generations of older people; and (c) developments in medical care and treatment mean that we can diagnose specific diseases earlier and offer more effective interventions. It is not that there are necessarily more people with condition X, it is just that now we can identify condition X at an earlier stage. Thus, when interpreting long-term trends, especially in diagnosed conditions, we also have to be alert to the problems of changes in diagnostic capabilities. Parker and Thorslund (2007) confirm that, internationally, we can observe this paradox of an increase of diagnosed illness and chronic conditions accompanied by decreases in disability. There is the potential for further complexity as these are very broad macro-level, largely national-level trends. Thus, Robine and Michel (2007) propose that the trends between the 'young' old and the 'oldest' old may be different as well as by gender, class and/or ethnicity. We shall return to this important point after we have considered the macro-level issues and reviewed in more detail the evidence for changes in morbidity over time and future prospects for both mortality and morbidity.

Has the prevalence of disability in old age changed over time?

It is in terms of the prevalence of disability that we can see evidence that supports the compression of morbidity hypothesis most strongly. Using US data for the period 1982 to 2004, Manton et al (2008) suggest that chronic disability rates for the older population may have decreased by up to 1.5% per annum over the two decades studied. In this study, disability was defined as (I)ADL and the greatest improvement over time was illustrated by those aged 65-74 in terms of the performance of IADL activities (Schoeni et al, 2005). Freedman et al (2008), using five sweeps of the US Health and Retirement Survey (HRS) over a decade, report that the prevalence of difficulties with ADL tasks declined from 30% in 1995 to 26% in 2004 for the population aged 75 and over: an annual percentage decrease in prevalence of 1.46%, which is very similar to that reported by Manton et al (2008). The analysis of Freedman et al (2008) shows some impressive decreases in specific ADL tasks such as toileting (9.8% reporting difficulties in 1995 and 5.8% in 2004), getting in/out of bed (10.1% to 6.6%), dressing (15.4% to 13.4%) and bathing (15.3% to 11.8%). If 'real', these are very important changes as it is difficulties with these key personal care tasks that compromise quality of life, challenge autonomy and independence and place individuals at risk of entry into long-term care. However, while these data are suggestive of overall decreases in levels of disability, they do not enable us to comment on changes to the modal age of disability onset. Indeed, most of the information is presented in terms of broad prevalence rather than 'onset', partly because of the difficulties of determining onset of disability in any meaningful way.

However, we must be cautious in placing too much confidence in the support of the compression of morbidity hypothesis on the basis of evidence generated by a single country. Do countries other than the US show both low mortality rates and the compression of mortality? Sulander et al (2009) report that there have been substantial decreases in the proportion of men aged 65 and over reporting ADL limitations of 5% and 10% for women in Finland during the 10 years 1993-2003. However, if there is any veracity to the propositions of Fries or Olshansky then we would expect to see evidence for the compression of morbidity across a broad range of countries. Lafortune et al (2007) reviewed existing studies of trends in ADL-based disability measures (that is, bathing, dressing and eating) for the population aged 65 and over across the 12 developed countries of the Organisation for Economic Co-operation and Development (OECD) during the 1990s. This produced two sets of conclusions. First, the prevalence of ADL disability for these populations varies considerably from 7% for the Netherlands to 18% for Britain (see Lafortune et al, 2007). This raises a key question when attempting to interpret trends in disability across countries, which is: are these differences 'real'? Are rates of ADL-based disability really more than twice as high in Britain as in the Netherlands? Are British older people really so much less 'healthy' and more dependent than their continental cousins? Alternatively, are these differences an artefact of methodological study design issues? Are the differences explained in terms of the composition of the study populations, such as exclusion/inclusion of the most frail either by design or biased response? Do these differences reflect variability between countries in the contextual factors that influence responses to such ADL-type questions? When we use these ADL questions we are asking about the difficulties respondents experience when undertaking them. So one explanation for the variability across countries is that older people have less difficulties with these tasks because they are being helped to undertake them, by services (both statutory and voluntary), family, friends or the use of technological aids or there are culturally defined thresholds for determining the responses to such questions. At what point along a continuum from 'not a problem with performing a task' to 'impossible to perform a task' do older people report task-related difficulties and do these vary between (and within) populations and over time? So to return to the low rates of ADL disability reported in the Netherlands, does this reflect a very high culturally ascribed norm for the threshold at which older people decide that they must accede independence and accept that they have some task-related difficulties? Clearly, examining these variations between countries is a fruitful area for research but one that is rather neglected.

Given the potential problems in interpreting these data, are there consistent trends in the prevalence of ADL-based disability over time across the OECD countries? There are five countries that show a clear and consistent trend of decline in disability: Denmark, Finland, Italy, the Netherlands and the US (see Table 7.3). The pattern for both Australia and Canada is stable while Belgium, Japan and Sweden demonstrate a trend of increasing disability rates, although in Sweden this recent rise follows a very long period of declining prevalence and thus might reflect the influence of a 'floor effect'. We need to consider the initial rate of disability. There is less potential for disability decline in a low rate country than a high rate one, which might explain the situation for Sweden. For some social indicators we observe, as noted above, what are termed 'floor effects' – the measures are not sensitive enough to detect changes below certain levels. Two countries, France and the UK, show a fluctuating pattern over the time period studied. Thus, a picture of declining rates of disability generated by US data is not as generalisable as we might expect and demonstrates the value of using cross-national data to develop a broader perspective.

Focusing on the UK, we can examine, in more detail, data relating to limiting long-term illness available from the GHS and estimates of disability from four surveys across 15 years combined with responses to the self-rating health questions from these surveys. Using these datasets, there is no obvious evidence of an increase in the percentages of older people reporting long-standing and limiting illness or rating their health as not good – it has remained stable at about 12% since 1977. Similarly, estimates of disability derived from four national surveys do not show any evidence of a clear trend in either direction nor does there seem to be any clear evidence of changes in disability severity overall or within age/gender

Table 7.3: Changes in the prevalence of disability by gender, population aged 65+, selected OECD countries

Country	Time period	% change in severe disability – all	% change in severe disability – M	% change in severe disability – F
Australia	1998-03	+0.1	–0.2	+0.3
Belgium	1997-04	+3.4	+3.8	+3.3
Denmark	1987-05	–1.7	–2.3	–1.3
Finland	1980-00	–2.0	–2.2	–1.9
France	1990-91-1998/99	–2.0	–1.1	–2.3
	1991/92-2002/03	+0.2	n/a	n/a
Italy	1991-99/00	–1.3	–3.5	–0.2
Netherlands	1996-03	–2.2	n/a	n/a
UK – GHS data	1994-02	–2.1	n/a	n/a
UK – HSE data	1995-01	+1.1	n/a	n/a
US	1992-04	–1.4	n/a	n/a

Note: GHS = General Household Survey; HSE = Health Survey for England.

Source: Lafortune et al (2007, table 3.13)

groups. So these data tend to support the conclusion of Lafortune et al (2007) of no obvious disability prevalence trends in the UK older population.

Thus far our analysis of trends in disability has been conducted at the aggregate or macro level, that is, we have been examining trends at the level of the whole population. However, we know that health and illness (and indeed, disability) are not equally distributed across the population. Hence, we might expect that improvements in morbidity as measured by disability or long-term health problems would not be equally distributed across the population. This has not been investigated systematically across countries. Where gender data are available for both Denmark and Finland, declines in disability have been greatest for men as opposed to women while for the US there is no obvious gender-based difference. In Australia, the overall stability of disability masks a slight improvement for men and a slight decrease for women. Examining the longer-term downward trend for Sweden we can see that the improvements are most marked for men and the more recent increases in disability are borne disproportionately by women. Sulander et al (2009) examined changes in disability prevalence in Finland in relation to education – a proxy measure of social status/social class and an aspect of disability prevalence change that is under-researched (see Freedman et al, 2002). Sulander et al (2009) demonstrate that, while there were decreases in disability prevalence evident across the educational spectrum, those with the most education benefited most and the gap between groups was, at best, stable. However, it does seem probable that if disability is decreasing overall for the older population, then it seems likely that some groups – men and those from the most privileged backgrounds – are benefiting disproportionately at the expense of others. Indeed, where the macro trend is of either stable or decreasing morbidity it seems that this may well mask a highly variable pattern of change between different groups based around class, gender and ethnicity. Hence, we must not presume that what is happening at the national population level is an accurate representation of the experience of the different subgroups within the older population.

What is causing these observable declines in disability? If the thesis of Fries is correct then these changes should result from changes in risk factors for the major sources of mortality (heart and circulatory diseases, cancer and respiratory disease). It is not clear that this is correct given the limited overlap between sources of mortality and morbidity. In particular, major causes of morbidity such as arthritis and dementia (and depression) have a large number of non-modifiable risk factors (such as age and gender). Cutler (2001) proposes that reductions in disability reflect improved healthcare interventions, behavioural changes and the growth of adaptive/assistive technology. Freedman et al (2002, 2007, 2008) consider that declines in disability reflect changes in the natural history in terms of changes in the pattern of onset of disability and/or changes in recovery. Using the HRS, Schoeni et al (2008) demonstrate a decrease in disability onset from 16.8% for the period 1995-98 to 15% for the period 2002-04 and 'recovery' from ADL disability increased from 16.9% to 21%. Again, further work is needed to tease out the differential contribution these factors are making to changing rates in disability and how they may (or may not) be experienced differentially by different groups within the population. Indeed, one of the key research areas is to look at how changes in disability are differentially distributed across the various subgroups that constitute the older population.

Will these observed declines continue into the future? Of course we need to be cautious in projecting what are, after all, historical declines in disability forward to future generations of older people. Lafortune et al (2007) examined data describing the prevalence of four index conditions – arthritis, heart problems, dementia and diabetes – as these are the key diseases associated with disability in later life. There are issues of comparability across countries in how these data were collected. Consequently, comparisons between countries may be compromised because of methodological issues. However, the sources used prioritise consistency within countries and this suggests that the prevalence of these conditions has increased over time, although the rate of increase varies between countries. However, again this raises the issue of better detection/identification versus a 'real' increase in prevalence and it is almost certainly the case that better detection/identification underpins much of the observed increase, especially for diabetes and hypertension (see Table 7.4).

Obesity across the OECD countries illustrates a growth rate of about 3% per annum over a period of about a decade. In Chapter Five we saw the high levels of obesity characteristic of contemporary older people and it is well established that obesity is linked with disability and a range of other negative health outcomes.

Table 7.4: Trends in the prevalence of selected conditions, population aged 65+, selected OECD countries, 1990-2004 (%)

Country	Arthritis	Heart disease	Diabetes	Hypertension	Obesity
Australia	0.3	0.9	6.8	3.3	n/a
Belgium	0.1	0.3	5.1	3.2	1.1
Canada	1.6	3.0	3.7	3.9	2.9
Denmark	n/a	n/a	3.3	n/a	n/a
Finland	−0.6	n/a	0.4	0.7	1.4
Italy	2.3	1.1	0.6	6.3	3.0
Japan	1.4	2.4	5.3	1.0	n/a
Netherlands	1.8	3.0	1.2	1.8	3.8
Sweden	n/a	n/a	0.9	0.9	2.0
UK	n/a	n/a	7.4	n/a	3.2
US	0.6	−0.3	2.2	1.5	3.5

Note: negative values = decline in prevalence

Source: Lafortune et al (2007, table A3.1)

Sturm et al (2004) have used Health and Retirement Survey data to examine the link between obesity and limitations in ADL. For those with a 'normal' Body Mass Index (BMI), 1.8-2.5% reported difficulties with ADL; this increased to 6.8% for the 'overweight' (BMI of 25-30), 10% for the moderately obese (BMI of 30-35) and 20% for the severely obese (BMI of 35+). Sturm and colleagues calculate that if current trends for obesity are continued and everything else is unchanged then overall disability rates for the population aged 50-69 will increase by approximately 1.4% for men and 1.7% for women (to 9.3% and 9.5% respectively) in 2020. This demonstrates that the maintenance of current trends cannot be taken for granted. Furthermore, we may see that future generations entering old age may be more 'disabled' than current cohorts, as Lakdawalla et al (2004) report that rates of disability in Americans aged 30-59 have increased due to obesity, at least in part. Thus, increases in the mortality profile resultant, directly or indirectly, from increases in obesity may well halt (or even reverse) the pattern of increasing life expectancy at birth observed over the last century.

Living longer but in worse health?

Another way of examining the issue of changes in the prevalence of disability in old age is to use combinations of mortality and morbidity data to calculate measures of 'healthy' or 'disability-free' life expectancy. This approach has the merit of combining information about survival rates with data concerning the health status of survivors and so we can combine in a single measure information about both quantity and quality of life. Thus, we can consider whether we are living longer but in better (or worse) health (see Turner, 2009). There are several measures that can be used to describe this concept including disability-free life expectancy, disability-adjusted life expectancy and healthy life expectancy. Despite the variation in the names of these measures and in the detail of the methods of calculation, they all express a related, and rather fundamental, concept. How many years (or what percentage) of our expected duration of life will be healthy or free from disability, dementia or dependency? We extend this question by considering trends over time (Are we living longer but in poorer health?) and between and within populations (Are countries such as the US benefiting more than China? Are the rich benefiting more than the poorer groups?). Two sets of data are required for the calculation of such measures: mortality and morbidity. We have already seen that Britain (and other Western societies) is well served by comprehensive and reasonably robust mortality data. However, measures of morbidity used to determine the expected likelihood of disability-free or healthy life expectancy are rather less robust, as indicated earlier. Consequently, we need to look carefully at the data on which these measures are based before accepting their utility and their arguments that healthy life expectancy has increased/decreased. Two measures are often used in the calculation of this measure in the UK: health rating as good (or better) (termed healthy life expectancy) or limiting long-term illness (as a proxy for disability) (termed disability-free life expectancy). Data for 2004-06 indicate that for Britain, life expectancy at birth was 76.9 years for males and 81.3 years for females, while it was 16.9 and 19.7 years respectively at age 65 (see Table 7.5). Focusing on males, we can see that 68.2 years (88.7%) would be classed as 'healthy' and 62.5 years (81.3%) as 'disability free' (see Table 7.5). We can see that women, although having a longer life expectancy, can expect less life classified as 'healthy' (86.7%) or disability free (77.7%). So from these data, we can conclude that women in Britain live longer but in worse health. We can also use these measures to look at changes over time. Life expectancy at birth increased by 5.7 years for men and 4.2 years for women for the period 1981-2004/06. In 1981, the average man could expect to live for 6.43 years in 'poor health' and 12.75 years with a 'disability'; by 2004-06 these had increased to 8.7 years and 14.4 years respectively. Similar trends are observable for women. For the UK, both life expectancy and 'healthy' life expectancy have increased while there has been a marginal increase in the percentage of life spent in poor health or disability and men have benefited more than women in terms of the 'health benefit' of the extra life years gained. We may speculate that the greatest 'health gain' has been recorded by those from the most privileged social backgrounds.

We should also note the limited nature of the definition of health and/or disability used in the above examples, which does not include for example, psychological wellbeing (see Pérès et al, 2008) or cognitive function, both of which can have a highly deleterious effect on quality of life. To address the issues of defining the health indicators used in these measures, Jagger and colleagues (2005) have been working towards developing an EU wide methodology for calculating healthy life years. This is an attractive proposition because, again, it will facilitate cross national comparisons. Jagger and the EHEMU (2005) note that 50

Table 7.5: Disability-free and healthy life expectancy by gender, Great Britain, 1981-2004 (%)

	At birth		At age 65	
Life expectancy	M	F	M	F
1981	70.8	76.8	12.9	16.9
2004	76.9	81.3	16.9	19.7
Healthy life expectancy				
1981	64.4	66.7	9.9	11.8
2004	68.0	70.3	12.5	14.5
Disability-free life expectancy				
1981	58.1	60.8	7.5	8.5
2004	62.3	64.0	9.9	10.7

Source: Smith et al (2008)

countries have estimates of health expectancy but that methodological differences limit robust comparisons between them. As an illustration of the potential benefits of using a common methodology across a range of countries, Jagger and the EHEMU (2005) have calculated health expectancies at birth and age 65 for 15 states of the European Union (EU) using a disability question from the European Community Household Panel (ECHP). This analysis shows considerable variation between the member states and some inconsistencies between the genders in terms of trends in disability-free life expectancy between 1995 and 2001. Three groups of countries are identified: those with reducing disability (for example Belgium and Italy [both male and female]); those with increasing disability (the Netherlands and the UK [males]); and those where there is no change (Spain and the UK [females]).

Ageing people in an ageing world

A key and enduring stereotype of old age is that it is a time of universal ill-health. In this book we have presented a range of data from different sources that have profoundly challenged this stereotype. While it is clear that the prevalence of ill-health and disability is age related, the levels do not reach the universality suggested by the popular stereotype (even in the oldest age groups). Indeed, we have demonstrated that in terms of mortality, disability and chronic illness, the health of older people in the UK is improving or, at worst, remaining stable. That there is the potential for further improvements is demonstrated by the health indicators for older people reported for other countries such as Japan. Indeed, cohort-based life expectancy population projections presume the continuation over the next four decades of current mortality improvements.

Within this apparently broadly stable pattern, there may well be changes within specific groups that are obscured by the macro-level analysis. We may speculate that within an overall pattern of 'no significant change', some groups may have 'improved' (perhaps those from privileged social class groups) while others may have deteriorated or remained stable. Indeed, the observation of detailed changes between people of different ages and genders within an apparent pattern of no overall change suggests that it is unlikely that either the compression or expansion of morbidity hypotheses would operate in a monolithic fashion. Rather, it may well be the case that any benefits/disadvantages will be spread differentially across the distinct components of the older population thereby maintaining, and possibly accentuating, inequalities in health status characteristic of the younger age groups. Thus, we can see evidence in terms of both mortality and morbidity that men are reducing the gender differentials in health status and are demonstrably recording greater 'health gains' than women. It seems unlikely that, given the nature of British society, the most privileged are not disproportionately benefiting in terms of health gain. Our lack of knowledge concerning the current (and future) experience of ageing and health for British minority ethnic communities remains one of the greatest 'knowledge gaps' in terms of understanding the experience of ageing and later life in contemporary Britain.

We cannot predict with any degree of accuracy the health experience of future generations of older people, nor the access, availability and quality of health and social care services (although Wanless, 2006, examined aspects of the demand for care). Current predictions for life expectancy at birth for 2031 suggest 84 years (period-based projections) or 92 years (cohort-based projections) (approximate interpolations of data from Table 7.6) with life expectancy at age around eight years compared with around six years for 2006. However, we can be (fairly) certain of the numbers of older people in 2026 as we are already born (unless there is a major compromise of mortality rates). Thus, the demographic imperative will inevitably result in changes in the absolute disease burden. Wanless (2006) calculated the (estimated) numbers of people aged 65 and over defined as having difficulties with two (or more) ADL under three scenarios of no change, increased disability and improved disability. Under the 'no change' scenario in 2026 there would be 921,000 people in this category, under the 'improved' scenario estimates there would be 851,000 people and in the 'worse case' scenario there would be 951,000 people compared with 551,000 in 2002. Thus, population change with no change in prevalence will result in a 67% increase in the numbers in this category while 'the best case scenario' will result in an increase of 54%!

In this book we have focused, inevitably on the UK. However, in thinking about ageing in the future we need to broaden our horizons and include the developing world, which is rapidly experiencing population ageing. This is now a globalised phenomenon with the largest concentration of the world's older citizens in the developing countries (see Victor, 2010a). It is in China and Asia that we find the largest absolute numbers of older people, along with the consequent implications for the numbers of people experiencing the health problems associated with old age, such as dementia and impaired mobility. It is in these countries where demographic change will also be profound. There are an estimated 35.6 million people worldwide living with dementia in 2010 and this number is estimated to virtually double every two decades to 65.7 million in 2030 and 115.4 million in 2050 (Alzheimer's International, 2009). The engine driving this increase is the numbers of people with dementia in middle- and low-income countries. Alzheimer's International (2009) reports that approximately 58% of the total population with dementia live in low- and middle-income countries and this is expected to rise to 63% in 2030 and 71% in 2050. Thus, responding to the health needs of older people is not simply the preoccupation of the developed world but a global challenge.

Table 7.6: Cohort and period life expectancy projections by age and gender, UK, 2031

	Period-based calculation		Cohort-based calculation	
Expectation of life	M	F	M	F
At birth	82.7	86.2	91.3	94.2
Age 15	68.2	71.6	75.0	78.1
Age 65	21.7	23.9	23.2	25.5
Age 75	14.2	15.8	15.0	16.6
Age 85	8.2	8.9	8.5	9.3

Source: Bray (2008, table 7.5)

Key points

In this book we have looked at the health of older people from a population perspective in order to complement and contextualise the books that focus on the clinical care and management of older people. As such, we have demonstrated the presence of a number of key themes in our analysis, as follows.

While many chronic conditions show a pattern of age-related increase, the stereotype of old age being a time of universal ill-health is inappropriate.

The distribution of chronic health problems, disability and mortality are all intimately linked with social factors such as social class, gender and (probably) ethnicity. This reminds us that (ill-) health is not simply a matter of biology but that social and environmental factors are also important. Consequently, a greater understanding of how these factors are linked with health in later life may offer a range of opportunities for improving the health of older people outwith the arena of genes and genetic manipulation.

Indicators such as life expectancy have demonstrated an almost unbroken pattern of improvement in the UK. That such improvements are not inevitable and should not be 'taken for granted' are illustrated by the declines in these parameters demonstrated by other countries worldwide. We must always be cautious when forward projecting current trends.

There remain many challenges in terms of how best to provide services for an older population that is becoming increasingly diverse. Which are the best models of care for older people? How can we develop a 'welfare state' that can respond to issues of frailty and chronic illness?

As a society there are many ethical and moral dimensions that accompany an 'ageing' society. Do we strive to continually extend life or do we focus on quality rather than quantity of life? Is a long and healthy life only the privilege of the few at the expense of the many? Is a short life a happy one?

Population ageing is often represented as a 'social disaster'. Yet as we have seen, this demographic phenomenon reflects the triumph of public health in reducing mortality, especially infant mortality. Those who represent population ageing in a highly negative light might want to consider the positive social benefits in terms of health and wellbeing that this demographic revolution represents.

Old age for Phat-hotep cited in the Introduction was 'the worst misfortune that can befall a man'. Hopefully in this volume we have dispelled some of the myths and stereotypes that abound about the health of older people and convinced readers that 'old age is better than the alternative' (an apocryphal saying attributed to Maurice Chevalier among others).

Activity

▶   What do you know about global ageing? Take part in a quiz at www.isu.edu/nursing/opd/ geriatric/friday/Global_Aging_Quiz.pdf

Further reading

Bowling, A. (2007) Aspirations for older age in the 21st century: what is successful aging? *The International Journal of Aging and Human Development*, 64(3), 263-97.

Bowling, A. and Gabriel, Z. (2007) Lay theories of quality of life in older age. *Ageing and Society*, 27(6), 827-48.

Phillipson, C. (2001) *The family and community life of older people: Social networks and social support in three urban areas.* London: Routledge.

Phillipson, C., Baars, J., Dannefer, D. and Walker, A. (eds) (2006) *Aging, globalisation and inequality: The new critical gerontology.* New York: Baywood Press.

Useful websites

• *Ageing and life course (World Health Organization):* www.who.int/ageing/ publications/active/en/

• *World population trends (United Nations):* www.un.org/popin/wdtrends.htm

Bibliography

Aboderin, I., Kalache, A., Ben-Shlomo, Y., Lynch, J. W., Yajnik, C.S., Kuh, D. and Yach, D. (2002) *Life course perspectives on coronary heart disease, stroke and diabetes: Key issues and implications for policy and research*. Geneva: World Health Organization.

Ainsworth, B.E., Haskell, W.L., Whitt, M.C., Irwin, M.L., Swartz, A.M., Strath, S.J., O'Brien, W.L., Bassett, D.R. Jr., Schmitz, K.H., Emplaincourt, P.O., Jacobs, D.R. Jr., and Leon, A.S. (2000) Compendium of physical activities: an update of activity codes and MET intensities. *Medicine & Science in Sports & Exercise*, 32(9), Suppl., pp S498–S516, 2000.

Albrecht, R. (1951) The social roles of older people. *Journal of Gerontology*, 6(2), 138-45.

Ali, R., Binmore, R., Dunstan, S., Greer, J., Matthews, Dl, Murray, L. and Robinson, S. (2009) *General Household Survey 2007: Overview report*. London: ONS (General Household Survey data available at: www.statistics.gov.uk/StatBase/Product. asp?vlnk=5756).

Alzheimer's International (2009) *World Alzheimer Report* (www.alz.co.uk/research/ files/WorldAlzheimerReport.pdf)

Anderson, R.M., Shanmuganayagam, D. and Weindruch, R. (2009) Caloric restriction and aging: studies in mice and monkeys. *Toxicology and Pathology*, 37(1), 47-51.

Andre, C. and Velasquez, M. (2010) *Age-based health care rationing*. Santa Clara, CA: Markkula Center for Applied Ethics, Santa Clara University (www.scu.edu/ ethics/publications/iie/v3n3/age.html).

Arber, S. and Attias-Donfut, C. (1999) *The myth of generational conflict*. London: Routledge.

Armour, J. (2007) Early perceptions of the role of community matrons. *Nursing Times*, 103(923), 32-3.

Askham, J. (2003) Interpreting measures of activities of daily living. In Bytheway, W. (ed) *Every day living in later life*. London: Centre for Policy on Ageing.

Avlund, K., Holstein, B., Osler, M., Damsgaard, T., Holm-Pedersen, P. and Rasmussen, N. (2003) Social position and health in old age: the relevance of different indicators of social position. *Scandinavian Journal of Public Health*, 31(2), 126-36.

Bajekal, M., Harries, T., Breman, R. and Woodfield, K. (2004) *Review of disability estimates and definitions*. In-house report 128, London: Department for Work and Pensions.

Bajekal, M., Primatesta, P. and Prior, P. (2003) *Health Survey for England, 2001*. London: The Stationery Office (www.archive2.official-documents.co.uk/ document/deps/doh/survey01/skf/skf.htm).

Baltes, P. (1993) The aging mind: potential and limits. *The Gerontologist*, 33, 580-94.

Baltes, P.B. and Baltes, M.M. (1990) Psychological perspectives on successful aging: the model of selective optimization with compensation. In Baltes, P.B. and Baltes, M.M. (eds) *Successful aging: Perspectives from the behavioural sciences.* Cambridge: Cambridge University Press.

Banks, J. and Leicester, A. (2006) Expenditure and consumption. In Banks, J., Breeze, E., Lessof, C., and Nazroo, J. (eds) *Retirement, health and relationships of the older population in England: The 2004 English Longitudinal Study of Ageing: Wave 2.* London: Institute of Fiscal Studies.

Barker, D.J. (1995) Fetal origins of coronary heart disease. *British Medical Journal,* 311, 171-4.

Barker, D.J. (1998) *Mothers, babies and health in later life.* Edinburgh: Churchill Livingstone.

Barker, D.J., Gluckman, P.D., Godfrey, K.M., Harding, J.E., Owen, J.A. and Robinson, J.S. (1993) Fetal nutrition and cardiovascular disease in adult life. *Lancet,* 341, 938-41.

Batchelor, I.R. and Napier, M.B. (1953) Attempted suicide in old age. *British Medical Journal,* 2(4847), 1186-9.

Battino, M. and Ferreiro, M.S. (2004) Ageing and the Mediterranean diet: a review of the role of dietary fats. *Public Health Nutrition,* 7(7), 953-8.

Beekman, A.T., Deeg, D.J., Geerlings, S.W., Schoevers, R.A., Smit, J.H.and van Tilburg, W. (2001) Emergence and persistence of late life depression: a 3-year follow-up of the Longitudinal Aging Study Amsterdam. *Journal of Affective Disorders,* 65(2), 131-8

Ben-Shlomo, Y. and Kuh, D. (2002) A life course approach to chronic disease epidemiology: conceptual models, empirical challenges, and interdisciplinary perspectives. *International Journal of Epidemiology,* 31, 285-93.

Beveridge, W. (1944) *Social insurance and allied services* (the Beveridge Report). HMSO, London.

Bianco, A., Pileggi, C., Rizza, P., Greco, M.A. and Angelillo, I.F. (2006) An assessment of inappropriate hospital bed utilization by elderly patients in southern Italy. *Aging Clinical and Experimental Research,* 18(3), 249-56.

Biggs, S., Manthorpe, J., Tinker, A., Doyle, M. and Erens, B. (2009) Mistreatment of older people in the United Kingdom: findings from the first National Prevalence Study. *Journal of Elder Abuse and Neglect,* 21(1), 1-14.

Biggs, S., Phillipson, C., Money, A.-M. and Leach, R. (2008) The mature imagination and consumption strategies: age & generation in the development of a UK baby boomer identity. *International Journal of Ageing & Later Life,* 2(2), 31-59.

Binney, E.A., Estes, C.L. and Ingman, S.R. (1990) Medicalization, public policy and the elderly: social services in jeopardy? *Social Science and Medicine,* 30(7), 761-71.

Binstock, R. (2003) The war on 'anti-aging medicine'. *The Gerontologist,* 43, 4-14.

Binstock, R. (2004) Anti-aging medicine: the history: anti-aging medicine and research: a realm of conflict and profound societal implications, *Journals of Gerontology Series A: Biological Sciences and Medical Sciences,* 59, 523-33.

Binstock, R.H., Juengst, E.T., Mehlman, M.J. and Post, S.G. (2003) Anti-aging medicine and science: an arena of conflict and profound societal implications. *Geriatrics and Aging*, 6(5), 61-3.

Black, D. (chair) (1980) *Inequalities in health*. London: HMSO.

Blackwell, L. (2000) Fragmented life courses: the changing profile of Britain's ethnic populations. *Population Trends*, 101, 4-10.

Blane, D., Netuveli, G. and Bartley, M. (2007) Does quality of life at older ages vary with socio-economic position? *Sociology*, 41, 717-26.

Blane, D., Higgs, P., Hyde, M. and Wiggins, R. (2004) Life course influences on quality of life in early old age, *Social Science and Medicine*, 58, 2171-9.

Blaxter, M. (2004a) *Health*. Cambridge: Polity Press.

Blaxter, M. (2004b) *Health and lifestyles*, London: Routledge.

Bloom, D. and Canning, D. (2005) *Global demographic change: Dimensions and economic significance*. Harvard Institute for Global Health Working Paper Series. Working Paper No. 1. Boston, MA: Harvard School of Public Health (available at www.hsph.harvard.edu/pgda/working/working_paper1.pdf).

Bond, J. and Corner, L. (2004) *Quality of life and older people*. Buckingham: Open University Press.

Bond, J. and Carstairs V. (1982) *Services for the elderly*. Scottish Health Service Studies. Edinburgh: Scottish Home and Health Department.

Bos, V., Kunst, A.E., Keij-Deerenberg, I.M., Garssen, J. and Mackenbach, J.P. (2004) Ethnic inequalities in age- and cause-specific mortality in The Netherlands. *International Journal of Epidemiology*, 33, 1112-19.

Bowling, A. (1995) What things are important in people's lives? A survey of the public's judgements to inform scales of health related quality of life. *Social Science and Medicine*, 41(10), 1447-62.

Bowling, A. (2004) Socioeconomic differentials in mortality among older people. *Journal of Epidemiology and Community Health*, 58, 438-40.

Bowling, A. (2005) *Ageing well: Quality of life in old age*. Maidenhead: Open University Press.

Bowling, A. (2006) Lay perceptions of successful ageing: findings from a national survey of middle aged and older adults in Britain. *European Journal of Ageing*, 3(3), 123-36.

Bowling, A. (2007) Aspirations for older age in the 21st century: what is successful aging? *International Journal of Aging and Human Development*, 64(3), 263-97.

Bowling, A. (2008) Enhancing later life: how older people perceive active ageing? *Aging and Mental Health*, 12(3), 293-301.

Bowling, A. (2009) *Research methods in health: Investigating health and health services*. Maidenhead: Open University Press.

Bowling, A. and Gabriel, Z. (2004) An integrational model of quality of life in older age: results from the ESRC/MRC HSRC Quality of Life Survey in Britain. *Social Indicators Research*, 69(1), 1-36.

Bowling, A. and Gabriel, Z. (2007) Lay theories of quality of life in older age. *Ageing and Society*, 27(6), 827-48.

Bowling, A., Bannister, D., Sutton, S., Evans, O. and Windsor, J. (2002) A multidimensional model of the quality of life in older age. *Aging and Mental Health*, 6(4), 355-71.

Bray, H. (2008) 2006-based national population projections for the UK and constituent countries. *Population Trends*, 131, 8-18.

Breeze, E., Sloggett, A. and Fletcher, A.E. (1999) Socioeconomic status and transition in old age in relation to limiting long-term illness measured at the 1991 Census: results of the Longitudinal Study. *European Journal of Public Health*, 9, 265-70.

Breeze, E., Fletcher, A.E., Leon, D.A., Marmot, M.G., Clarke, R.J. and Shipley, M.J. (2001) Do socioeconomic disadvantages persist into old age? Self-reported morbidity in a 29-year follow-up of the Whitehall Study. *American Journal of Public Health*, 91(2), 277-83.

Börsch-Supan, A., Brugiavini, A., Jürges, H., Johan Mackenbach, J., Siegrist, J. and Weber, G. (2005) Health, ageing and retirement in Europe - First Results from SHARE, Mannheim Research Institute for the Economics of Aging (MEA), Mannheim (www.share-project.org/t3/share/index.php?id=69).

Börsch-Supan, A., Brugiavini, A., Jürges, H., Kapteyn, A., Mackenbach, J., Siegrist, J. and Weber, G. (2008) *First results from the Survey of Health, Ageing and Retirement in Europe (2004-2007): Starting the longitudinal dimension*. Mannheim: Mannheim Research Institute for the Economics of Aging (www.share-project.org/t3/share/uploads/tx_sharepublications/BuchSHAREganz250808.pdf).

Bowler, M. (2009) Exploring patients' experiences of a community matron service using storybooks. *Nursing Times*, 105(24), 19-21.

Brouwer, W. and van Exel, N. (2005) Expectations about length and health related quality of life: some empirical results. *Social Science & Medicine*, 61(5), 1083-94.

Brown, K., Stainer, K. and Stewart, J. (2008) Older people with complex long-term health conditions: their views on the community matron service: a qualitative study. *Quality in Primary Care*, 16(6), 409-17.

Bryman, A. (2008) *Social research methods* (3rd edition). Oxford: Oxford University Press.

Burnham, A. (2009) *Shaping the future of care together*. London: DH (www.dh.gov.uk/en/Publicationsandstatistics/Publications/PublicationsPolicyAndGuidance/DH_102338).

Burnham, A. (2010) *Building a national care service*. London: DH (www.dh.gov.uk/en/Publicationsandstatistics/Publications/PublicationsPolicyAndGuidance/DH_114922).

Bury, M. (2005) *Health and illness*, Cambridge: Polity Press.

Bury, M. and Gabe, J. (eds) (2004) *The sociology of health and illness: A reader*. London: Routledge.

Bury, M. and Wadsworth, M. (2003) The 'biological clock'? Ageing, health and the body across the lifecourse. In Williams, S.J., Birke, L. and Bendelow, G.A. (eds) *Debating biology: Sociological reflections on health, medicine and society*. London: Routledge.

Bytheway, B. (2002) Positioning gerontology in an ageist world. In Anderson, L. (ed) *Cultural gerontology.* London: Greenwood Publishing Group.

Bytheway, B. (2005a) Ageism and age categorisation. *Ageism, Special Edition of the Journal of Social Issues,* 61(2), 359-72.

Bytheway, B. (2005b) Ageism. In Johnson, M.L., Coleman, P. and Bengtson, V. (eds) *The Cambridge handbook on age and ageing.* Cambridge: Cambridge University Press.

Bytheway, B. (2005c) Age-identities and the celebration of birthdays. *Ageing & Society,* 25(4), 463-77.

Bytheway, B. (2006) Age prejudice and discrimination. In Ritzer, G. (ed) *Encyclopedia of sociology.* Vol 1. Oxford: Blackwells.

Bytheway, B., Ward, R., Holland, C. and Peace, S.M. (2007) The road to an age-inclusive society. In Bernard, M. and Scharf, T. (eds) *Critical perspectives on ageing societies.* Bristol: The Policy Press.

Cabinet Office (2008) *Food matters: Towards a strategy for the 21st century.* London: Strategy Unit, Cabinet Office.

Calnan, M. and Gabe, J. (2001) From consumerism to partnership? Britain's National Health Service at the turn of the century. *International Journal of Health Services,* 31(1), 119-31.

Canudas-Romo, V. (2008) The modal age at death and the shifting mortality hypothesis. *Demographic Research,* 19(30), 1179-204.

Cardona, B. (2007) Anti-aging medicine and the cultural context of aging in Australia: preliminary findings from ongoing research on users and providers of 'anti-aging medicine' in Australia. *Annals of the New York Academy of Sciences,* 1114(1), 216-29.

Cardona, B. (2008) Healthy ageing policies and anti-ageing ideologies and practices: on the exercise of responsibility. *Medicine, Health Care and Philosophy,* 11(4), 489-94.

Cattell, H. (2000) Suicide in the elderly. *Advances in Psychiatric Treatment,* 6, 102-8.

Chapman, I.M. (2008) Obesity in old age. *Frontiers in Hormone Research,* 36, 97-106.

Chapman, L., Smith, A., Williams, V., and Oliver, D. (2009) Community matrons: primary care professionals' views and experiences. *Journal of Advanced Nursing,* 65(8), 1617-25.

Cheung, S.L.K. and Robine, J.-M. (2007) Increase in common longevity and the compression of mortality: the case of Japan. *Population Studies,* 61(1), 85-97.

Cheung, S.L.K., Robine, J.-M. and Caselli, G. (2008) The use of cohort and period data to explore changes in adult longevity in low mortality countries. *Genus,* LXIV(1-2), 101-29.

Cheung, S.L.K., Robine, J.-M., Tu, E.J.-C. and Caselli, G. (2005) Three dimensions of the survival curve: horizontalization, verticalization, and longevity extension. *Demography,* 42(2), 243-58.

Cheung, Y.B. (2002) A confirmatory factor analysis of the 12-item General Health Questionnaire among older people. *International Journal of Geriatric Psychiatry,* 17(8), 739-44.

Chief Medical Officer (2004) *On the state of the public health: Annual report of the Chief Medical Officer.* London: DH.

Cole, M.G. and Dendukuri, N. (2003) Risk factors for depression among elderly community subjects: a systematic review and meta-analysis. *American Journal of Psychiatry*, 60(6), 1147-56.

Craig, R. and Mindell, J. (2007) *Health Survey for England 2005: The health of older people.* London: National Centre for Social Research.

Craig, R., Mindell, J. and Hirani, V. (2009) *Health survey for England 2008: Physical activity and fitness.* London: NHS Information Centre (www.ic.nhs.uk/statistics-and-data-collections/health-and-lifestyles-related-surveys/health-survey-for-england/health-survey-for-england--2008-physical-activity-and-fitness).

Crimmins, E.M. (2004) Trends in the health of the elderly. *Annual Review of Public Health*, 25, 79-98.

Crimmins, E.M., Kim, J.K. and Seeman, T.E. (2009) Poverty and biological risk: the earlier 'aging' of the poor. *Journals of Gerontology, A: Biological and Medical Sciences*, 64(2), 286-92.

Cutler, D.M. (2001) The reduction in disability among the elderly. *Proceedings of the National Academy of Sciences*, 98(12), 6546–7

Davey Smith, G., Dorling, D., Mitchell, R. and Shaw, M. (2002) Health inequalities in Britain: continuing increases up to the end of the 20th century. *Journal of Epidemiology and Community Health*, 56, 434-5.

Davis, M.G. and Fox, K.R. (2007) Physical activity patterns assessed by accelerometry in older people. *European Journal of Applied Physiology*, 100(5), 581-9.

de Grey, A. (2008) *Ending aging.* London: St Martin's Press.

Demakakos, P., Nunn, S. and Nazroo, J. (2006) Loneliness, relative deprivation and life satisfaction: retirement, health and relationships of the older population in England. In Banks, J., Breeze, E., Lessof, C. and Nazroo, J. (eds) *The 2004 English Longitudinal Study of Ageing (wave 2).* London: Institute for Fiscal Studies.

DeSalvo, K.B., Bloser, N., Reynolds, K., He, J. and Muntner, P. (2006) Mortality prediction with a single general self-rated health question: a meta-analysis. *Journal of General and Internal Medicine*, 21(3), 267-75.

DH (Department of Health) (1999) *National Service Framework for Mental Health: Modern Standards and Service Models.* London: The Stationery Office.

DH (2000b) *Community Care (Direct Payments) Act 1996: Policy and Practice Guidance.* London: The Stationery Office.

DH (2002) *Fair access to care services: Guidance on eligibility criteria for adult social care*, London: DH (www.dh.gov.uk/en/Publicationsandstatistics/Publications/PublicationsPolicyAndGuidance/DH_4009653).

DH (2003) *The National Service Framework for Older People.* London: The Stationery Office.

DH (2005a) *Independence, well-being and choice: Our Vision for the future of social care in England.* London: DH.

DH (2005b) *Choosing activity: A physical activity action plan.* London: DH.

DH (2005c) *The National Service Framework for Long-Term Conditions*. London: DH.

DH (2006) *Our health, our care, our say: A new direction for community services*. London: Stationery Office.

DH (2007) *Putting people first: A shared vision and commitment to the transformation of adult social care*. London: DH (available at www.dh.gov.uk/en/Publicationsandstatistics/ Publications/PublicationsPolicyAnd).

DH (2009) *Government response to the Health Select Committee report on health inequalities*. London: The Stationery Office (available at www.dh.gov.uk/prod_ consum_dh/groups/dh_digitalassets/documents/digitalasset/dh_099782.pdf).

DH (2010) *Prioritising need in the context of Putting People First: A whole system approach to eligibility for social care – Guidance on eligibility criteria for adult social care*, England 2010. London: Department of Health (www.dh.gov.uk/en/ Publicationsandstatistics/Publications/PublicationsPolicyAndGuidance/ DH_113154).

Diehl, M., Marsiske, M., Horgas, A.L., Saczynski, J., Rosenberg, A. and Willis, S.L. (2005) The Revised Observed Tasks of Daily Living: a performance-based assessment of everyday problem solving in older adults. *Journal of Applied Gerontology*, 24, 211–30.

Djernes, J.K. (2006) Prevalence and predictors of depression in populations of elderly: a review. *Acta Psychiatrica Scandinavia*, 113(5), 372–87.

Dominguez, L.J., Barbagallo, M. and Morley, J.E. (2009) Anti-aging medicine: pitfalls and hopes. *Aging Male*, 12(1), 13–20.

Dowswell, T., Towner, E., Cryer, C., Jarvis, S., Edwards, P. and Lowe, P. (1999) *Accidental falls: Fatalities and injuries – An examination of data sources and a review of the literature of preventive strategies*. Gateshead: University of Newcastle upon Tyne

Doyle, Y., McKee, M., Rechel, B. and Grundy, E. (2009) Meeting the challenge of population ageing. *British Medical Journal*, 339, b3926.

Dugan, S.A. (2007) Exercise for health and wellness at midlife and beyond: balancing benefits and risks. *Physical medicine and rehabilitation clinics of North America,* 18, 555–75.

Dunnell, K. (2007) The changing demographic picture of the UK: National Statistician's annual article on the population. *Population Trends*, 130, 9–21.

DWP (Department for Work and Pensions) (2009) *The pensioners' incomes series 2007-08*. London: The Stationery Office.

Ebrahim, S. (2001) New beginning for care for elderly people? Proposals for intermediate care are reinventing workhouse wards. *British Medical Journal*, 323, 337–8.

Ebrahim, S. (2002) The medicalisation of old age. *British Medical Journal*, 324, 861–3.

Estes, C.L. (1979) *The aging enterprise*. San Francisco, CA: Jossey-Bass.

Estes, C.L. (1989) Aging, health and social policy: the crisis and the crossroads. *Journal of Aging and Social Policy*, 1, 17–32.

Estes, C.L. and Binney, E.A. (1989) The biomedicalization of aging: dangers and dilemmas. *The Gerontologist*, 29(5), 587–96.

Estes, C.L. (2001) *Social policy & aging: A critical perspective*. London: Sage Publications.

Estes, C.L., Biggs, S. and Phillipson, C. (2003) *Social theory, social policy and ageing: A critical introduction*. Maidenhead: Open University Press.

Evandrou, M. and Falkingham, J. (2006) Will the babyboomers be better off than their parents in retirement? In Vincent, J.A., Phillipson, C.R. and Downs, M. (eds) *Futures of old age*. London: Sage Publications/The British Society of Gerontology.

Falconer, M. and O'Neill, D. (2007) Profiling disability within nursing homes: a census-based approach. *Age and Ageing*, 36(2), 209-13.

Ferri, C.P., Prince, M., Brayne, C., Brodaty, H., Fratiglioni, L., Ganguli, M., Hall, K., Hasegawa, K., Hendrie, H., Huang, Y., Jorm, A., Mathers, C., Menezes, P.R., Rimmer, E., Scazufca, M. and Alzheimer's Disease International (2005) Global prevalence of dementia: a Delphi consensus study. *Lancet*, 366, 2112-17.

Fishman, J., Binstock, R. and Lambrix, M.A. (2008) Anti-aging science: the emergence, maintenance, and enhancement of a discipline. *Journal of Aging Studies*, 22(4), 295-303.

Flint, A.J. (2005) Generalised anxiety disorder in elderly patients: epidemiology, diagnosis and treatment options. *Drugs and Aging*, 22(2), 101-14.

Foucault, M. (1973) *The birth of the clinic: An archaeology of medical perception* (trans. A.M. Sheridan-Smith). London: Tavistock.

Frankl, S., Elwood, P., Sweetnam, P., Yarnell, J., Davey Smith, G. (1996) Birthweight, body mass index in middle age and incidence of coronary heart disease. *Lancet*, 348, 1478-80.

Freedman, V.A. (2004) Resolving inconsistencies in trends in old-age disability: report from a technical working group. *Demography*, 41(3), 417-41.

Freedman, V.A. and Martin, L.G. (2006) Commentary: dissecting disability trends – concepts, measures, and explanations. *International Journal of Epidemiology*, 35(5), 1261-3.

Freedman, V.A., Martin, L.G. and Schoeni, R.F. (2002) Recent trends in disability and functioning among older adults in the United States: a systematic review. *Journal of the American Medical Association*, 288(24), 3137-46.

Freedman, V.A., Martin, L.G., Schoeni, R.F. and Cornman, J.C. (2008) Declines in late-life disability: the role of early- and mid-life factors. *Social Science and Medicine*, 66(7), 1588-602.

Freedman, V.A., Schoeni, R.F., Martin, L.G. and Cornman, J.C. (2007) Chronic conditions and the decline in late-life disability. *Demography*, 44(3), 459-77.

Fries, J.F. (1980) 'Aging, natural death and the compression of morbidity'. *New England Journal of Medicine*, 303, 130-5.

Fries, J.F (1990) The sunny side of aging. *Journal of the American Medical Association*, 2, 263(17), 2354-5.

Fries, J.F. (2002) Successful aging: an emerging paradigm of gerontology. *Clinics in Geriatric Medicine*, 18(3), 371-82

Fries, J.F. (2003) Measuring and monitoring success in compressing morbidity. *Annals of Internal Medicine*, 2(139), 455-9.

Galloway, M.T. and Jokl, P. (2000) Aging successfully: the importance of physical activity in maintaining health and function. *Journal of the American Academy of Orthopaedic Surgery*, 8(1), 37-44.

Gilleard, C. (1996) 'Consumption and identity in later life: toward a cultural gerontology', *Ageing and Society*, 16, 489-98.

Gilleard, C. and Higgs, P. (1998) 'Older people as users and consumers of health care: a third age rhetoric for a fourth age reality', *Ageing and Society*, 18, 233-48.

Gilleard, C. and Higgs, P. (2000) *Cultures of ageing: Self, citizen and the body*. Harlow: Prentice Hall.

Gilleard, C. and Higgs, P. (2005) *Contexts of ageing: Class, cohort and community*. Cambridge: Polity Press.

Glasby, J., Littlechild, R. and Pryce, K. (2006) All dressed up but nowhere to go? Delayed hospital discharges and older people. *Journal of Health Services Research and Policy*, 11(1), 52-8.

Godden, S., McCoy, D. and Pollock, A. (2009) Policy on the rebound: trends and causes of delayed discharges in the NHS. *Journal of the Royal Society of Medicine*, 102(1), 22-8.

Goffman, E. (1961) *Asylums: Essays on the condition of the social situation of mental patients and other inmates*. Harmondsworth: Penguin.

Gompertz, B. (1825) On the nature of the function expressive of the law of human mortality, and on a new model of determining the value of life contingencies. *Philosophical Transactions of the Royal Society of London*, 115: 513–85 (http://visualiseur.bnf.fr/Visualiseur?Destination=Gallica&O=NUMM-55920).

Gooberman-Hill, R., Ayis, S. and Ebrahim, S. (2003) Understanding long-standing illness among older people. *Social Science and Medicine*, 56(12), 2555-64.

Gould, N. and Gould, E. (2001) Health as a consumption object: research notes and preliminary investigation. *International Journal of Consumer Studies*, 25(2), 90-101.

Gravelle, H., Dusheiko, M., Sheaff, R., Sargent, P., Boaden, R., Pickard, S., Parker, S. and Roland, M. (2007) Impact of case management (Evercare) on frail elderly patients: controlled before and after analysis of quantitative outcome data. *British Medical Journal*, 334(7583), 31.

Grenier, S., Préville, M., Boyer, R. and O'Connor, K. (2009) Scientific Committee of the ESA Study. *Journal of Anxiety Disorder*, 23(7), 858-65.

Grimley Evans, J. and Tallis, R.C. (2001) A new beginning for care for elderly people? *British Medical Journal*, 322, 807-8.

Grimley Evans, J., Franklin Williams, T., Lynn Beattie, B., Michel, J.P and Wilcock, G.K. (2000) *Oxford textbook of geriatric medicine* (2nd edition). Oxford: Oxford University Press.

Gruenberg, E.M. (1977) The failures of success. *Milbank Memorial Fund Quarterly*, 55(1), 3-24.

Gruman, G.J. (1996) *A history of ideas about the prolongation of life*. Philadelphia, PA: Philosophical Society.

Grundy, E. and Glaser, K. (2000) Socio-demographic differences in the onset and progression of disability in early old age: a longitudinal study. *Age and Ageing*, 29(2), 149-57.

Grundy, E. and Holt, G. (2001) The socioeconomic status of older adults: how should we measure it in studies of health inequalities? *Journal of Epidemiology and Community Health*, 55, 895-904.

Grundy, E. and Sloggett, A. (2003) Health inequalities in the older population: the role of personal capital, social resources and socio-economic circumstances. *Social Science and Medicine*, 56, 935-47.

Gullette, M. (2004) *Aged by culture.* Chicago, IL: University of Chicago Press.

Guralnik, J., Butterworth, S., Wadsworth, M.E.J. and Kuh, D. (2006) Childhood socioeconomic status predicts physical functioning a half century later. *Journal of Gerontology: Medical Sciences*, 61(7), 694-701.

Hammond, C.L., Pinnington, L.L. and Phillips, M.F. (2009b) A qualitative examination of inappropriate hospital admissions and lengths of stay. *BMC Health Services Research*, 9, 44.

Hammond, C.L., Phillips, M.F., Pinnington, L.L., Pearson, B.J. and Fakis, A. (2009a) Appropriateness of acute admissions and last in-patient day for patients with long term neurological conditions. *BMC Health Services Research*, 9, 40.

Harper, S. (2006) *Ageing societies.* London: Hodder Arnold.

Harris, T., Cook, D.G., Victor, C., DeWilde, S. and Beighton, C. (2006) Onset and persistence of depression in older people: results from a 2-year community follow-up study. *Age and Ageing*, 35(1), 25-32.

Harris, T.J., Owen, C.G., Victor, C.R., Adams, R. and Cook, D.G. (2009) What factors are associated with physical activity in older people, assessed objectively by accelerometry? *British Journal of Sports Medicine*, 43(6), 442-50.

Harwood, D.G. and Ownby, R.L. (2000) Ethnicity and dementia. *Current Psychiatry Reports*, 2(1), 40-5.

Harwood, R.H. (2007) Evaluating the impact of the National Service Framework for Older People: qualitative science or populist propaganda? *Age and Ageing*, 36, 483-5.

Hattersley, L. (1999) Trends in life expectancy by social class – an update. *Health Statistics Quarterly*, 2, 16-24.

Haycock, D.B. (2008) *Mortal coil: A short history of living longer.* Yale: Yale University Press.

Haynie, D.A., Berg, S., Johansson, B., Gatz, M. and Zarit, S.H. (2001) Symptoms of depression in the oldest old: a longitudinal study. *Journals of Gerontology B: Psychology and Social Sciences*, 56(2), 111-8.

Health Advisory Service (1982) *The rising tide: Developing services for mental illness in old age.* London: DHSS.

Heilbronn, L.K. and Ravussin, E. (2005) Calorie restriction extends life span – but which calories? *PLoS Medicine*, 2(8), e231.

Henderson, A.S., Korten, A.E., Jacomb, P.A., Mackinnon, A.J., Jorm, A.F., Christensen, H. and Rodgers, B. (2001) The course of depression in the elderly: a longitudinal community-based study in Australia. *Psychological Medicine*, 27(1), 119-29.

Herzlich, C. (1973) *Health and illness.* London: Academic Press.

Hicks, J. and Allen, G. (1999) *A century of change: Trends in UK statistics since 1900.* House of Commons Library Research Paper 99/11.

Higgs, P. and Jones, I.R. (2009) *Medical sociology and old age: Towards a sociology of health in later life.* London: Routledge.

Higgs, P.F., Hyde, M., Gilleard, C.J., Victor, C.R., Wiggins, R.D. and Jones, I.R. (2009) From passive to active consumers? Later life consumption in the UK from 1968-2005, *Sociological Review*, 57(1), 102-24.

Hildon, Z., Smith, G., Netuveli, G., Blane, D. (2008) Understanding adversity and resilience at older ages. *Sociology of Health and Illness*, 30(5),726-40.

Hildon, Z., Mongomery, S., Blane, D., Wiggings, R., Netuveli, G. (2010) Examining resilience of quality of life in the face of health-related and psychosocial adversity at older ages: what is 'right' about the way we age? *The Gerontologist,* 50(1): 36-47.

Hoeymans, N., Garssen, A., Westert, G. and Verhaak, P. (2004) Measuring mental health of the Dutch population: a comparison of the GHQ-12 and the MHI-5. *Health and Quality of Life Outcomes*, 2, 23-35.

Hofer, A.M. and Sliwinski, M.J. (2006) Design and analysis of longitudinal studies of ageing. In Birren, J. and Schaie, K. (eds) *Handbook of the psychology of aging* (4th edition). Bulington, MA: Elsevier Academic Press.

Huisman, M., Kunst, A.E. and Andersen, O. (2004) Socioeconomic inequalities in mortality among elderly people in 11 European populations. *Journal of Epidemiology and Community Health*, 58, 468-75.

Humphries, R., Forder, J. and Fernandez, J.-L. (2010) *Securing good care for more people: Options for reform.* London: King's Fund (www.kingsfund.org.uk/publications/securing_good_care.html)

Huppert, F., Gardener, E. and McWilliams, B. (2006) Satisfaction retirement, health and relationships of the older population in England. In Banks, J., Breeze, E. and Nazroo, J. (eds) *The 2004 English Longitudinal Study of Ageing (wave 2).* London: Institute for Fiscal Studies.

Illich, I. (1975) *Limits to medicine.* London: Marion Boyars Publishers.

Isaacs, B. (1965) *An introduction to geriatrics.* London: Balliere, Tindall and Cassell.

Isaacs, B. (1992) *The challenge of geriatric medicine.* Oxford: Oxford University Press.

Isaacs, B., Livingstone, M. and Neville, Y. (1972) *Survival of the unfittest: A study of geriatric patients in Glasgow.* London: Routledge & Kegan Paul.

Jagger, C. and the EHEMU (European Health Expectancy Monitoring Unit) team (2005) *Healthy life expectancy in the EU15.* Available at www.ehemu.eu/pdf/Carol_Budapest.pdf

Jagger, C., Gillies, C., Moscone, F., Cambois, E., Van Oyen, H., Nusselder, W., Robine, J.-M. and the EHLEIS team (2008) Inequalities in healthy life years in the 25 countries of the European Union in 2005: a cross-national meta-regression analysis. *Lancet*, 372(9656), 2124-31.

Janssen, I. (2007) Morbidity and mortality risk associated with an overweight BMI in older men and women. *Obesity*, 15(7), 1827-40.

Janssen, I. and Bacon, E. (2008) Effect of current and midlife obesity status on mortality risk in the elderly. *Obesity*, 16(11), 2504-9.

Janssen, I. and Mark, A.E. (2007) Elevated body mass index and mortality risk in the elderly. *Obesity Review*, 8(1), 41-59.

Jarman, B. and Aylin, P. (2004) Death rates in England and Wales and the United States: variation with age, sex, and race. *British Medical Journal*, 329, 1367-7.

Jefferies, J. (2005) The UK population: past, present and future. In *Focus on people and migration*. London: ONS (www.statistics.gov.uk/downloads/theme_compendia/fom2005/01_FOPM_Population.pdf).

Johansson, L.A. and Westerling, R. (2000) Comparing Swedish hospital discharge records with death certificates: implications for mortality statistics. *International Journal of Epidemiology*, 29(3), 495-502.

Johansson, L.A., Björkenstam, C., Westerling, R. (2009) Unexplained differences between hospital and mortality data indicated mistakes in death certification: an investigation of 1,094 deaths in Sweden during 1995. *Journal of Clinical Epidemiology*, 62(11), 1202-9.

Johansson, L.A., Westerling, R. and Rosenberg, H.M. (2006) Methodology of studies evaluating death certificate accuracy were flawed. *Journal of Clinical Epidemiology*, 59(2), 125-31.

Jones, I.R., Higgs, P. and Ekerdt, D.J. (2009) *Consumption and generational change: The rise of consumer lifestyles*. New Jersey, NJ: Transaction Publishers.

Jones, I.R., Hyde, M., Victor, C., Wiggins, R., Gilleard, C. and Higgs, P. (2008) *Ageing in a consumer society: From passive to active consumption in Britain*. Bristol: The Policy Press.

Jorm, J., Korten, A. and Henderson, A. (1987) The prevalence of dementia: a quantitative integration of the literature. *Acta Psychiatrica Scandinavia*, 76, 465-79.

Jylhä, M. and Luukkaala, T. (2006) Social determinants of mortality in the oldest-old: social class and individual way-of-life. In Robine, J.-M., Crimmins, E., Horiuchi, S. and Yi, Z. (eds) *Human longevity, individual life duration, and the growth of the oldest-old population*. Dordrecht: Springer.

Kane, R. and Huck, S. (2000) The implementation of the EverCare Demonstration Project. *Journal of the American Geriatrics Society*, 48, 218-28.

Kane, R.L., Flood, S., Keckhafer, G. and Rockwood, T. (2001) How EverCare nurse practitioners spend their time. *Journal of the American Geriatrics Society*. 49(11), 1530-4.

Kane, R., Keckhafer, G., Flood, S., Bershadsky, B. and Siadaty, M. (2003) The effect of Evercare on hospital use. *Journal of the American Geriatrics Society*, 51, 1427-34.

Karp, F. (ed) (2007) *Growing older in America: The Health and Retirement Survey*. Washington, DC: National Institute on Aging.

Katz, S. (1996) *Disciplining old age: The formation of gerontological knowledge*. Charlottesville, VA: University Press of Virginia.

Keill, J. (1706) 'An account of the death and dissection of John Bayles, of Northampton, reputed to have been 130 years old'. *Philosophical Transactions of the Royal Society*, 25, 2247-52.

Kermack, W.O., McKendrick, A.G. and McKinlay, P.L. (1934) Death rates in Great Britain and Sweden: some general regularities and their significance. *The Lancet*, 226, 698–703.

Koenig, H.G. and Blazer, D.G. (1992) Epidemiology of geriatric affective disorders. *Clinical Geriatric Medicine*, 8(2), 235–51.

Kuh, D., Hardy, R., Butterworth, S., Okell, L., Wadsworth, M.E.J., Cooper, C. and Aihie Sayer, A. (2006a) Developmental origins of adult grip strength: findings from a British birth cohort. *Journal of Gerontology: Medical Sciences*, 61(7), 702-6.

Kuh, D.J.L., Hardy, R., Butterworth, S., Okell, L., Wadsworth, M.E.J., Cooper, C. and Aihie Sayer, A. (2006b) Developmental origins of midlife physical performance: evidence from a British birth cohort. *American Journal of Epidemiology*, 164, 110-21.

Kydd, A., Duffy, T. and Duffy, F. (eds) (2009) *The care and wellbeing of older people: A textbook for healthcare students.* Exeter: Reflect Press.

Lafortune, G., Balestat, G. and the Disability Study Expert Group Members (2007) *Trends in severe disability among elderly people: Assessing the evidence in 12 OECD countries and future implications.* OECD Health Working Papers No. 26. Brussels: OECD.

Laing and Buisson plc (2008) *Care of elderly people market survey.* London: Laing and Buisson.

Lakdawalla, D.N., Bhattacharya, J. and Goldman, D.P. (2004) Are the young becoming more disabled? *Health Affairs (Millwood)*, 23(1), 168-76.

Lakkireddy, D.R., Basarakodu, K.R., Vacek, J.L., Kondur, A.K., Ramachandruni, S.K., Esterbrooks, D.J., Markert, R.J. and Gowda, M.S. (2007) Improving death certificate completion: a trial of two training interventions. *Journal of General Internal Medicine*, 22(4), 544-8.

Lang, I., Llewellyn, D., Alexander, K. and Melzer, D. (2008) Obesity, physical function, and mortality in older adults. *Journal of the American Geriatrics Society*, 56, 1474–8.

Lee, M. (2006) *Promoting mental health and well-being in later life: Services and support for older people with mental health problems.* London: Age Concern England..

Lee, M. (2007) *Improving services and support for older people with mental health problems.* London: Age Concern England.

Leighton, Y., Clegg, A. and Bee, A. (2008) Evaluation of community matron services in a large metropolitan city in England. *Quality in Primary Care*, 16(2), 83-9.

Leung, L.P. and Fan, K.L. (2010) Who should be admitted to hospital? Evaluation of a screening tool. *Hong Kong Medical Journal*, 14(4), 273-7.

Lewis, J. (2001) Older people and the health social care boundary in the UK: half a century of hidden policy conflict. *Social Policy and Administration*, 35(4), 343-59.

Lillyman, S. and Saxon, A. (2009) Community matrons and case managers: who are they? *British Journal of Community Nursing*, 14(2), 70-3.

Lucke, J.C. and Hall, W. (2005) *Who wants to live forever?* European Molecular Biology Organisation Report 6, 98–102 (www.ncbi.nlm.nih.gov/pmc/articles/PMC1299249/).

Lucke, J.C. and Hall, W. (2006) Strong and weak lifespan extension: what is most feasible and likely? *Australasian Journal on Ageing*, 25(2), 58-62.

Lucke, J., Ryan, B. and Hall, W. (2006) What does the community think about lifespan extension technologies? The need for an empirical base for ethical and policy debates. *Australasian Journal on Ageing*, 25(4), 180-4.

Luthy, C., Cedraschi, C., Herrmann, F., Kossovsky, M., Perrin, E., Chopard, P., Michel, J.P. and Allaz, A.F. (2007) Appropriateness of hospital use: comparison between elderly patients' point of view and a structured questionnaire. *Age and Ageing*, 36(6), 681-4.

McCoy, D., Godden, S., Pollock, A.M. and Bianchessi, C. (2007) Carrot and sticks? The Community Care Act (2003) and the effect of financial incentives on delays in discharge from hospitals in England. *Journal of Public Health*, 29(3), 281-7.

Macintyre, S., McKay, L. and Ellaway, A. (2006) Lay concepts of the relative importance of different influences on health: are there major socio-demographic variations? *Health Education Research: Theory and Practice,* 21, 731-9.

Mahmood, A. and Martin-Matthews, A. (2008) Dynamics of carework: boundary management and relationship issues for home support workers and home care recipients. In A. Martin-Matthews and J. Phillips (eds) *Aging and caring at the intersection of work and home life: Blurring the boundaries*. New York: Taylor and Francis.

Mann, A. (2000) Depression in the elderly: findings from a community survey. *Maturitas*, 38(1), 53-8.

Manthorpe, J., Biggs, S., McCreadie, C., Tinker, A., Hills, A., O'Keefe, M., Doyle, M., Constantine, R., Scholes, S. and Erens, B. (2007a) The U.K. national study of abuse and neglect among older people. *Nursing Older People*, 19(8), 24-6.

Manthorpe, J., Clough, R., Cornes, M., Bright, L., Moriarty, J., Illiffe, S. and OPRSI (Older People Researching Social Issues) (2007b) Four years on: the impact of the National Service Framework for Older People on the experiences, expectations and views of older people. *Age and Ageing*, 36(5), 501-7.

Manton, K. (1999) Dynamic paradigms for human mortality and aging. *Journal of Gerontology: Biological Sciences*, 54A, B247-B254.

Manton, K.G. (1986) Cause specific mortality patterns among the oldest old: multiple cause of death trends 1968 to 1980. *Journal of Gerontology*, 41(2), 282-9.

Manton, K.G. and Gu, X. (2001) Changes in the prevalence of chronic disability in the United States black and nonblack population above age 65 from 1982 to 1999. *Proceedings of the National Academy of Sciences of the United States of America*, 98, 6354-9.

Manton, K.G., Gu, X. and Lowrimore, G.R. (2008) Cohort changes in active life expectancy in the U.S. elderly population: experience from the 1982-2004 National Long-Term Care Survey. *Journal of Gerontology Series B: Psychological and Social Science*, 63(5), S269-S281.

Marmot, M. (chair) (2008) *Closing the gap in a generation*. Report of the WHO Commission on Social Determinants of Health. Geneva: World Health Organization (available at www.who.int/social_determinants/en/).

Marmot, M., Banks, J., Blundell, R., Lessof, C. and Nazroo, J. (2003) *Health, wealth and lifestyles of the older population of England: The 2002 English Longitudinal Survey of Ageing*. London: Institute of Fiscal Studies.

Marmot, M., Shipley, M., Brunner, E. and Hemingway, H. (2001) Relative contribution of early life and adult socioeconomic factors to adult morbidity in the Whitehall II study. *Journal of Epidemiology & Community Health*, 55, 301-10.

Marsiske, M., Franks, M.M. and Mast, B.T. (1998) Psychological perspectives on aging. In Kunkel, S. and Morgan, L. (eds) *Frames of reference: Sociological perspectives on age and aging* (pp 145-206). Thousand Oaks, CA: Pine Forge Press.

Martin, L.G., Freedman, V.A., Schoen, R.F. and Andreski, P.M. (2009) Health and functioning among baby boomers approaching 60. *The Journals of Gerontology Series B: Psychological Sciences and Social Sciences*, 64B(3), 369-77.

Martin, L.G., Schoeni, R.F., Freedman, V.F. and Andreski, P. (2007) Feeling better? Trends in general health status. *Journal of Gerontology: Social Sciences*, 62B, S11-S21.

Martin-Matthews, A. (2004) Aging and families: ties over time and across generations. In N. Mandell and A. Duffy (eds) *Canadian families: Diversity, conflict and change* (3rd edn). Toronto: Harcourt Brace.

Martin-Matthews, A. and Phillips, J. (eds) (2008) *Aging and caring at the intersection of work and home life: Blurring the boundaries*. London: Taylor and Francis.

Martin-Matthews, A. and Sims-Gould, J. (2008) Employers, home support workers and elderly clients: identifying key issues in delivery and receipt of home support. *Healthcare Quarterly*, 11(4), 69-75.

Mathers, C.D., Ma Fat, D., Inoue, M., Rao, C. and Lopez, A.D. (2005) Counting the dead and what they died from: an assessment of the global status of cause of death data. *Bulletin of the World Health Organisation*, 83, 171-7.

Mayer, K.U., Maas, I. and Wagner, M. (2001) Socioeconomic conditions and social inequalities in old age. In Baltes, P.B. and Mayer, K.U. (eds) *The Berlin Aging Study: Aging from 70 to 100*. Cambridge: Cambridge University Press.

Means, R. (2007) The remedicalisation of later life. In Bernard, M. and Scharf, T. (eds) *Critical perspectives on ageing societies*. Bristol: The Policy Press.

Means, R. and Smith, R. (1998) *From Poor Law to community care*. London: Routledge.

Means, R., Richards, S. and Smith, R. (2008) *Community care* (4th edition). Basingstoke: Palgrave Macmillan.

Melzer, D., Lan, T.-Y., Deeg, D. and Guralnik, J. (2004) Variation in thresholds for reporting mobility disability between national population sub-groups and studies. *The Journals of Gerontology Series B: Psychological Sciences and Social Sciences*, 59(12), 1295-303.

Melzer, D., McWilliams, B., Brayne, C., Johnson, T. and Bond, J. (2000) Socioeconomic status and the expectation of disability in old age: estimates for England. *Journal of Epidemiology and Community Health*, 54, 286-92.

Metchnikoff, E. (1903) *The nature of man*. New York: G.P. Putnam & Sons.

Metz, D. and Underwood, M. (2005) *Older richer fitter: Identifying the consumer needs of Britain's ageing population*. London: Age Concern Books.

Mitchell, R., Dorling, D. and Shaw, M. (2000) *Inequalities in life and death: What if Britain were more equal?* York: Joseph Rowntree Foundation.

Mitchell, R., Dorling, D. and Shaw, M. (2002) Population production and modelling mortality: an application of Geographic Information Systems in health inequalities research. *Health & Place*, 8: 15-24.

Moody, H. (2002) Who's afraid of life extension? *Generations*, Anti-Aging: Are You For It Or Against It?, Special edition, 25(4), 33-7.

Moody, H.R. (2008) Aging America and the boomer wars, Book review, *Gerontologist*, 48: 839-44.

Morley J.E. (2004) A brief history of geriatrics. *Journals of Gerontology Series A: Biological Sciences and Medical Sciences* , 59: 1132-52.

Murata, C., Kondo, T., Tamakoshi, K., Yatsuya, H. and Toyoshima, H. (2006) Determinants of self-rated health: could health status explain the association between self-rated health and mortality? *Archives of Gerontology and Geriatrics*, 43(3), 369-80.

Murphy, E. (2004) Case management and community matrons for long term conditions. *British Medical Journal*, 329, 1251-2.

Murphy, E. and Isaacs, B. (1982) The post-fall syndrome: a study of 36 elderly patients. *Gerontology*, 28, 265-70.

Mykytyn, C.E. (2006a) Anti-aging medicine: a patient/practitioner movement to redefine aging. *Social Science and Medicine*, 62, 643-53.

Mykytyn, C.E. (2006b) Contentious terminology and complicated cartography of anti-aging medicine. *Biogerontology*, 7(4), 279-85.

Mykytyn, C.E. (2008) Medicalizing the optimal: anti-aging medicine and the quandary of intervention. *Journal of Aging Studies*, 22(4), 313-21.

Mykytyn, C.E. (2010) A history of the future: the emergence of contemporary anti-ageing medicine. *Sociology of Health and Illness*, 32(2), 181-96.

Nascher, I.L. (1914) *Geriatrics: The diseases of old age and their treatment*, Philadelphia: P. Blakiston's Son & Co (reprinted in 1979 by Ayer Publisher, New Hampshire; 1919 second edition published by Kegan Paul available to read online: www. archive.org/stream/geriatricsdiseas00nascuoft#page/n5/mode/2upshire).

Nazroo, J., Goodman, J., Marmot, M. and Blundell, R. (2009) *Inequalities in health in an aging population: Patterns, causes and consequences*. London: ESRC (www. esrcsocietytoday.ac.uk/esrcinfocentre/viewawardpage.aspx?awardnumber=R ES-000-23-0590).

Netuveli, G. and Blane, D. (2008) Quality of life in older ages. *British Medical Bulletin*, 85, 113-26.

Netuveli, G., Wiggins, R.D., Hildon, Z., Montgomery, S.M. and Blane, D. (2006) Quality of life at older ages: evidence from the English Longitudinal Study of Aging (wave 1). *Journal of Epidemiology and Community Health*, 60, 357-63.

NHS Information Centre (2009a) *Statistics on alcohol: England 2009*. Leeds: NHS Information Centre (www.ic.nhs.uk/pubs/smoking09).

NHS Information Centre (2009b) *Statistics on smoking: England 2009*. Leeds: NHS Information Centre (www.ic.nhs.uk/statistics-and-data-collections/health-and-lifestyles/smoking/statistics-on-smoking-england-2009).

NHS Information Centre (2009c) *Community care statistics*. Leeds: NHS Information Centre.

NHS Information Centre (2009d) *Trends in consultation rates in general practice: 1995-2009*. Leeds: NHS Information Centre.

NHS (National Health Service) Information Centre (2009e) *Statistics on obesity, physical activity and diet: England*. February. Leeds: NHS Information Centre.

Nowak, H. and Hubbard, R.E. (2009) Falls and frailty: lessons from complex systems. *Journal of the Royal Society of Medicine*, 102, 98-102.

O'Loughlin, J., Dugas, E., Maximova, K., Kishchuk (2006) Reporting of ethnicity in research on chronic disease: update. *Postgraduate Medical Journal*, 82, 737-42, doi:10.1136/pgmj.2005.048074

Oeppen, J. and Vaupel, J.W. (2002) Broken limits to life expectancy. *Science*, 296, 1029-31.

Oliver, M. (1996) *Understanding disability: From theory to practice*. Basingstoke: Macmillan.

Olshansky, S.J. (1985) Pursuing longevity: delay vs elimination of degenerative diseases. *American Journal of Public Health*, 75(7), 754-7.

Olshansky, S.J. (2005) Projecting the future of U.S. health and longevity. *Health Affairs (Millwood)*, 24(suppl 2), W5R86-9.

Olshansky, S.J., Carnes, B.A. and Cassel, C. (1990) In search of Methuselah: estimating the upper limits to human longevity. *Science*, 250(4981), 634-40.

Olshansky, S.J., Hayflick, L. and Carnes, B. (2002a) No truth to the fountain of youth. *Scientific American*, 286(6), 92-5.

Olshansky, S.J., Hayflick, L. and Carnes, B.A. (2002b) Position statement on human aging. *The Journals of Gerontology Series A: Biological Sciences and Medical Sciences*, 57A, B292-B297.

ONS (Office for National Statistics) (2006) *Mortality statistics* (Series DH1), no 39, table 4. London: ONS.

ONS (2008) *Trends in life expectancy by social class 1972-2005*. London: ONS (www.statistics.gov.uk/downloads/theme_population/Life_Expect_Social_class_1972-05/life_expect_social_class.pdf)

ONS (2009) *Population trends*, 28. London: ONS.

ONS (2010) *Family spending: A report on the 2008 Living Costs and Food Survey*. Basingstoke: Palgrave Macmillan (www.statistics.gov.uk/downloads/theme_social/Family-Spending-2008/FamilySpending2009.pdf).

Parker, M.G. and Thorslund, M. (2007) Health trends in the elderly population: getting better and getting worse. *The Gerontologist*, 47(2), 150-8.

Peace, S., Holland, C. and Kellaher, L. (2005a) *Environment and identity in later life*. Maidenhead: Open University Press.

Peace, S., Holland, C. and Kellaher, L. (2005b) Making space for identity. In Phillips, D.R. and Andrews, G. (eds) *Ageing and place*. London: Routledge.

Pérès, K., Jagger, C. and Matthews, F.E. (2008) Impact of late-life self-reported emotional problems on Disability-Free Life Expectancy: results from the MRC Cognitive Function and Ageing Study. *International Journal of Geriatric Psychiatry*, 23(6), 643-9.

Pew Research Center (2009) *Growing old in America: Expectations vs. reality*. Washington, DC: Pew Research Center (available at http://pewresearch.org/pubs/1269/aging-survey-expectations-versus-reality).

Phillips, J. (2007) *Care*. Cambridge: Polity Press.

Phillipson, C., Leach, R., Money, A. and Biggs, S. (2008) Social and cultural constructions of ageing: the case of the baby boomers. *Sociological Research Online*, 13(3).

Philp, I. (2002a) The National Service Framework – suggestions about priorities for policy development welcome. *Age and Ageing*, 31(5), 411.

Philp, I. (2002b) Developing a National Service Framework for older people. *Journal of Epidemiology and Community Health*, 56(11), 841-2.

Philp, I. (2004) *Better health in old age: Report from Professor Ian Philp*. London: DH.

Philp, I. (2006) *A new ambition for old age: Next steps in implementing the National Service Framework for Older People: A resource document*. London: DH.

Player, S. and Pollock, A.M. (2001) Long term care: from public responsibility to public good. *Critical Social Policy*, 21(2), 231-55.

Ploubidis, G.B. and Grundy, E. (2009) Later-life mental health in Europe: a country-level comparison. *The Journals of Gerontology Series B: Psychological Sciences and Social Sciences*, 64B(5), 666-76.

Pollock, A.M., Player, S. and Godden, S. (2001) How private finance is moving primary care into corporate ownership. *British Medical Journal*, 322(7292), 960-3.

Post, S.G. and Binstock, R.H. (2004) *The fountain of youth: Cultural, scientific, and ethical perspectives on a biomedical goal*. Oxford: Oxford University Press.

Powell, A.P. (2005) Issues unique to the masters athlete. *Current Sports Medical Reports*, 6, 335-40.

Préville, M., Boyer, R., Grenier, S., Dubé, M., Voyer, P., Punti, R., Baril, M.C., Streiner, D.L., Cairney, J. and Brassard, J. (2008) Scientific Committee of the ESA Study: the epidemiology of psychiatric disorders in Quebec's older adult population. *Canadian Journal of Psychiatry*, 53(12), 822-32.

Propper, C. (2002) The demand for private health care in the UK. *Journal of Health Economics*, 19, 855-76.

Propper, C. and Green, K. (2001) A larger role for the private sector in financing UK health care: the arguments and the evidence, *Journal of Social Policy*, 30, 685-704.

Propper, C., Rees, H. and Green, K. (2001) The demand for private medical insurance in the UK: a cohort analysis. *Economics Journal*, 111, C180-C200.

Prus, S.G. (2007) Age, SES, and health: a population level analysis of health inequalities over the lifecourse, *Sociology of Health and Illness*, 29(2), 175-296.

Puts, M.T.E., Shekary, N., Widdershoven, G., Heldens, J. and Deeg, D.J.H. (2010) The meaning of frailty according to Dutch older frail and non-frail persons. *Journal of Aging Studies*. In press.

Quetelet, M.A. (1968) *A treatise on man and the development of his faculties*. New York: Burt Franklin. (Original work published in 1835 by Bachelier, Imprimeur-Libraire.)

Quine, S., Bernard, D. and Kendig, H. (2006) Understanding baby boomers' expectations and plans for their retirement: findings from a qualitative study. *Australasian Journal of Ageing*, 25(3), 145–50.

Rahkonen, O. and Takala, P. (1998) Social class differences in health and functional disability among older men and women. *International Journal of Health Services*, 28(3), 511–24.

Ramsay, S.E., Morris, R.W., Lennon, L.T., Wannamethee, S.G. and Whincup, P.H. (2008) Are social inequalities in mortality in Britain narrowing? Time trends from 1978 to 2005 in a population-based study of older men. *Journal of Epidemiology and Community Health*, 62, 75–80.

Rao, C., Yang, G., Hu, J., Ma, J., Xia, W. and Lopez, A.D. (2007) Validation of cause-of-death statistics in urban China. *International Journal of Epidemiology*, 36(3), 642–51.

Redfern, S. and Ross, F. (eds) (2006) *Nursing older people* (4th edition). Edinburgh: Churchill Livingstone Elsevier.

Reyes-Ortiz, C.A., Ostir, G.V., Pelaez, M. and Ottenbacher, K.J. (2006) Cross-national comparison of disability in Latin American and Caribbean persons aged 75 and older. *Archives of Gerontology and Geriatrics*, 42(1), 21–33.

Rich-Edwards, J.W., Stampfer, M.J., Manson, J.E., Rosner, B., Hankinson, S.E., Colditz, G.A. et al (1997) Birth weight and risk of cardiovascular disease in a cohort of women followed up since 1976. *British Medical Journal*, 315, 396–400.

Rickards, L., Fox, K., Roberts C., Fletcher, I. and Goddard, E. (2004) *Living in Britain: Results from the 2002 General Household Survey*. London: The Stationery Office (www.statistics.gov.uk/downloads/theme_compendia/lib2002.pdf).

Robine, J.-M. and Michel, P.J. (2007) Looking forward to a general theory on population aging. *Tijdschrift voor Gerontologie en Geriatrie*, 37(4), 29–37.

Robine, J.-M., Cheung, S.L.K., Horiuchi, S. and Thatcher, A.R. (2008) Is the compression of morbidity a universal phenomenon? Presented at the Living to 100 and Beyond Symposium, Orlando, Florida, 7–9 January (www.soa.org/library/monographs/retirement-systems/living-to-100-and-beyond/2008/january/mono-li08-04-cheung.pdf).

Robine, J.-M., Jagger, C., Van Oyen, H. and Cambois, E. (2009) Increasing healthy life expectancy and reducing longevity gaps between European countries. In EU Task Force on Health Expectancies, *Healthy life years in the European Union: Facts and figures 2005*, Brussels: European Commission (http://ec.europa.eu/health/ph_information/reporting/docs/hly_en.pdf).

Rockwood, K. (2005) Frailty and its definition: a worthy challenge. *Journal of the American Geriatrics Society*, 53(6), 1069–70.

Roebuck, J. (1979) When does old age begin? The evolution of the English definition. *Journal of Social History*, 12(3), 416–28.

Roehrig, B., Hoeffken, K., Pientka, L. and Wedding, U. (2007) How many and which items of activities of daily living (ADL) and instrumental activities of daily living (IADL) are necessary for screening. *Critical Reviews in Oncology/Haematology*, 62(2), 164–71.

Rowe, J. and Kahn, R. (1997) Successful aging. *The Gerontologist*, 37(4), 433-40.

Rutter, M. (1987) Psychosocial resilience and protective mechanisms. In J. Rolf, A. Masten, D. Cichetti, K. Nuechterlein and S. Weintraub (eds) *Risk and protective factors in the development of psychopathology* (pp 181-214) New York: Cambridge University Press.

Sainsbury, P. (1961) Suicide in old age. *Proceedings of the Royal Society of Medicine*, 54, 266-8.

Salihu, H.M., Bonnema, S.M. and Alio, A.P. (2009) Obesity: what is an elderly population growing into? *Maturitas*, 63(1), 7-12.

Sanderson, W.C. and Scherbov, S. (2005) Average remaining lifetimes can increase as human populations age. *Nature*, 435, 811-13.

Sarkisian, C.A., Lee-Henderson, M.H. and Mangione, C.M. (2003) Do depressed older adults who attribute depression to 'old age' believe it is important to seek care? *Journal of General Internal Medicine*, 18(12), 1001-5.

Schaie, K.W. (1996) Intellectual development in adulthood. In Birren, J.E. and Schaie, K.W. (eds) *Handbook of the psychology of aging* (4th edition). San Diego, CA: Academic Press.

Scheffer, C., Schuurmans, M.J., van Dijk, N., van der Hooft, T. and de Rooij, S.E. (2008) Fear of falling: measurement strategy, prevalence, risk factors and consequences among older persons. *Age and Ageing*, 37(1), 19-24.

Schoeni, R.F., Freedman, V. and Martin, L.G. (2008) Why is late-life disability declining? *Milbank Quarterly*, 86, 47-89.

Schoeni, R.F., Martin, L.G., Andreski, P.M. and Freedman, V.A. (2005) Persistent and growing socioeconomic disparities in disability among the elderly: 1982-2002. *American Journal of Public Health*, 95(11), 2065-70.

Self, A. and Zealey, L. (2007) *Social trends no. 37*. London: ONS.

Shah, A. (2007a) The relationship between suicide rates and age: an analysis of multinational data from the World Health Organization. *International Psychogeriatrics*, 19(6), 1141-52.

Shah, A. (2007b) The impact of the Community Care (Delayed Discharge) Act 2003 on the length of stay and bed occupancy in old age psychiatry units in England. *International Journal of Geriatric Psychiatry*, 22(11), 1164-5.

Shah, A.K., Oommen, G. and Koshy A. (2009) Ethnic elders and their needs. *Psychiatry*, 8(9), 358-62.

Shannon, K., Kerr, T., Strathdee, S.A., Shoveller, J., Montaner, S.J. and Tyndall, M.W. (2007) Prevalence and correlates of obsessive-compulsive disorder among older adults living in the community. *British Medical Journal*, 334, 316-30.

Sheldon, J.H. (1948) *The social medicine of old age*. Oxford: Nuffield.

Sidell, M. (1995) *Health in old age: Myth, mystery and management*. Buckingham: Open University Press.

Sink, K.M., Covinsky, K.E., Newcomer, R. and Yaffe, K. (2004) Ethnic differences in the prevalence and pattern of dementia-related behaviors. *Journal of the American Geriatrics Society*, 52(8), 1277-83.

Smith, A. (2009) *Ageing in urban neighbourhoods: Place attachment and social exclusion.* Bristol: The Policy Press.

Smith S.M., Allwright S. and O'Dowd T. (2007) Effectiveness of shared care across the interface between primary and specialty care in chronic disease management. *Cochrane Database of Systematic Reviews*, 3, art. no. CD004910. DOI: 10.1002/14651858.CD004910.pub2.

Smith, M., Edgar, G. and Groom, G. (2008) Health expectancies in the United Kingdom, 2004-2006, *Health Statistics Quarterly* 40, 77–80 (www.statistics.gov.uk/statbase/Product.asp?vlnk=6725) (www.statistics.gov.uk/StatBase/Product.asp?vlnk=12964).

Sproston, K. and Mindell, J. (2006) *Health Survey for England 2004: The health of minority ethnic groups.* Leeds: NHS Information Centre (www.ic.nhs.uk/statistics-and-data-collections/health-and-lifestyles-related-surveys/health-survey-for-england/health-survey-for-england-2004:-health-of-ethnic-minorities--full-report).

Stein, C.E., Fall, C., Kumaran, K., Osmond, C., Cox, V. and Barker, D.J.P. (1996) Fetal growth and coronary heart disease in South India. *The Lancet*, 348: 1269-73.

Stoddart, H., Donovan, J., Whitley, E., Sharp, D. and Harvey, I. (2001) Urinary incontinence in older people in the community: a neglected problem? *British Journal of General Practice*, 51(468), 548–52.

Strehler, B. (1962) *Time, cells and aging.* New York: Academic Press.

Sturm, R., Ringel, J.S. and Andreyeva, T. (20040 Increasing obesity rates and disability trends. *Health Affairs (Millwood)*, 23(2), 199-205.

Sulander, T., Rahkonen, O., Nummela, O. and Uutela, A. (2009) Ten year trends in health inequalities among older people, 1993-2003. *Age and Ageing*, 38(5), 613-7.

Sutherland, S. (chair) (1999) *With respect to old age: Long term care – rights and responsibilities.* A Report by the Royal Commission on Long Term Care. London: The Stationery Office.

Thane, P. (2000) *Old age in English history: Past experiences, present issues.* Oxford: Oxford University Press.

Thane, P. (2005) *The long history of old age.* London: Thames & Hudson.

Townsend, P. (1961) A provisional measure of incapacity for self-care. In Donahue, W., Tibbits, C. and Williams, R.H. (eds) *Psychological and sociological processes of ageing: An international research seminar.* New York: Columbia University Press.

Townsend, P. (1962) *The last refuge: A survey of residential institutions and homes for the aged in England and Wales.* London: Routledge & Kegan Paul.

Tromans, N., Jefferies, J. and Natamba, E. (2009) Have women born outside the UK driven the rise in UK births since 2001? (pp 28-43). *Population trends 136.* Basingstoke: Palgrave Macmillan.

Tulle, E. (2003) Sense and structure: towards a sociology of old bodies. In Biggs, S., Lowenstein, A. and Hendricks, J. (eds) *The need for theory: Critical approaches in social gerontology.* Amityville, NY: Baywood Publishing.

Tulle, E. (2007) Running to run: embodiment, structure and agency amongst veteran elite runners. *Sociology*, 41(2), 329-46.

Tulle, E. (2008a) *Ageing, the body and social change.* Basingstoke: Palgrave Macmillan.

Tulle, E. (2008b) Acting your age? Sports science and the ageing body. *Journal of Aging Studies*, 22(4), 291–4.

Tulle, E. (2008c) The ageing body and the ontology of ageing: athletic competence in later life. *Body & Society*, 14(3), 1–19.

Turner, B.S. (2009) *Can we live forever? A social and moral inquiry.* London: Anthem Press.

Twigg, J. (1997) Deconstructing the 'social bath': help with bathing at home for older and disabled people. *Journal of Social Policy*, 26(2), 211–32.

Twigg, J. (2000a) Carework as bodywork. *Ageing and Society*, 20, 389–411

Twigg, J. (2000b) *Bathing, the body and community care.* London: Routledge.

Twigg, J. (2002a) The body in social policy: mapping a territory. *Journal of Social Policy*, 31(3), 421–40.

Twigg, J. (2002b) The bodywork of care. In Andersson, L. (ed) *Cultural gerontology.* Westport, CT: Greenwood.

Twigg, J. (2003) 'The body and bathing: help with personal care at home. In Faircloth, C.A. (ed) *Ageing bodies: Images and everyday experiences.* Walnut Creek, CA: Altamira Press.

UN (United Nations) (2008) *Demographic Yearbook 2004.* New York: UN Statistics Division, Department of Economic and Social Affairs.

Underwood, M., Bartlett, H.P. and Hall, W.D. (2007) Community attitudes to the regulation of life extension. *Annals of the New York Academy of Sciences*, 1114, 288–99.

Underwood, M., Bartlett, H.P. and Hall, W.D. (2009a) Professional and personal attitudes of researchers in ageing towards life extension. *Biogerontology*, 10(1), 73–81.

Underwood, M., Bartlett, H.P., Partridge, B., Lucke, J. and Hall, W.D. (2009b) Community perceptions on the significant extension of life: an exploratory study among urban adults in Brisbane, Australia. *Social Science and Medicine*, 68(3), 496–503.

Vetter, N. (2003) Inappropriately delayed discharge from hospital: what do we know? *British Medical Journal*, 326, 927–8.

Victor, C.R. (1991) Continuity or change: inequalities in health in later life. *Ageing and Society*, 11, 23–39.

Victor, C.R. (1997) *Community care and older people.* Cheltenham: Stanley Thornes.

Victor, C.R. (2005) *The social context of ageing.* London: Routledge.

Victor, C.R. (2007) Researching ageing. In Bond, J., Peace, S., Dittmann–Kohli, F. and Westerhof, G. (eds) *An ageing society.* London: Sage Publications.

Victor, C.R. (2008) Consuming health in later life. In Jones, I.R. Hyde, M., Victor, C., Wiggins, R., Gilleard, C. and Higgs, P. (2008) *Ageing in a consumer society: From passive to active consumption in Britain.* Bristol: The Policy Press.

Victor, C.R. (2009) The future of social care in England. *British Medical Journal*, 339, 3384.

Victor, C.R. (2010a) The demography of ageing. In Danefer, D. and Phillipson, C. (eds) *The Sage handbook of social gerontology,* London: Sage.

Victor, C.R. (2010b) Where now for social care in England? *British Medical Journal*, 340, c2017.

Victor, C., Bond, J. and Scambler, S. (2009) *The social world of older people*. Maidenhead: Open University Press [★ in text = data hitherto unpublished but which informed the research in this 2009 publication].

Villareal, D.T., Apovian, C.M., Kushner, R.F. and Klein, S. (2005) Obesity in older adults: technical review and position statement of the American Society for Nutrition and NAASO, The Obesity Society. *Obesity Research*, 13(11), 1849–63.

Vincent, J.A. (2003a) *Old age*. London: Routledge.

Vincent, J.A. (2003b) What is at stake in the 'war on anti-aging medicine'? *Ageing and Society*, 23, 675–84.

Vincent, J.A. (2006) Ageing contested: anti-ageing science and the cultural construction of old age. *Sociology*, 40(4), 681–98.

Vincent, J.A. (2008) The cultural construction old age as a biological phenomenon: science and anti-ageing technologies. *Journal of Ageing Studies*, 22(4), 331–9.

Vincent, J.A., Phillipson, C. and Downs, M. (eds) (2006) *The futures of old age*. London: Sage Publications.

Vincent, J.A., Tulle, E. and Bond, J. (2008) Editorial: the anti-ageing enterprise: science, knowledge, expertise, rhetoric and values. *Journal of Aging Studies*, 22(4), 340–7.

Wadsworth, M.E.J., Butterworth, S.L., Hardy, R., Kuh, D.J., Richards, M., Langenberg, C., Hilder, W.S. and Connor, M. (2003) The life course prospective design: an example of benefits and problems associated with study longevity. *Social Science and Medicine*, 57(11), 2193–05.

Wanless, D. (2006) *Securing good care for older people*. London: King's Fund (www.kingsfund.org.uk/publications/securing_good.html).

Ward-Griffin, C., and Marshall. V. (2003) Reconceptualizing the relationship between 'public' and 'private' eldercare. *Journal of Aging Studies*, 17, 189–208.

Warren, M.W. (1943) Care of the chronic sick: a case for treating chronic sick in blocks in a general hospital. *British Medical Journal*, 2: 822–3.

Weir, D. (2007) Are baby boomers living well longer? In Madrian, B., Mitchell, O.S. and Soldo, B.J. (eds) *Redefining retirement: How will boomers fare?* (pp 95–111). New York: Oxford University Press.

Welch, S.S. (2001) A review of the literature on the epidemiology of parasuicide in the general population. *Psychiatric Services*, 52, 368–75.

Werner, P. and Heinik, J. (2008) Stigma by association and Alzheimer's disease. *Aging and Mental Health*, 12(1), 92–9.

White, A. (ed) (2002) *Social focus in brief: Ethnicity*. London: ONS (available at www.statistics.gov.uk/downloads/theme_social/social_focus_in_brief/ethnicity/ethnicity.pdf).

White, C. (2009) An update to measuring chronic illness, impairment and disability in national data sources. *Health Statistics Quarterly*, 42, 40–53.

WHO (World Health Organization) (1946) Preamble to the Constitution of the WHO as adopted by the International Health Conference, New York, 19–22 June, 1946; signed on 22 July 1946 by the representatives of 61 States (Official Records of the WHO, no. 2, p 100) and entered into force on 7 April 1948 (www.who.int/about/definition/en/print.html/).

WHO (1980) *International classification of impairments, disabilities and handicaps.* Geneva: WHO.

WHO (2008) *Global burden of disease: 2004 update,* Geneva: WHO (www.who.int/healthinfo/global_burden_disease/2004_report_update/en/index.html).

Wick, G. (2002) 'Anti-aging' medicine: does it exist? A critical discussion of 'anti-aging health products. *Experimental Gerontology,* 37, 1137–40.

Wilkinson, R. and Pickett, K. (2009) *The spirit level: Why more equal societies almost always do better.* London: Allen Lane.

Williams, R. (1990) *A protestant legacy: Attitudes to death and illness among older Aberdonians.* Oxford: Clarendon Press.

Williamson, J., Stokoe, I.H., Gray, S., Fisher, M., Smith, A., Mcghee, A. and Stephenson, E. (1964) Old people at home: their unreported needs. *The Lancet,* 1(7343), 1117–20.

Winter, L., Lawton, M.P. and Ruckdeschel, K. (2003) Preferences for prolonging life: a prospect theory approach. *International Journal of Aging and Human Development,* 56, 155–70.

Wright, K., Ryder, S. and Gousy, M. (2007) An evaluation of a community matron service from the patients' perspective. *British Journal of Community Nursing,* 12(9), 398–403.

Zunzunegui, M.V., Alvarado, B.E., Béland, F. and Vissandjee, B. (2009) Explaining health differences between men and women in later life: a cross-city comparison in Latin America and the Caribbean. *Social Science and Medicine,* 68(2), 235–42.

Zunzunegui, M.V., Minicuci, N., Blurnstein, T., Noale, M., Deeg, D., Jylhä, M. and Pedersen, N.L. (2007) Gender differences in depressive symptoms among older adults: a cross-national comparison – the CLESA project. *Social Psychiatry and Psychiatric Epidemiology,* 42, 198–207.

Index

Note: The letter t following a page number indicates a table